Dapper & Deadly

The True Story of Black Charlie Harris

Taylor Pensoneau

Downstate Publications

Edited by Liz Pensoneau
Book design by Jerry Hutmacher

Downstate Publications
P.O. Box 320
New Berlin, IL 62670
www.downstatepublications.com
downstatepublications@mchsi.com

Publisher's Cataloging-in-Publication
(Provided by Quality Books, Inc.)

Pensoneau, Taylor.
    Dapper & deadly : the true story of Black Charlie
Harris / Taylor Pensoneau.
    p. cm.
    Includes bibliographical references and index.
    LCCN 2009935942
    ISBN-13: 978-0-9710718-2-7
    ISBN-10: 0-9710718-2-9

    1. Harris, Charles Bryan, 1896-1988. 2. Gangsters--
Illinois--Biography. 3. Gangsters--Illinois--History--
20th century.   I. Title. II. Title: Dapper and deadly.

HV6248.H225P47 2010   364.1'092
                    QBI09-600181

Also by Taylor Pensoneau

Dan Walker: The Glory and the Tragedy (coauthor Bob Ellis)
Governor Richard Ogilvie: In the Interest of the State
Brothers Notorious: The Sheltons
The Summer of '50 (fiction)
Powerhouse: Arrington from Illinois

Contents

Contents

Prologue

Charles (Black Charlie) Harris was not only the last of the big-name desperadoes from southern Illinois, the FBI viewed him as a lethal figure in American crime.

However, many persons who knew him on his home ground in Wayne County, Illinois, found him engaging, even captivating. They were loyal friends and followers until his involvement in sensational murders in his own neighborhood.

Like the notorious Shelton brothers, with whom Harris had a deadly falling-out, he captured the imagination of individuals who never ceased to be amazed at the gangsters dominating the legends and lore of the Prairie State.

Some persons even sensed that the stories of Harris and other southern Illinois gangsters approached the realm of myth. If so, the mythology emanated from the dark side of life.

It was a gross exaggeration, nothing short of balderdash, to suggest that Harris and comparable figures defined their neck of the world—part of the expansive region south of Chicago covered by author Baker Brownell in his book *The Other Illinois*.

Yet, there was no denying that Harris and the others certainly added spice to their times.

Acknowledgments

After the publication of *Brothers Notorious: The Sheltons* in 2001, it was suggested that I should follow up with a book on Charles Bryan Harris, who like the Shelton brothers dominated headlines for many years. The writing and publication of two other books intervened before I started work on one about Harris in early 2008. I soon became completely absorbed by my fascination with the life of the man known as Black Charlie.

Getting his story down on paper would not have been possible without the assistance of many persons. They were diverse individuals because all did not view Harris in the same light—meaning that a number saw him as something other than an unrepentant criminal. Nevertheless, there was unanimous agreement that his life had the makings of a book.

The actions of Harris greatly affected the lives of numerous individuals. Two of them, Beatrice Riley of Elkhart, Kansas, and Carolyn Sue Bland of Fairfield, Illinois, graciously consented to lengthy interviews. Their contributions included salient photographs, one being the illustration on the book's cover. Used with the permission of Mrs. Riley, it shows Harris sitting for a formal photo as a young man in Arizona.

Tracing the family history of Harris was a challenge—a task that only was accomplished because of the perseverance of Doris Bland Thompson of Fairfield, a genealogist par excellence. Mrs. Thompson also was overly generous in the time she spent securing newspaper articles and other sources of important information.

As with the Shelton book, many individuals in Fairfield were helpful in one or more ways in bringing the book to fruition. They included Richard C. Cochran, Sheila Zurliene, Judith Puckett, Rhonda Simpson, Bettie Laws, Bill E. Taylor, Billie J. Taylor and William L. Schmitz.

Tom Mathews Jr., the publisher and editor of the *Wayne County Press*, and Preston Mathews, head of the newspaper's commercial printing business, were again important resources. Coverage of Harris' activities by the *Press* was a valuable source of information. Background also was gleaned from columns on Harris in the *Evansville Courier & Press* by Len Wells, the newspaper's southern Illinois correspondent. Previously, I knew Len only in his other role as the news director of Radio Station WFIW in Fairfield and as the good-natured Murvis on the station's morning show with sidekick Woody Long (Kirk Wallace).

J. David Dickey unhesitatingly shared his knowledge of Wayne County. A onetime treasurer of the county and operator of a meat packing plant in Fairfield, David also wrote poems to his wife Nina and on other subjects that he eventually collected in a book, *The Door is Always Open*.

Numerous individuals outside of Wayne County also contributed to my effort: Gary and Judy DeNeal of Herod, Illinois, publishers of *Springhouse* magazine; longtime confidant Jeff Prugh of Chattanooga, Tennessee; friend Mark Vincent of New Berlin, Illinois; Murphysboro, Illinois, attorney Richard White; Kim Underwood, a onetime state regulator of Illinois coal mining; and former Wayne County residents Ron Peddicord of Chatham, Illinois, and Patsy Sheraden Musgrave of Springfield, Illinois.

When researching the book, the assistance of three individuals was crucial. They were John Reinhardt, archival program administrator at the Illinois State Archives at Springfield; Charles E. Brown, assistant director of the St. Louis Mercantile Library at the University of Missouri-St. Louis; and Bill Clutter, a Springfield private investigator. Among other things, Bill paved the way for my receipt of extensive documents on Harris in the files of the Federal Bureau of Investigation in Washington, D.C.

Subsequently, records necessary for the Harris story were obtained from the Arizona State Archives by Kay Harris, a historical researcher at Springfield. Documents on Harris' criminal trial in Detroit were supplied by Donald W. Jackanicz, archivist at the Great Lakes Region office in Chicago of the National Archives and Records Administration. Likewise, a dossier on Harris' years in the federal penitentiary at Leavenworth, Kansas, was forwarded by Mary Burtzloff of the National Archives office at Kansas City.

Each of these individuals and entities earned my appreciation for helping to track the unending twists and turns in the tumultuous life of Black Charlie. If his story fails to hold one's attention, no one is to blame but the author.

Taylor Pensoneau
January 2010

1

Going Home

July 1963

I t must have been around midnight when bullets zinged out of the darkness on a warm night in the dangerous Pond Creek neighborhood of Wayne County, Illinois. Betty Newton screamed to her fifteen-year-old daughter, Carolyn Sue, to get her younger sisters and brothers under the bed in a back bedroom of a house known as the Hodge Place.

"I was really scared, trying to keep the little kids under control," Carolyn said decades later. "But, I don't think any of the shots came into the house, and nobody was wounded. The bullets (which left numerous holes in two cars in front of the house) may have been little more than a scare tactic."

One of the cars was driven by the Newton family; the other by Charles Bryan (Charlie) Harris.

The mysterious shooter, or shooters, quickly vanished into the blackness. Decades later, Carolyn could not remember whether her father, Charles Newton, or Harris returned the fire. Both could have. Her father always carried a pistol, sometimes a double-barreled derringer, and Harris never went anywhere without a weapon from his private arsenal.

"Charlie," Carolyn recalled, "had enemies." That was an understatement.

Just a few hours before the gunfire erupted, the Newton family had arrived at the Hodge house after an exhausting drive from Phoenix, Arizona. Betty and her husband had started unpacking and were being assisted in settling in by Harris, who owned the home. Harris was, after all, the person who'd persuaded the Newtons to end their yearlong stay in the Southwest and return to working for him in Wayne County.

The move to Phoenix had been prompted mainly by concerns over the health of Charles, who'd suffered lung damage on a ship in World War II. However, Harris had journeyed to Arizona to offer Newton a job that he, Newton, considered fairly attractive. Newton would say afterward that he and Betty had been considering a return to Illinois anyway.

As the years passed, though, Carolyn continued to harbor a feeling that her mother was anything but excited about going back to Illinois. Betty had gotten a job in a bar in Phoenix, and certainly was aware that Harris was the subject of considerable controversy back home. Only a few days before approaching the Newtons in Phoenix, Harris had been acquitted of a murder charge in a highly publicized trial in Wayne County. He had become a polarizing figure, a man admired by a good number and hated by just as many. Regardless of the camp one fell into, all knew that trouble, serious trouble, usually awaited those who crossed the man.

Young Carolyn was not aware back in 1963 that—if gossip and even court testimony later on were to be believed—her mother and Harris had engaged in an affair prior to the Newton family departure for Arizona. Years down the line, when she was Carolyn Bland in married life, she still entertained doubt that such a relationship existed.

In her words, "He may have been enamored with my mother, but I do not think it was reciprocal."

As events would show, there would be little doubt of Harris' infatuation with Betty Newton. It would have been better for all concerned if she and her husband had stayed in Arizona.

Twenty-five Years Later

On June 20, 1988, rural Elkhart, Kansas, was enduring a day of sweltering heat. The old man who lived some miles out of town on the property of Bea Riley, his niece, had been out in the oppressive air all afternoon, probably not a wise move for a person approaching his ninety-second birthday.

Here, Charles Bryan Harris was known to most as the "nice little old uncle" of one of the most respected, and unique, members of the Elkhart community. Bea Riley had built a reputation as a giving, sharing individual since moving to Elkhart in the early 1950s. The days of her youth in Wayne County were part of the past, as were the years there in which her uncle had made quite a name for himself.

Those times for Harris were history now—buried history as far as the world of Elkhart knew.

On this particular day in June 1988, the routine was normal around dinner time at Bea's home in the midst of a celebrated grassland region. Uncle Charlie had laid down on a couch in her home for his daily rest before the evening meal. Yet, Bea noticed that he hadn't taken off his shoes, which was unusual. She took it as a sign that he was abnormally tired, most likely a result of too many hours that day in the Kansas sun.

With the time to sit down for supper drawing near, she thought he'd fallen asleep, and she could see that he did not have his teeth in his mouth. So, she asked her grandson to fetch the teeth from Charlie's nearby trailer. When the boy returned, Charlie raised his head a bit and said: "Son, put the teeth right there." Complying, the youngster placed the dentures on a coffee table by the couch.

Those were the last words ever uttered by Harris.

2

Legendary Pond Creek

A fter the violence finally ebbed, writers went to great lengths to paint a picture for readers of the land named after the most famous creek in Illinois.

Charles Gibson North declared in *Master Detective* magazine that the Pond Creek region not only was a "desolate land," but also "a slash of primitive beauty."

Reporter James Sprehe observed in the *St. Louis Post-Dispatch* that the "prevailing force in the wild and beautiful Pond Creek bottoms now is the heavy foliage which has moved in to cover all traces of human violence."

"Without a guide or prior knowledge of the incidents," Sprehe concluded, "it would be impossible to guess what had occurred...."

But, there would be no guide, no road maps, to direct curiosity seekers to the sites where events made the bottoms a legend in criminal lore. As the years went on, and the twentieth century gave way to the new millennium, one only could muster images of the ghosts of the Shelton brothers and Charles Bryan Harris among the scrub timber, hedgerows, rusted oil pumps and scattered farm fields of the Pond Creek neighborhood.

For Harris, there had been no divorcing his twisted saga from the bottoms southeast of the Wayne County seat of Fairfield.

By 1965, when a late-in-life prison sentence finally forced departure from his home territory, Harris had done more than his share to carve the name of Pond Creek into the lexicon of infamy.

To link lawbreaking with Pond Creek in the same breath as accounts of the hellfire doings in East St. Louis, or of the bloodthirsty pillaging at not too distant Cave in Rock, might have seemed unfair. Such a sordid image hardly squared with many of the down-to-earth farmers, oilmen and others earning an honest living in the bottoms of Wayne County.

Yet, there was no erasing the memory of the Sheltons, the onetime kings of downstate Illinois racketeering, and their nemesis, Harris, the person primarily linked to the demise of the brothers. Forever, they remained the main actors in the Pond Creek drama, a tragedy revolving around sensational murders, arson in the dead of night and fractured loyalties that pitted neighbors and even family members against each other.

Newspapers spellbound readers for years by headlining the rise and fall of Carl, Big Earl and Bernie Shelton, who emerged from rural obscurity to reach the top of their chosen profession. As for Harris, he made enough front pages in the last half of his life to become a household name—mainly by the monikers of Black Charlie or Blackie.

He couldn't escape being identified as the last of the big-name gangsters south of Chicago, a tag he ridiculed as a gross exaggeration. Hardly ever did he admit or own up to any of the wrongdoing linked to him.

To the contrary, Harris saw himself as far from a mobster. He claimed that he was a descendant of southern Illinois pioneers, a man proud to be among those labeled Pond creekers. He savored a sometime reputation as a defender of his neighbors against bullying by the Sheltons. While acknowledging missteps in his life, he avowed to never have wanted anything more than to be a respected farmer and land owner.

One thing was certain. Harris was a very dapper man of the land and a fellow capable of considerable charm. He was a veritable clothes-horse, which further accentuated the impression of him, religiously held by many, of a mannerly gentleman. He was of short stature, but it hardly diminished his appeal to women—single or married. He made a game of romance throughout his long life, and its end often resulted in conquest.

His best years—which assuredly did not include the more than twenty-five years consumed by three prison terms—were among those spent in the Pond Creek bottoms. At least, for a while, they were trouble free.

Leech Township

Harris' backyard was Leech Township, the place where Pond Creek ended in the Little Wabash River. Actually, the creek was a rather unremarkable waterway that meandered in a southeasterly direction from Fairfield to the river. It traversed first Barnhill Township and then part of Leech, the township in the southeastern corner of Wayne. Way back, before dredging occurred, the creek spawned a region of ponds. Hence, the given name was easy to understand.

For persons looking on the brighter side of life, the history of Leech Township was extolled in an affectionate portrait drawn by writer Lelah Allison in a manuscript published in 1954.

She painted a picture of the first white settlers in Wayne County, hardy folks largely from Kentucky, Tennessee and other points south, who put down roots in what was to become Leech Township.

They were people who literally lived off the land and the abundance of wild animals, not unlike the early residents of other southern Illinois counties. Food was not scarce. Wild animals, berries, honey and nuts were plentiful. Some men killed four or five bears in a week. When a deer was harvested, it was not uncommon to skin it, fill the skin with honey, tie the ends together and lug all of it home. When corn was grown (raising wheat in the early days was difficult), corn meal and hominy supplemented the diet surrounding venison and bear meat.

As for apparel, Allison wrote that "clothes were made from deer hides; sometimes the skins, after being tanned, were dyed red or yellow. The women knew how to make dyes from herbs in the forest. When tanned properly, the skin was soft and pliable. Women wore narrow deer skin skirts and deer skin blouses. Men wore…breeches of buckskin. The moccasins were made of bear hide, the fur turned inward in the winter."

Fireplaces were a big deal because they were the only means for heating a cabin and cooking. Since just flint and tinder were available to make fires, they had to be kept burning all the time. A crisis might set in if a settler "happened to be so unfortunate as to let his fire die out," Allison noted.

In that case, she added, "he went to a neighbor, if he had one, to borrow some coals to restart his fire."

An interesting part of Allison's work covered the families instrumental in the settlement of Leech. It is here that the role of pioneering Harris family members came into play. In fact, the author cited the significant contribution of Charles Harris in delving into Harris family history. A photograph in the book showed a Harris family reunion around 1900—a pic that revealed little Charlie in his mother's lap. Another was of Charles Harris' home in the mid 1950s.

Allison pretty much romanticized life in Leech until the end of the document, when she acknowledged "troubles," some caused by "ignorance or viciousness." She mainly recounted heated differences over election contests as well as other disputes that she found common in most places.

However, she did mention, if only briefly, "more serious difficulties"— happenings "rare, not the usual thing." She alluded to murderous "machine gun play" in Leech "that caused the sensational reporters of the city papers to print long write-ups as if all in Leech carried guns, participated in gang warfare and lived on dirt roads in a backward state of civilization."

The killings of several of the Shelton brothers in particular, she lamented, provided fertile food "for those reporters who made Pond Creek a symbol of gangsterism, instead of…a thriving community of stable citizens…."

Nevertheless, she surely knew that a few bad apples were all that was needed to spoil a barrel.

3

Charlie's Roots

How ironic.

Charles Bryan Harris was born July 26, 1896. Exactly twelve years later, on July 26, 1908, President Theodore Roosevelt issued an order authorizing a small detective force in the United States Department of Justice that eventually would be called the Federal Bureau of Investigation. Besides sharing a birthday, Harris and the FBI would come to know each other quite well.

They didn't get acquainted, though, until many years down the road. By then, the world was far removed from the nineteenth century's final decade, the Gay Nineties, during which Wayne County farmer John Michael Harris' wife, Talitha, gave birth to little Charlie in the Pond Creek bottoms.

Charlie was one of John and Talitha's six children. As is frequently the case with the youngest in a large family, he was doted upon by his parents and his older siblings. This was saying a lot. When the offsprings of his mother and father by previous marriages were totaled, Charlie was the youngest of as many as twenty-two children.

Many of them, married by the time Charlie was born, remembered him as a polite and handsome boy. The lad, whose face one day would appear on FBI wanted posters, often was dressed for family outings in little velvet suits—modeled perhaps after the black velvet suits worn by Little Lord Fauntleroy, the hero of a popular children's novel at the time.

The Wayne County that Charlie knew as a boy, as he later related to Indiana's *Evansville Courier*, was "just peaceful farmland and open space." There was, in his words, "no roughness" as he rubbed shoulders with other young men in the county—including sons of another farm couple, Benjamin and Agnes Shelton. Harris even joined one or more of the Shelton brothers in Sunday school at the Union Church bordering the Pond Creek neighborhood.

Faith played a role in the life of Harris' parents. They were believers, what Harris called "religious people—not fanatics, but good, churchgoing people." He recalled to the *Courier* cold winter nights in his home when his father and an itinerant Baptist preacher hashed over the Bible in front of the fireplace.

For Charlie, though, religion was inconsequential in the long run. Sitting in a church pew on Sunday morning was not his cup of tea.

Freeda Williams, the wife of Fairfield automobile dealer Ray Williams, remembered once asking Charlie to join her and her husband at an upcoming revival at the First Baptist Church in the city. Several days later, Charlie told Ray Williams that this was the first time anyone had asked him to go to church since he had reached adulthood. However, he was a no-show.

More important to Harris than religion was his ancestry. Beyond claiming to be a descendant of southern Illinois pioneers, he insisted that his father's lineage was traceable to the first white settler in Wayne County. He was darn near right.

Based on various accounts, a man named Isaac Harris from Kentucky was credited with being the first white settler in what would become Wayne County. He achieved this distinction when he moved in 1814 to the area later designated as Leech Township to build a home for his family. The house, a one-room log cabin in which bear skins covered the dirt floor, was raised on a bluff at the west edge of the Little Wabash bottoms. A large spring at the foot of the bluff made the location very desirable. Subsequently, according to Lelah Allison's history, Isaac's property was identified as the Atteberry farm. By the 1950s, she added, the farm was in the hands of none other than Charlie Harris. And, the former site of Isaac's cabin was occupied by a white house in which Charlie resided.

Back to Isaac Harris. Before he settled permanently in Wayne, he and a brother, Gilham, had been in and out of the area for several years with herds of hogs. They had found the woods there to be a plentiful source of mast for the animals. However, at one point, Isaac had a quarrel with one of the Indians who often camped along the Little Wabash. Isaac killed the Indian, an unlawful act. This prompted Isaac to go on the lam for a spell; a period in which he fought with American partisans against the British in the War of 1812. With the end of the conflict in sight, Isaac accurately assumed that sufficient time had elapsed since the murder of the Indian for him to return safely to the Little Wabash area.

When he came back in 1814 to put down roots, he was accompanied by Gilham and another brother, Elijah. In the ensuing years, relatives of Isaac who would migrate to the county included a cousin, Thomas Harris. He'd live there with a son, Alexander.

More important to the Charlie Harris story, though, was another son of Thomas named John Michael, who was born May 8, 1829, at Bowling Green, Kentucky. Records uncovered by Doris Bland Thompson, a Fairfield genealogist, revealed the last name of John Michael's mother to be Newton.

On December 18, 1879, John Michael married Talitha Jane (Jennie) Standerfer in Wayne County, twenty-seven years after he moved to the county and settled in Leech Township. It was the second marriage for each. He was fifty years old at the time and she was twenty.

Talitha was born August 28, 1859, in Illinois' rural Moultrie County, a daughter of Joseph Standerfer and a woman, apparently his wife, named Sarah Moon. Said to be part Cherokee, Talitha endeavored throughout her life to play down the Native American part of her ancestry. She initially was married to Isaac S. Harris, a grandson of the original white settler in Wayne. They had two children, Lemuel and Elizabeth (and a daughter, Rosa, who died in infancy), before Isaac's death in 1878. Lemuel, born nineteen years before Charlie, would be Charlie's favorite brother, although they were only half brothers.

Late in Charlie's life, people reportedly observed tears in his eyes when he thought of Lem, who died in 1953. Lem, a farmer and musician who could make a French horn talk, got the highest accolade from Charlie. "I loved Lem," he related to the *Courier*. "He was a good man."

As for John Michael Harris, his first wife was Sarah Courtney Parker, who was born February 26, 1836, in Tennessee and died March 24, 1877, in Wayne County. Before she was buried there in Union Cemetery, it was her union with John that produced enough half brothers and half sisters to enable Charlie to state that he was, overall, the youngest of twenty-two children.

Prior to the birth of Charlie, John Michael and Talitha had a daughter, Cora Mabel, and three sons, Cleveland, James and Oliver. They also had a daughter who died in early childhood. Cora, who preferred to be called by her middle name, was the only one of the five—outside of Charlie—to remain in Wayne County as an adult. Five years older than Charlie, she remained close to him through thick and thin.

Charlie's early years were dominated by a journey hard enough to test the endurance of any family. As he recounted to Bea Riley in later years, his parents decided to leave Leech Township to start a new life in Oklahoma. This occurred about 1900, when Oklahoma still was a territory not yet admitted to statehood.

Departing southern Illinois for a region still very much part of the Wild West was a bold move possibly motivated, at least in part, by economics. The reputation of the 1890s as a decade of excitement, upheaval and striking contradictions with little parallel never diminished. Charlie Harris entered a world of wrenching and even violent tensions between the rich and poor, capitalists and labor, and white and black. The plight of the poor grew even more serious during a severe economic depression that began in 1893 and lasted for four years.

Not to be forgotten was that the early 1890s marked the end of the Gilded Age; years in which the spread of the Industrial Revolution to the United States created factory-dominated cities populated by an ethnically diverse working class beholden to super rich industrialists and financiers. They were people with names like Vanderbilt, Rockefeller, Carnegie and J. P. Morgan. Fair or not, they were lambasted by critics as "robber barons." No question, they were an elite class that overpowered society with sometimes ruthless success and shady financial manipulations.

Among the many having a tough go of it in the 1890s were independent farmers, individuals such as John Michael Harris and others in southern Illinois. Even before the onset of the depression, the average farmer in the country was typically isolated and, consequently, denied many advantages and conveniences that fellow Americans in the growing urban centers took for granted.

The Gay Nineties were anything but that for the large number of farmers hit by mortgage foreclosures. By the decade's end, the number of persons working farms as tenants rather than owners had noticeably increased. This was not surprising in view of the thousands of business failures, hundreds of bank closures and numerous railroad bankruptcies during the depression. For a while, bands of jobless men, loosely organized into "armies," roamed the countryside.

Some historians questioned, in looking back, whether the labeling of the 1890s as the Gay Nineties was a misnomer. (The appellation was not coined until the 1920s, the so-called Jazz Age, when many Americans living it up seemed to recall the 1890s as a similar period of merriment and frivolity. And, this notion probably was true for many of the wealthy.)

On the brighter side, only three years before Charlie Harris was born America and the rest of the civilized world were titillated by the massive Columbian Exposition in Chicago, the 1893 world's fair commemorating (one year late) the four hundredth anniversary of the discovery of America. In 1898, two years after his birth, the self-confidence and expansionist aims of the United States were bolstered by the decisive defeat of Spain in the Spanish-American War.

In the end, though, the extravagant displays of wealth in the Gay Nineties increasingly accentuated the widening disparities between the haves and the have-nots. This led, on the political front, to the emergence of a strong populist movement, which primarily represented agrarian interests and advocated the free coinage of silver and government control of monopolies.

Charlie was born during the one term of Illinois' first liberal governor, Democrat John Peter Altgeld. In years to come, Charlie would take pride in his own middle name because he insisted it came from William Jennings Bryan, the "Great Commoner" from nearby Salem, Illinois, who ran unsuccessfully for president in 1896. Bryan, who overall lost three presidential elections as the nominee of the Democratic Party, claimed to be a candidate of the ordinary American.

John and Talitha Harris seemingly were among the droves looking for a greener pasture as the 1890s wound down. Most leaving farms went to the big cities and sought industrial jobs. John and Talitha not only bucked this trend by heading for Oklahoma, but they did so in an amazing manner.

Since access to one of those newfangled motorized vehicles was out of the question, the family embarked on its trek in a covered wagon pulled by oxen. The glorified years of covered wagons heading west may have been past, but the Harris clan still faced many of the same rigors encountered by earlier pioneers traversing hundreds of miles by such a lumbering mode of transportation.

There was much to consider. Planning ahead had to take into account weather conditions, food for the family and oxen and supplies of water. Dealing with the myriad of housekeeping chores starting before daylight and continuing into the night, the family was lucky to make ten to fifteen miles per day. When rain turned the roads and trails into mud, advancing one mile in a day was an accomplishment.

Passing through still sparsely populated regions, the journey offered virtually none of the amenities then available to travelers in some other parts of the country. Since much of the terrain between southern Illinois and Oklahoma was rough, riding in the wagon was so bumpy that older members of the family usually walked behind it.

As the trek neared an end, its stress was heightened when several Indians on horseback followed the wagon in what the family feared to be a threatening manner. The Indians did not scatter until Cleveland Harris fired a shot over their heads.

The family finally reached its destination of Tulsa, a small town originally part of Indian Territory near the Arkansas River. Within a few years after the Harris family arrived, Tulsa—which only had been incorporated since 1898—began its explosion into an oil boomtown. John and Talitha were not around for the excitement, though. After a short time in the city on the edge of the Great Plains, they decided it was not what they wanted and returned to Wayne County.

Still, the exposure to the American West whetted the appetite of some family members for that part of the country. Oliver Harris returned to Oklahoma and served at Tulsa as an Indian agent. His brother Jim ended up in Arizona, where the places he called home included Phoenix and a small mining town, most likely Globe or Miami. It was in Phoenix that Jim and his wife Molly ran a hotel.

Charlie too was not immune to the lure of the West. As a young man, he spent time in Arizona, much of it under less than pleasant circumstances. But, that is getting ahead of the story.

After returning to Wayne County from Oklahoma, John Michael structured a comfortable existence for his family. According to a 1910 atlas and plat book, he owned 110 acres in Leech Township. He was identified in the records as a retired farmer, and also as a man who had served as a school director and highway commissioner.

In the years after his parents came back from Oklahoma, Charlie attended the Wagner School, a one-room schoolhouse in Pond Creek.

Records showed that he did not attend school consistently, but rather off and on. Helping out on the family farm often took precedence over schooling, a matter substantiated by records in Wayne County's School District 101. Harris was shown to be seventeen years old, but doing only sixth grade work in 1913-1914, his final period in school. All in all, his grades were about average in spelling, writing, grammar and geography. Reading and arithmetic were another matter. He was graded very poorly in reading, while simultaneously receiving a perfect rating in arithmetic.

His strong command of numbers was recognized early on in his years at Wagner. For instance, his second grade teacher, Wylie Keen, gave him one of the top grades in the school in arithmetic in 1905-1906. In 1908-1909, when he was a fifth grader, his grades were far from the best in school—with one exception. In a report that year, teacher Frank Harlan gave him the highest score in geography.

Irrespective of his decent marks, Charlie never graduated from grade school. As with so many other situations later in his life, a good thing came to an abrupt end.

4

A Young Man in Trouble

No question, there were telltale signs that Charlie might be the black sheep of his family.

If recollections were accurate, the young man from Pond Creek was good-looking, captivating and hot-tempered. Smaller than many of his male contemporaries, he did not stack up as a bully—unlike several of the Shelton brothers, his older friends in the neighborhood that he openly admired. Just the same, nobody picked on Harris, who early on exhibited the willingness to respond fearlessly to even the slightest provocation. He had a mean streak, alright, always hovering under that gentlemanly veneer. Yet, there were, and always would be, persons who saw only his courteous side.

His quicksilver temper was ignited easily, and it may have been the reason he was kicked out of the Wagner School during the 1913-1914 school year. One could not be sure, though, because the report of his teacher, Elma Karr, stated only that Charlie "was expelled at (the) end of (the) 4th month."

His tempestuous nature led to early run-ins with the law. He still may have been in grade school—since he was seventeen years old when expelled—at the time of one incident. Local law officers wanted to question him about something. When they approached him at the Union Church, of all places, he jumped into a horse-drawn buggy and departed in an all-out gallop. A chase ensued, but to no avail. Charlie was not to be overtaken in the narrow byways of Pond Creek that he knew so well. Those who swear to the veracity of the story could not say if Harris ever was called to account for the escapade.

As Harris moved through his teenage years, his surface urbanity camouflaged a penchant for mischief, a rascality that might be affable but also capable of irresponsibility. Rebelliousness underneath the skin endeared him to some other young men in Wayne County, a number of which were to find themselves hunkered down in trenches in Europe after the United States entered World War I.

Joining the military would cross Charlie's mind as the war continued, but his latter days as a teen were spent as a budding farmer and young buck sampling the pleasures of more than a few younger women in his backyard. Back then, he already fancied himself as a ladies' man, and he showed enough makings of an aspiring Don Juan to back it up.

There was one young gal, though, who captured his permanent attention. She was Lelah J. Smith, a daughter of William A. and Martha Eva Hodge Smith, a Leech Township farm couple. His affection for her was apparently mutual because they were married February 14, 1915, when Charlie was eighteen years old and she sixteen. On August 10, 1916, they had a son, Howard W. Harris.

The marriage did not last.

During the same month that their son was born, Harris skipped out on Lelah. He left not only his wife, but also Illinois. His destination was Arizona, a state only admitted to the Union in 1912; a vast land of desert and mountains with a relatively handful of people scattered in dusty crossroad settlements, copper mining towns and whistle-stops on railroads. The image of Arizona in the minds of many Americans was of a place where hard-riding cowboys took off after Indians and where the sun sank slowly behind gigantic saguaro cactuses. In truth, when Harris' self-professed "urge to roam" took him to Arizona, the state had a lot of folks who could recall real fights with Apaches.

Harris' first years in Arizona were spent in Phoenix and the mining region to its east. Although far from a large city then, Phoenix was the commercial center for that part of the country, as well as the site of Harris brother Jim's hotel. In Charlie's words, he endeavored to earn his own living out there as "a common laborer."

During 1918, the course of his life in Arizona changed markedly. Interestingly enough, Harris' depiction of that period contrasted sharply with the picture painted by public records still available for scrutiny many years later.

According to a 1983 story in the *New Harmony Times*, an Indiana newspaper, Harris related in an interview with James (Harry) Linville, a retired barber and historian, that he tired of making a living as a laborer in Arizona and decided to return to the Midwest—but to Detroit instead of Wayne County.

Six years earlier, he was quoted in the *Evansville Courier* as saying that he joined the navy in July 1918 in Phoenix. Maria Pojeta, the reporter interviewing Harris, went on to write that he "enlisted for the duration of World War I" and subsequently was discharged when the armistice ending the fighting was signed in November 1918. After that, she wrote, he traveled for several years before ending up in 1922 in Detroit, where he said he became a carpenter's apprentice.

Harris did indeed wind up living in Detroit in the early 1920s. However, he omitted in these interviews revelation of a major interlude in his life before leaving Arizona. Evidence of this discrepancy surfaced after his wife Lelah sued December 16, 1918, in Wayne County Circuit Court for divorce and custody of their son.

A petition in support of Lelah's filing charged that Harris had deserted her and neglected to contribute anything toward the support of her and little Howard. Even though Harris left her shortly after Howard's birth, he must have stayed around long enough for her to contend in the petition that Charlie was a person who used "profane and indecent language in the hearing and presence" of the baby boy. Moreover, she claimed, her husband simply was "a man of bad habits."

Harris never responded to the divorce action, and a document filed with the circuit court on January 20, 1919, gave the reason. In an affidavit or sworn statement, submitted to the court the day before it granted Lelah the divorce and custody of the youngster, she stated that she had been informed by a law enforcement authority in Phoenix that Harris was incarcerated at the time in the state penal system in Arizona.

This was news to folks in Wayne County, with the possible exception of certain family members who—while aware of the imprisonment—had not disclosed it publicly. Harris himself never talked about it openly. From the start, his incarceration in Arizona was, and would remain, well-closeted.

So, what transpired in the desert state that landed him behind bars?

Documents in the History and Archives Division of the Arizona State Library in Phoenix reveal that Harris was arrested and charged with felonious "assault by means likely to produce great bodily harm" as a result of a clash with a Phoenix police officer August 15, 1918.

Asked about the accusation during the author's visit to her Kansas home in 2008, Bea Riley said that, to the best of her memory, Charlie had signed up for the navy in mid-1918. A few days before he was to report for duty, she said, he was visiting a woman in a house she occupied in Phoenix. Without warning, two men entered the residence. The intruders were not recognized by Harris or the woman. One made the mistake of attempting to manhandle Harris. Reacting, Harris produced a knife and plunged it into the man.

"He (Harris) cut the fellow up pretty bad, or so I understood," said Bea. "But, I never really knew much more about it."

Just as she mentioned, Harris was shown by archival records to have joined the navy not long before the incident. Facing induction into the military as World War I entered its final months, he opted to enroll as an apprentice seaman in the United States Naval Reserve Force. He was to have entered active duty shortly after the day of the stabbing, but the arrest curtailed his military service. He was discharged, as he told the Evansville newspaper later in his life, but the records do not indicate whether his release was honorable.

The prosecution's version of the altercation, as spelled out in files of the superior court for Maricopa County (the seat of which is Phoenix), contended the following:

On the day of the alleged felony, Phoenix cops Lew Mickey and Roscoe Broyles, both in plain clothes, were staking out a house used as a residence by Myrtle Thorner Swartz—described in the prosecution's statement of facts as "a notorious woman." They were said to be enforcing a Phoenix ordinance, approved in 1916, that made it unlawful for "any person or persons to occupy any room or premise for the purposes of fornication or adultery or other immoral practices." Violation of the ordinance was a misdemeanor.

Mickey and Broyles saw Harris and Myrtle enter the house. Several minutes later, the policemen entered the place and arrested them for purported flouting of the ordinance. The pair was ordered to accompany the officers to a police station.

At that juncture, according to the statement, "Harris suddenly drove a knife into the side of Mickey, stabbing him severely, without any warning, and without any cause whatsoever." It was added that Mickey recovered from the stabbing after a short time.

Harris pled not guilty to the assault, and the case went to trial before a jury in the superior court.

He was defended by attorney Hubert W. Clark, who argued vigorously that the arrest of Harris was illegal. Mickey was not, in Clark's words, "clothed with due and legal process...the crime for which the defendant was to be arrested was a misdemeanor, if anything at all, and the arrest was made in the night time and without a warrant."

Clark also maintained that Mickey started the rough stuff by slugging Harris in the eye, forcing Charlie to protect himself with the knife. Therefore, Harris "did not use any more force than was necessary to repel the illegal arrest," Clark insisted.

The jury didn't buy the defense argument. It found Harris guilty of the assault charge December 10, 1918. Three days later, he was sentenced to a term of two to six years in the Arizona state prison at Florence. Prison records, held by the Pinal County Historical Society, show that he entered the prison on the last day of 1918—the start of the first of the three prison terms in his life.

The "description of convict" segment of the records described Harris (prisoner number 5263) as 5 feet, 5 inches tall, dark complected and weighing 141 pounds. Mention was made of several gold crowns or fillings in his upper front teeth, a noticeable feature of Harris' smile through the years. He was identified as a farmer and sailor, not as a laborer. It also was noted that he was a married man with one child, a person who could read and write and a user of tobacco (but not opium).

The prison at Florence, an early stagecoach stop and mining supply shipping center 65 miles east of Phoenix, was about a decade old when Harris arrived. The pen was built by inmates who lived in tents during its construction. It replaced the territorial prison at Yuma down by the Mexican border.

Penologists found Florence to be a distinct improvement over the conditions faced by inmates at Yuma. Nevertheless, the prison soon was known for its death chamber and a fearsome place called "the snakes." It was an underground cell for solitary confinement for unruly prisoners; a hellhole to be avoided even more so because of the reptiles that regularly slithered into it. Whether Harris spent any time there was questionable.

More likely, he was among the prisoners used as a cheap source of labor to build roads through nearby mountains. This at least may have been the case during a two-month stretch in 1919 when Harris was taken from the prison for incarceration at a place called the Clifton road camp.

The conviction of Harris was appealed to the Arizona Supreme Court after he arrived at Florence. However, in a ruling handed down in June 1919, D. L. Cunningham, the chief justice, said no grounds existed for a nullification of the guilty verdict in the lower court.

Harris remained in the prison until February 19, 1920, when he was paroled—some ten months shy of the two-year minimum sentence he'd been handed.

After Harris' release from Florence, the ensuing chapter of his life in Detroit would become embroiled in unlawful activity leading to his second prison term.

As noted earlier, Harris told the *Evansville Courier* in 1977 that his arrival in Detroit in 1922 followed several years of travel. There was no question he was living in Detroit in 1923—based on a legal document recorded in the clerk's office of the Wayne County Circuit Court.

The filing listed the heirs and amounts each received from the estate of Charlie's mother, Talitha, who passed away November 29, 1919, at the age of sixty (Harris' father, John Michael, died earlier that same year on January 17, a few months short of his ninetieth birthday). The estate, administered by Harris' brother, Oliver, provided the grand sum of $110 as Charlie's inheritance—and it was delivered to him January 20, 1923, in Detroit.

Harris went to Detroit to learn carpentry under the tutelage of Henry Vernon Sloan, whose wife, Emma, was Charlie's half sister.

An interesting twist during his early stage in the Motor City was the accompaniment of his second wife, who happened to be Myrtle Swartz— the woman of supposedly ill repute who was with him the day of his arrest in Phoenix. The time or place of their marriage could not be ascertained. Clearly she disliked the harsh winter climate of Detroit and wanted to return to warmer surroundings. Presumably, this meant either the copper boomtown of Miami, Arizona, where she'd spent part of her life, or Los Angeles, to where her parents had moved. When Charlie nixed leaving Detroit, she left without him, and the marriage ended in his second divorce.

Harris did seem to have reason to feel good about Detroit. Based on information he supplied to the *Courier*, he worked as an apprentice and then journeyman in Detroit's Local 19 of the carpenters' union. When Linville interviewed him, he said that he had achieved success as a master carpenter. He'd kept his nose to the grindstone in his trade, he contended, except for periodic visits to southern Illinois to see family and friends. Among those in the latter group was one or more of the Shelton brothers.

As the 1920s unfolded, the Shelton boys were no longer the poor young men that Harris had rubbed shoulders with in his boyhood days. The onset of Prohibition had spawned a new category of illegal business-men labeled bootleggers, and the Sheltons had established themselves vir-tually overnight as monarchs of the breed.

Who would have guessed before the onset of the 1920s that the Shel-tons would be among the decade's nationally recognized figures? Not in anyone's wildest imagination did the thought emerge that newspaper readers from coast to coast would devour details of the Sheltons' bloody exploits in establishing and maintaining a far-flung criminal empire.

Each decade in American history is a different story, but few featured the colorful energy and once unthinkable change of the 1920s. The sobri-quet of the Jazz Age or even Flapper Era certainly fit, but the nickname most cast in stone had to be the Roaring Twenties. Apt it was.

This was the decade that started off with a great surge of optimism— America's doughboys had come home in a sea of victorious confidence that they'd fought "the war to end all wars"—and ended on a disastrously sour note with the stock mark crash leading to the Great Depression. Before the downfall, though, unprecedented numbers believed that the possibilities of getting ahead were boundless, and although not everybody engaged in the proliferation of get-rich-quick schemes, the majority earnestly adhered to the title of the hit song "Look for the Silver Lining."

To celebrate the speculative spirit, which for a time had the well-to-do and less well-off looking more alike, Americans partied and partied. And how. Most noticeably, women no longer took a backseat. Finally allowed to vote nationally at the start of the decade, they were symbolized in the 1920s by flappers kicking up their heels in the Charleston or Black Bottom with hair bobbed, glittering skirts up to knees and, for the first time in public, cigarettes in hand. Booze, too.

Prohibition may have been a "noble" experiment seeking the betterment of society, but it was widely ignored. Banning the production and drinking of liquor actually led to an increase in its consumption and to general lawlessness. As never before, Americans of all classes openly and knowingly patronized crime by flooding speakeasies and other venues for illicit hooch.

Supplying the suddenly voracious thirst was big business; a requisite met by the emergence of organized crime on a grand scale. Its denizens became household names. Outstanding examples were Al Capone in Chicago and the Sheltons in downstate Illinois. Surprising numbers saw these individuals, not as villainous lawbreakers, but as heroes satisfying the public's appetite. As they fueled the alcoholic craze, the excitement of the gangsters' operations contributed greatly to the decade's moniker of the Roaring Twenties.

Guns, murder, corruption of public officials and, of course, greed were hallmarks of the networks ruled by Capone and the Sheltons. Yet, it was clear that these individuals were, if still outside the law, sound businessmen. To succeed, they employed armies of people necessary for the manufacture and distribution of the prohibited beverages. The black market in liquor also saw the importation of some of the best stuff from countries where it was made legally. Getting these spirits into the country was challenging, especially for gangsters like the Sheltons whose bootlegging empire in the heartland was far from the nation's borders.

It was a predicament that led Charlie Harris to serious involvement with the Sheltons.

Although not without their own stills, the Sheltons hardly could stock the city speakeasies and rural roadhouses in their territory without imported liquor. Much of it was smuggled into the country at isolated beaches on the Florida coast, often at the personal direction of Big Earl Shelton. Another major point of entry for the whiskey, wine and beer smuggling was the then bustling city of Detroit, sitting across the river by that same name from Canada.

As hard as it was to believe, some insisted that illegal liquor sales were second only to the growing automobile industry in spurring Detroit's economy. In the words of one commercial fisherman in the waters near Detroit, "I could make more money running one load of booze than I could in a year on the fishing boats."

Since Detroit was such a plum as a port for receiving the products legally manufactured by Canadian distilleries and breweries, the Sheltons had no hesitation about trying to secure a share of the pie. To do so, they— like other big-time bootleggers—needed a person on the scene to handle their interests—an individual they could trust. They felt they had their perfect man in Harris, their friend going back to years past in the Pond Creek neighborhood.

In later decades, Charlie talked sparingly of his years in Detroit in the 1920s. Furthermore, when he did, he denied working there for the Sheltons, insisting that he stuck to carpentry. In the 1977 interview with the *Courier*, he declared that he'd "never hauled booze for myself or anyone else."

And, he took offense at those describing him in his Detroit years as a "Shelton henchman" or "Shelton lieutenant" or even a "Shelton follower."

However, whatever the terminology, Harris did become the Sheltons' purchasing agent in Detroit. Shelton family sources told this author that he bought liquor shipments from Canada for distribution to the Sheltons' pubs. After the booze was secured, it was transported by Shelton men driving fast cars to East St. Louis and other Shelton operating points. Talk had it that Charlie himself sometimes wheeled one of the autos, but he contended he never left Detroit.

Because bootlegging in Detroit was so lucrative, individual or independent players like Harris faced risks on more than one front. The watchful eyes of Prohibition enforcement agents were everywhere. He also had to be wary of organized criminal groups like the ascending Purple Gang, an exceptionally violent mob of bootleggers and hijackers, mostly Jewish immigrants, who started out as a gang of young delinquents on Detroit's lower east side.

Besides bootlegging, the gang engaged in extortion, jewelry thefts and armed robberies. The outfit's name supposedly came from a conversation between two Detroit market owners, each a victim of the gang. The mob was rotten, one of the owners observed, "purple like the color of bad meat."

As the 1920s moved along, the gang set a standard for ruthlessness in killing untold numbers of rival gang members in wars to achieve supremacy in Detroit bootlegging. By the dawn of 1927, crime historians agreed, the Purple Gang was heading for control of Detroit's underworld. That's when the gang no longer might have tolerated the go-it-alone types, little guys like Harris operating as sort of free-lancers.

Nothing ever suggested, though, that Harris' dealings amounted to enough to attract the attention of the Purple Gang. Anyway, by the end of 1927, the year the gang completed its bloody march to the top, Harris was gone from Detroit.

For many Americans, 1927 was a year to remember for a lot more than bootlegging wars and the red-hot economy. Charles Lindbergh Jr., the "Lone Eagle," became an international hero by making the first nonstop, transatlantic flight from New York to Paris. New York Yankees' slugger Babe Ruth belted a then record 60 home runs in one season. The first successful full-length talkie, *The Jazz Singer* featuring Al Jolson, hit the movie screens. Stars Greta Garbo, Tom Mix and John Gilbert enthralled moviegoers, and the Ziegfeld Follies were all the rage.

But, 1927 was not kind to Harris. It would leave a scar on his relationship with the Sheltons. A searing memory not to be erased.

5

The Sheltons

"**P**eople never ask me if I've known any prominent citizens, any bankers, ministers or merchants," Charlie Harris lamented to a reporter late in his life. "They only ask if I've known the Sheltons."

There was no dodging the question, and there shouldn't have been. His interaction with the Shelton brothers defined Harris in the public eye during his elevation from criminal obscurity to a household name. While the exact extent of his involvement in the rise and fall of the Sheltons remained shrouded, the inexorable link of Harris to the brothers had all the makings, in the sad end, of a Greek tragedy.

After it was over, one had to marvel at the improbable success of the Sheltons in progressing from underdog farm boys in Wayne County to nationwide attention-getters. Even though they pulled it off through lawbreaking bathed in bloodshed, it was still the stuff of legends. Their story was a remarkable one, and Harris was part of it—despite his protestations to the contrary.

As best could be determined, Harris went to work for the Sheltons in Detroit in the mid-1920s. He was among many doing their bidding during one of the most sensational chapters in the Sheltons' rise to power in American bootlegging.

Numerous months, in a period running from late 1923 into early 1926, were scandalized in southern Illinois by an all-out war between the Ku

Klux Klan and bootleggers over the enforcement of Prohibition. Put simply, the KKK wanted Prohibition enforced and took it upon itself to try to attain this goal in vigilante fashion when many local law officers and duly elected officials refused to do so. Combating the Klansmen—with either open or covert approval of some authorities—were bootleg gangs orchestrated by the Sheltons and their lieutenants.

Each side was a formidable force, leading to killings, reigns of terror gripping whole towns, mobilization of troops to preserve order and widespread mayhem. When religious antagonism tied to hostility between immigrants and native-born citizens was added to the fire, the social ills from the Klan war lingered in downstate Illinois for years after the folks in white hoods and robes disappeared from the scene.

Nobody should have been surprised that southern Illinois, already known at the time for its coal belt, was as ripe for bootlegging as any other area. Matter of factitively speaking, drinking was part of life. Many who came up from Kentucky, Tennessee and other southern states left behind a culture ingrained with intoxicating liquor, much of it moonshine. Immigrants to southern Illinois from Europe carried with them their old world predilection for beer and wine. Coal towns routinely revolved around two institutions that were not exactly soul mates: saloons and churches.

Violence sparked by Prohibition flared in many parts of the United States, but the episodes in southern Illinois served to inflame a reputation for lawlessness already well in place. Not that long before the Klan conflict, the country was astounded by the Herrin Massacre in Williamson County. Occurring June 22, 1922, it claimed twenty-three victims, the bulk of them mine guards and strikebreakers slaughtered by striking miners and their sympathizers.

More than sensational, some of the encounters in the Klan war were downright bizarre. Take the time early in 1924 when Klansmen put Herrin's hospital under siege in an attempt to bring out bootlegger-allied officials who had taken refuge in the institution. During the onslaught, which lasted until military troops arrived and ordered the attackers to scatter, the Klansmen turned the hospital into a shooting gallery, shattering windows and sending terrified patients and medical personnel to the floor. Miraculously, nobody was hit by a bullet.

In the aftermath of this incident, Herrin was under a KKK dictatorship for a few days, with the fiery leader of the Klan forces, S. Glenn Young, presiding in city hall, acting as police chief, swearing in deputy policemen and ordering the arrests and jailing of certain persons. Conversely, more than a few towns in southern Illinois were under the heels of the gangsters for lengthy periods—days in which the dictums of Carl Shelton, the leader of his gang, carried more weight than the words of any mayor or cop.

Whole areas in southern Illinois were battlegrounds, and, as in any war, one side or the other would have an upper hand in each locale in the manner of an occupying army. Carl and his brothers felt they could do without the publicity they were receiving, but their main nemesis, Klan leader Young, relished the reputation as a controversial man of the hour that he gained virtually overnight.

Well built but short, Seth Glenn Young was aptly labeled the "little Napoleon" of Williamson County during his brief time on center stage. His appearance alone, with puttees and other military-like garb, the pearl-handled side arms and the submachine gun often in his grip, made him a standout as he led raids on roadhouses and stills. Young's arrogance, though, cemented his hatred by the Shelton boys and their followers.

So it was that on May 23, 1924, the Sheltons and several of their men ambushed Young and his wife as they were driving from Herrin to East St. Louis. Shots fired in the attack, which occurred after the Dodge touring car of the Sheltons caught up with Young's Lincoln sedan in the remote Kaskaskia River bottoms near Venedy, left Young wounded and his wife blinded. The Sheltons escaped prosecution for the attempted assassination, just as they were left off the hook or not prosecuted for their roles in other highly publicized gunfights in that period.

The Sheltons finally were free of Young when he died during a spectacular shoot-out in January 1925 at a hotel cigar store in Herrin. Also killed as a result of the clash were Ora Thomas—the chief deputy sheriff of Williamson County and a friend of the Sheltons—as well as two of Young's henchmen. This episode brought the Klan conflict in southern Illinois to a peak. Subsequently, the hostilities subsided, save for one more bloody gun battle in Herrin in early 1926 which, for all purposes, was the final attempted show of force by a declining Klan.

But, the demise of the KKK in the open warfare business soon was followed by another span of widespread terror in southern Illinois, a vicious gang war triggered by a fallout between the Sheltons and fellow bootlegger Charlie Birger of Saline County.

If anybody came close to challenging the Sheltons, especially Carl, for marquee billing among downstate Illinois gangsters in the 1920s, it was Birger. Born in Russia, Birger, a handsome Jew, was an enigmatic figure ingrained with Jekyll and Hyde qualities. A killer not hesitant to dispose of those impeding or perceived to be threatening his unlawful enterprises, Birger just as readily could demonstrate a winning folksiness and charitable demeanor.

Like Carl Shelton, Birger ingratiated himself with many law officers in his territory—not just with payoffs but also through an ability to preserve order among other lawless elements around, thereby curtailing loose ends otherwise spelling headaches for sheriffs and local police. Unquestionably, most of the lesser lights in lawbreaking dreaded the Sheltons or Birger in the 1920s more than they did the fellows with badges.

Judging by the unending fascination of the public with the Shelton-Birger conflict, later generations might have been surprised to learn that the clash lasted only a matter of months—from the summer of 1926 into the early days of 1927. However, it was time enough for Americans to see nefarious reputations further cemented and more than one new twist introduced into gangsterism. Besides the heavy body count on both sides, the Sheltons directed an unparalleled civilian bombing raid on Birger's Shady Rest headquarters, and each gang converted a truck into a homemade tank. These war wagons sparked both amusement and fear as they lumbered over narrow southern Illinois highways. No doubt, newspaper readers couldn't wait each day to read about the latest high jinks in the war.

Back in the fight against the Klan, the Sheltons and Birger were allies against a common enemy. When the KKK subsided, the bootleggers and other assorted scofflaws appeared to have carte blanche to expand their undertakings in downstate Illinois, including illegal gambling.

Yet, the tenuous alliance of the gangsters could not help but be strained as each became free to cast greedy eyes on new territory. For Birger that meant, among other things, pursuits in parts of Williamson County long staked out by the Sheltons. At the same time, the Sheltons surmised that some of Birger's haunts no longer were off limits to them.

Still, sorting out the exact reason or reasons for the Shelton-Birger split was difficult. Fallouts among gangsters were common throughout the country, and the coveting by one outfit of another's domain usually was the main motive.

In the Shelton-Birger imbroglio, though, additional reasons were cited. One centered around a woman named Helen Holbrook, a buxom babe with money who lived in a mansion in Shawneetown and who could not resist sexual liaisons with gangsters. Strong rumor had it that Holbrook, while involved with Birger, shacked up with Carl Shelton when Birger was in Florida buying liquor. Certainly it was true that Carl, like his younger friend Charlie Harris, fancied himself as a ladies' man.

Irrespective of what inflamed the feud, scorekeepers had to conclude that the Sheltons won the war after Birger was hanged in 1928 at Benton, Illinois, for the shooting death of Shelton ally Joe Adams, the mayor of nearby West City (a crime that Birger did not commit but orchestrated).

With Birger out of the way, and having put several major criminal trials and a short prison stay in their past, the Sheltons were at the top of their game at the end of the 1920s.

Their reputations had been even more enhanced by the gauntlets they had survived. They appeared fearsome and extremely calculating, and suddenly they had no more challengers. They had more on their plates than they ever could have imagined in their wildest dreams during their early years in Wayne County.

In bootlegging alone, they were the undisputed kingpins of the trade in downstate Illinois; so secure in their hold on their widespread territory that the Capone organization in Chicago kept at a respectful distance. They became big wholesalers, middlemen acquiring shipments of booze and reselling them for a tremendous profit. The business required a payroll of drivers and guards for the cars, trucks and secret storehouses. A need also existed for individuals to represent Shelton interests in the garnering or receipt of illegal beverages away from Illinois—folks such as Harris in places like Detroit.

In sizing up the history of the Shelton gang, 1930 well may have been the year that Carl, Earl and Bernie reached a zenith in fame and fortune. At least, that seemed to be the conclusion in a report three decades after the onset of Prohibition by a special United States Senate committee to investigate organized crime chaired by Senator Estes Kefauver of Tennessee.

"A careful estimate of their income at the peak of their success in 1930," the committee reported, "was that they were collecting $2,000,000 a year from slot machines, $1,500,000 from handbooks and $1,000,000 from other gambling, such as dice...and $250,000 from vice. Estimates were that they had collected approximately $5,000,000 a year, and after paying for protection and other costs of operation, the Sheltons netted between $1,500,000 and $2,000,000 each year." Two points had to be made about the findings. First, the income listed from vice was questionable in that the brothers maintained they avoided drug dealing and prostitution. Second, the committee listed no money from bootlegging, even though the Sheltons were world-beaters at it.

From 1930 on, for at least two more decades, the Sheltons remained in the public eye. They encountered highs and lows. Their base in East St. Louis eroded in the 1930s with the end of Prohibition and their failure in attempting to gain a foothold in labor racketeering. They rebounded during World War II when they gained power up north in wide-open Peoria, Illinois. That was their last hurrah; their final time to ride high before their precipitous downfall via murders and family denigration. Many viewed the windup for the Sheltons as apt retribution, assumably including those who subscribed to the onetime characterization of the Shelton gang by *The Saturday Evening Post* as America's "bloodiest."

Calling the Sheltons the bloodiest guys in the criminality born out of Prohibition may have been an exaggeration given the high numbers of casualties tied to bootlegging in Chicago and other parts of the United States. Without argument, though, the brothers were adept at exploiting the societal maelstrom or turbulence triggered by Prohibition, and violence was a means to that end.

A great number of lives were affected, some destroyed, by the Sheltons. There were on one hand the otherwise respectful citizens who enjoyed the fruits of the Shelton endeavors. Then there were those directly involved with the boys—either through working for them or standing in their way. For the obstructionists, the end often was unfortunate. Even many succumbing to a place in the world of the Sheltons paid a price. Charlie Harris was one of them, or at least he liked to think so.

Harris even maintained that the Sheltons stuck him with the nickname Black Charlie, which he disdained. He viewed it as a put-down, although he usually only smiled when addressed as Black Charlie or, sometimes, as Blackie. (Another explanation for the moniker, according to a few old-timers, was that, as Harris was growing up, two Charlie Harrises lived in

Pond Creek. One, redheaded and light skinned, was called Sandy Charlie. The other was dubbed Black Charlie because of his dark hair and swarthy complexion.)

Of those whose lives were touched by the Sheltons, Harris was one of the few who knew the brothers up close. More than being aware of where they came from, he had a good idea of the likes and dislikes of each, of their individual character traits.

Carl, Earl and Bernie, the hierarchy of their gang, were three of the seven children of Ben and Agnes Shelton growing to adulthood. Of the five boys, Roy, the oldest, spent a good part of his life in prison for offenses apart from those of his brothers' gang. The other son, Dalta, was a farmer with no connection to the headline-making activities of his brothers. The youngest of the seven children were daughters Hazel Katherine and Lula. Unlike Katherine, Lula would be vulnerable to the trouble encompassing the family at the end of its road in Illinois.

For the most part, Ben and Agnes were associated with the little village of Merriam, five miles east of Fairfield, where they worked their share of largely unproductive tracts in addition to tilling acreage in or near river bottoms in the area.

Ben had the reputation of a decent, God-fearing man, an individual ashamed of the course in life of most of his sons. One of those who admired Ben was none other than Harris. He himself called the Shelton family patriarch God-fearing during a taped interview in the late 1970s, a period when Harris was an inmate at the Illinois prison at Vienna.

"I think Mr. Shelton was a good, God-fearing man," said Harris. "If he wasn't, he was sure deceitful, because he lived, to the best of my knowledge, a good Christian life." In Harris' words, Ben "prayed as good a prayer as you would ever want to hear in church."

To Harris, Ben was Uncle Ben Shelton. Although they were not related, Harris said he called Ben uncle "with respect to his age and because so many people called him uncle."

If Ben had a problem, Harris observed, it was "just that he had no control over those boys."

Likewise, Agnes Shelton appeared to have little control over her sons. Her husband was another matter. She was a strong-willed person who wore the pants in the marriage. A holy terror when upset, she was given a wide berth by Ben and others as she struggled for years to keep her family's head above water. As remembered by ones who knew her, she could be disdainful toward those who saw her gangster sons as criminals because, to Agnes, her boys really were not bad fellows.

Financial insecurity dissipated for Agnes and her husband in their later years, but they shunned any showiness that might have been possible as a result of the money raked in by their sons. Beginning in the early 1900s and continuing through and beyond the heyday of the Shelton gang, Ben and Agnes called home an unpretentious house where the Merriam Road crossed State Highway 15. There was nothing fancy about their lifestyle.

In their younger days, the sons of Ben and Agnes helped their father with farm chores. But, neighbors also recalled them as troublemakers and bullies who learned to handle guns early in life. Carl, Earl and Roy, and maybe Bernie too, gave coal mining a try. However, as opposed to so many other young guys in southern Illinois, they didn't hang around the mines very long, believing there were better ways to make money.

So it was that Carl, Earl and Bernie shifted their focus from the coal fields to East St. Louis, where they got their hands on a saloon in roughly the same time frame as the onset of Prohibition (which began January 20, 1920). It was there—in that rough and tumble industrialized city with a wicked underbelly by the Mississippi River—that the Sheltons soon displayed a ready knack for running up illegal liquor from the south, not only for their own place, but for other bars in town as well.

Subsequent events put the Sheltons on the map of public recognition. First off, by rapidly expanding their bootlegging beyond East St. Louis, the brothers could claim authority within a few years over the distribution of booze in a broad terrain that eventually included much of Illinois south of Peoria. Next, as noted earlier in this chapter, their reputation further skyrocketed as a result of their leadership in the bootleggers' war against the KKK. And that was followed by their volatile clash with Birger.

One thing that kept tongues wagging was the differing perceptions of Carl, Earl and Bernie.

All recognized that Carl was the leader of the gang. The second oldest of the five Shelton boys, he was handsome, attractive to women, likable and capable of gracious sophistication, if only superficially. He and

Earl were reliable to do business with, and both were pleasant enough as long as matters went their way. When they didn't, the ruthless side of Carl emerged with a murderous cunning, a quality found in every big-time mobster.

Clearly, Carl maneuvered with a velvet glove whenever he could, or until a situation dictated otherwise. Besides supplying the brains for his gang, he was its ambassador, a role he played well.

Earl, or Big Earl as he was known, had enough ornery craftiness to make him as dangerous as Carl. But, he much preferred tending to business accounts, an area in which he was notably proficient during his rum-running days and in his aboveboard, successful dealings later in life. Besides not coveting notoriety, Earl was always a farm kid at heart.

Bernard, or Bernie, was another story. The youngest of the boys, he was a tough cookie from the get-go, frequently surly and armed with a hair-trigger temper. Unlike the others, he was a practitioner of the shoot first and talk afterward school. Understandably, he was quite successful in convincing saloon keepers supplied by the Sheltons to also purchase protection from the brothers—protection from not only the law but also other bootleggers as ambitious as the Sheltons.

Caring little what people thought, Bernie's priorities, according to one who knew him well, were to have "good clothes, a big automobile, gaudy diamonds and to go out with a gal and have a hell of a time." He accomplished every bit of this, and always with a .45-caliber automatic stuck under his belt. He just never craved the across-the-board respectability sought by Carl.

When the assorted talents of Carl, Bernie and Big Earl were combined under one roof, it was easy to see that the Sheltons were able to ward off virtually any challenge to their illegal empire by rival lawbreakers. Actually, there were few gangsters in Illinois south of Chicago with the wide name recognition or talents of the Sheltons.

One who might have given Carl Shelton a run for the money, had things turned out differently, was racketeer John Looney of Rock Island, Illinois, another widely known city of dubious repute on the Mississippi.

Looney's ignoble career flourished in two stages, the first in the early 1900s when he presided over a vice network that also encompassed the old haven of sin dubbed Bucktown in Davenport, the Iowa city across the

Mississippi. Looney's crime lordship had several uncommon twists. He was a practicing lawyer and, even more unusual for a gangster, he started a newspaper, *The Rock Island News*. Besides throwing the paper into bitter competition with its rival, *The Rock Island Argus*, which Looney figured was out to get him, he used the *News* to recklessly slur people he considered his enemies.

At least once, in 1912, the success of Looney and his followers in spurring riotous turmoil in Rock Island forced Governor Charles Deneen to dispatch National Guard troops to the city as it was placed under martial law. Afterward, Looney left Rock Island and did not return until 1921, when he embarked on his second period as a crime potentate.

That stint as criminal king of the hill lasted only a few years—during the same span in which the Shelton brothers were beginning to make their name in southern Illinois. On this go-around, Looney ruled bootlegging, brothels and gambling in a region extending from the Wisconsin border to a point far south of Rock Island. As the Sheltons would do, Looney became adept at extorting "protection" money from businesses to help defray the payoff costs in securing immunity from police and other officials for unlawful activities.

However, Looney had nothing near the staying power of the Sheltons. In 1925, he first was convicted of conspiring to protect wagering, prostitution and illegal booze trafficking in Rock Island, and then, in another trial, he was found guilty of murder. After his release in 1934 from a term in Illinois' Stateville prison, he lived as a broken man until his death in 1942—a year in which the Sheltons were cementing their hold on Peoria's underworld.

In the territory more closely associated with the Sheltons, only the gangs in St. Louis were as familiar to the public as the brothers. In the 1920s, and off and on in following years, the Sheltons had dealings with these mobs, as well as with certain individual racketeers in the Missouri metropolis. It wasn't always hunky-dory.

Gangland-speaking, St. Louis was or had been the home of Egan's Rats, the Hogans, the Cuckoos, the Russo outfit and some vicious Italian mobsters. Naturally, they all desired a piece of the lucrative action during Prohibition on the East Side, the slang name for St. Clair and Madison, the Illinois counties across the Mississippi from St. Louis and solid Shelton turf. More than once, Carl Shelton maneuvered successfully to blunt attempted incursions into the East Side by the St. Louisans, a matter of no small doing.

The gang getting along best with the Sheltons, for a time, was the one with the silly name, Cuckoo. The report by the Kefauver panel pointed out that part of the Cuckoo bunch "worked with the Shelton gang as guards for stills, (and) guards for trucks hauling bootleg liquor, and performed other duties incident to large-scale crime operations."

Nationally, the best known of the St. Louis gangs during the Roaring Twenties was Egan's Rats, a band of thugs mainly coming out of the poor Irish immigrant enclave of "Kerry Patch" north of downtown St. Louis. When the gang finally fell apart in the mid-1920s, many of its members who had escaped prison went on their own to commit robberies, kidnappings and contract murders throughout the Midwest.

One ex-Rat, Fred (Killer) Burke, an early user of submachine guns in bank stickups, turned up as a hired killer for Al Capone in the late 1920s and reportedly was among those taking part in the infamous St. Valentine's Day Massacre of seven men in Chicago in 1929. Burke also teamed up with another former Rat, Milford Jones, in kidnappings, often of rival Italian mobsters. For a while, Burke and Jones based their "snatch racket" in Detroit.

Two other erstwhile Rats, Pete and Thomas Licavoli, found their way to Detroit and set up the River Gang, a bootlegging outfit that gained a share of the booze running in the Motor City as well as Toledo, Ohio. This was possible since room for more players in the hierarchy of Detroit crime opened up in the early 1930s with the self- destruction of the ruling Purple Gang through internal quarrels and jealousies.

All considered, Detroit was host to some of the biggest names in American criminal history during the 1920s and afterward: The Purple Gang; The River Gang; Fred Burke; Milford Jones; and numerous others.

Obviously, the lexicon of standouts in Detroit lawlessness never included Charlie Harris. To have heard him tell it, he was not even a two-bit player. Maybe not exactly an innocent bystander, but close to it.

He never owned up to what befell him in Detroit.

6

Guilty in Detroit

H arris insisted that Detroit bootlegger Patrick Walsh was a snake in the grass, and that he had no idea what the hell Walsh was talking about when he claimed to have sold whiskey to Harris. If he was guilty of anything, Harris later held, it was letting himself be duped by the Shelton brothers, whom he felt had betrayed him. Their trickery, he was convinced, cost him precious years of freedom.

Walsh was a key witness against Harris in a counterfeit money conviction in 1927 that landed Charlie back behind bars, this time in the federal penitentiary at Leavenworth, Kansas.

Try as hard as he might, Harris failed to unravel the case against him put together by prosecutors in United States District Court in Detroit.

They charged the following:

On December 12, 1926, Harris visited Walsh's house on Sixteenth Street in Detroit between 8 and 8:30 P.M. to arrange a purchase of whiskey. The following night, Harris returned to Walsh's home and parked his car in the garage. The liquor then was brought from the upper floor of the residence and loaded into the auto by Harris, Walsh and a young man working for Walsh. After that, Harris handed Walsh $1,280 in currency.

When Walsh attempted to deposit the money in the Peninsular State Bank in Detroit, he was told it was counterfeit by teller Thomas Wolfenden and Claude Shafer, the manager of the facility.

Subsequently, on January 21, 1927, the then thirty-year-old Harris requested lodging at a Detroit rooming house ran by a woman named Mrs. Alma Harl. She assigned Harris to a room on the second floor. The next day, Harris was arrested around noon while seated at Mrs. Harl's dining room table. He was charged in a multiple-count indictment with possession and passing of phony dough.

The case against Harris was bolstered, prosecutors continued, by a discovery made by William Spriggs, a Detroit police officer and cousin of Mrs. Harl. Spriggs said that, on a visit to the rooming house by himself and another Detroit cop two days after Harris' arrest, he discovered counterfeit bills in the room briefly occupied by Harris. He said the fake money was visible in an envelope in a slightly opened drawer of a dresser. According to Spriggs and Mrs. Harl, the room had not been occupied since the arrest of Harris.

Spriggs' finding, the prosecution concluded, left no doubt about Harris' culpability. The feds rested their case.

Consequently, Harris was found guilty in a trial before a jury May 11, 1927, conducted during a session at which two United States district judges, Arthur J. Tuttle and Charles C. Simons, were present. On the same day, Simons sentenced Harris to a ten-year term in Leavenworth and fined him $5,000.

Harris steadfastly denied his guilt, insisting that the witnesses for the prosecution—Walsh and his young helper along with Mrs. Harl and Spriggs—were downright liars.

The only thing admitted by Harris was his arrest at Mrs. Harl's place when he showed up for a noon meal. He denied occupying a room there, thus making it impossible for him to know of fake money being discovered in the upstairs room.

Harris labored for years to refute the case against him. However, the day eventually arrived when he acknowledged having dough sent by the Sheltons in his possession in Detroit. The money was not intended for the purchase of illegal booze, he held, but for other unspecified business dealings. He also maintained that he had no idea the money was counterfeit, stressing he never assumed the Sheltons would have pulled such a stunt on him.

The feeling of being deceived by the brothers stuck in his craw—although he did not completely sever his friendship with them until sometime after the completion of his stay in Leavenworth.

Not long after the start of his imprisonment, Harris began to mount a vigorous attempt to have his conviction set aside in trying to secure approval by the federal court for a new trial. In support of this effort, he produced a number of affidavits or sworn statements from individuals that directly contravened the testimony of the prosecution witnesses.

Had these persons been given an opportunity to testify at his trial as rebuttal witnesses, Harris argued, he would have been acquitted of the charges against him. But, he contended that he was denied ample time to line up defense witnesses prior to the trial. He also claimed that he lacked competent legal counsel at the trial, a main assertion in his belief that he was railroaded from the time of his arrest through his conviction.

Harris spelled out his disgust with his legal representation in the written argument supporting his move for a new trial. In the document, signed by Harris and part of the Detroit case records on file in Chicago at the Great Lakes Region office of the National Archives and Records Administration, he charged that the attorney "entered the case...unprepared, ignorant and disdainful of the interests of the defendant." It was not clear whether the unnamed lawyer was hired by Harris or appointed by the court. Rumor had it that the Sheltons funneled some money to Harris to help him defend himself. But, it could have been just that—a rumor.

Harris wanted the trial delayed until he could summon his witnesses. However, the court refused to grant a continuance because, in Harris' words, "the attorney did not fully inform the court that he was not prepared to proceed." The attorney failed to tell the court of potential defense witnesses, said Harris, and "what he expected to prove by them if they were present...."

He added that the lawyer "did not question the validity of the purported indictment on which defendant was convicted" and "recorded no exceptions to any evidence or proceedings."

The main thrust of Harris' appeal consisted of the sworn statements of individuals that, if true, could or should have exonerated him. Those submitting the affidavits included: Mrs. Corine Sanders; Miss Marie Murphy; Ira B. Ellis and his wife, Prinna; Ivan Windlan; Fred Windlan and his wife, Emma Lee; Mrs. William Gordier; and Miss Ella Gordier.

Mrs. Sanders and Miss Murphy, sisters living in Detroit, said in their statement, dated January 30, 1929, that Harris was in their company from late afternoon until about 10:30 P.M. on December 12, 1926. During that time, the three ate dinner together and went to a movie.

After leaving the sisters, Harris proceeded to an apartment on Third Street in Detroit occupied by Ira and Prinna Ellis, according to an affidavit signed by the two. Ira and Prinna, who noted that they had known Harris since his childhood, said that he stayed during the night at their place, "sleeping on a featherbed on the floor of their room."

Then, on the morning of the following day, December 13, they said Harris left their apartment in the company of her nephew, Ivan Windlan, for a drive to the home of Windlan's parents, Fred and Emma, in Anderson, Indiana.

Harris and Ivan arrived during the afternoon, and Harris spent the night at the Windlan home before departing the morning of December 14 for a visit to Illinois—according to affidavits from the three Windlans.

Based on these statements, Harris declared that Walsh clearly was lying when testifying that Harris visited him on the nights of December 12 and 13, 1926, to arrange and then carry out the pickup of the unlawful whiskey.

Harris also produced an affidavit that contradicted the testimony of Alma Harl. In a statement signed by the two women with the surname Gordier, they stipulated they were well acquainted with Harris, and that he spent the evening of January 21, 1927, in their Detroit apartment instead of the Harl boarding house. The Gordier affidavit substantiated Harris' claim that he never occupied a room at Mrs. Harl's place.

Another affidavit in defense of Harris was submitted by William O. McKee of Detroit, a builder who had employed Harris as a carpenter. In the words of McKee, "I had found him (Harris) straight and on the square in all his dealings and believed him innocent of the crime charged."

McKee was in the courtroom for Harris' trial. When he saw that Harris "would be forced to go to trial without witnesses for the defense," McKee stated, "I volunteered to go to the addresses he had given to ask those who could testify to hurry to the courtroom." However, McKee couldn't find any of the Detroit residents at home who later submitted statements in support of Harris.

In spite of the belated affidavits of those who apparently would have testified for Harris at his trial, the federal bench never granted Harris a new day in court. He was denied a retrial even though the affidavits were accompanied by detailed outlining of legal precedents purporting to show that the indictment, prosecution and conviction of Harris amounted to a miscarriage of justice.

Judging by the expertise evident in the filings supporting Harris' argument for a second trial, he seemingly had access to assistance or advice from one or more legally adept individuals after he went behind bars. The case records do not indicate whether the lawyerly aid was gratis. They do reveal that Harris depicted himself as "a poor person" lacking the funds to pay the court costs incurred in filing his appeal.

No reference was made to a belief by some that the Sheltons put up $1,500 to help Harris defend himself either before or after his trial. Of course, an equal number felt that the brothers simply abandoned Harris from day one, starting off by looking the other way as he dangled in the wind with the counterfeit money.

Documents in Leavenworth's file on Harris indicate that the Sheltons may not have totally ignored his plight in prison—at least in the beginning.

Shortly after entering Leavenworth two days following his conviction and sentencing, Harris began an exchange of telegrams with Edmund Burke, a prominent attorney in Springfield, Illinois. The Sheltons may have been responsible for the Burke contact since he also served as a defense lawyer for the brothers when they were facing charges in several major criminal trials.

A onetime state's attorney of Sangamon County, Burke had become a principal legal honcho for many well known individuals. Besides representing the Sheltons, Burke was a personal attorney for John L. Lewis, the legendary president of the United Mine Workers of America, during Lewis' years in Springfield.

A sign that Burke might be retained in Harris' appeal of his conviction was evident in a telegram dated August 7, 1927, to Charlie from his half brother, Lem Harris.

"Mr. Burke will be out to see you Wednesday," Lem said in the Western Union communiqué. "Rest assured that we will do all there is possible for you. Tell Mr. Burke that we will take care of the expenses on anything that you want him to do."

This was not the last time Harris would seek defense counsel in a criminal proceeding from a big-time lawyer. On each occasion, though, Harris did not end up with the help he desperately wanted.

If Burke remained in Harris' corner, Leavenworth records on Charlie don't show it. To the contrary, in a May 18, 1928, letter to a relative, Harris signified displeasure with Burke.

"Later," Harris wrote, "when I get back in court, I can...go after Burke, that attorney in Springfield...about taking...money and lieing (sic) to us."

It may have been that Harris was aided in preparing paperwork for his appeal by a person identified as Edward Harris of Michigan. In a letter to the warden of Leavenworth at the end of 1928, Emma Sloan, Harris' half sister in Detroit, said that Edward Harris, a nephew who was a law student, at least did "the preliminary work...necessary for presentation (of the appeal) to the court."

Irrespective of who may have done what in aiding Harris on his appeal, the undertaking went for naught.

Failure to win a retrial was par for the course for Charlie in the dreary confinement of Leavenworth. Bright spots were few and far between.

One good thing concerned his extremely itchy skin. Harris long had suffered from a vexing condition that left his skin cracking and often bleeding. Not long after Charlie entered the pen, C. A. Bennett, a doctor at the institution, treated the irritation with, first, a certain "brown salve" and then an "orange ointment" that eliminated the problem and left no scars. Charlie was grateful.

Another ray of sunshine occurred about the time he arrived at Leavenworth. The wearing of the traditional but belittling striped clothing by inmates was abandoned. Instead, they switched to standard uniforms of dark blue cotton.

It was something at least.

Leavenworth

L eavenworth may have been dubbed "The Big Top," but the penitentiary was far from a circus for Harris.

The United States Penitentiary at Leavenworth, Kansas, usually referred to as just Leavenworth, was the flagship of the federal prison system by the time Harris entered it May 13, 1927. He arrived the year after the attainment of a milestone in the pen's construction—the placement of a grand dome on top of the newly built administration building. Since the dome apparently reminded some of a big top, the main tent of a circus, Leavenworth's nickname was born.

This was not a big top featuring clowns, wild animals and trapeze artists. It enclosed a burgeoning inmate population that included a number of hardened criminals; persons widely known and justifiably feared. Harris would rub shoulders with many of them, including big city gangsters—a breed seldom found in Leavenworth before the enforcement of Prohibition in the 1920s.

However, for every Frank (Jelly) Nash or George (Machine Gun) Kelly, bank robbers of considerable repute and fellow prisoners of Harris, Leavenworth lodged mainly run-of-the-mill scofflaws. Harris recalled some of them later in asserting to the *Evansville Courier* that a surprising number of his fellow inmates really didn't seem to mind being cooped up there after the Great Depression triggered hard days. For them, prison apparently was preferable to skid row.

"I knew something was wrong out there," he related. Some guys, he observed, were "checked in…for little things, like stealing a car because they were tired of walking. Times were bad, and they were sent in for just little sentences."

The only upside of his years in Leavenworth, he acknowledged, was not having to face, for a good part of the 1930s, the economic pitfalls of the Depression. Still, that was hardly enough to diminish his hatred of incarceration.

Down the line, he repeatedly turned away questions about his Leavenworth stay, keeping almost as mum about it as he was about his earlier period behind bars in the prison at Florence, Arizona. That pen was about ten years old when Harris was admitted whereas Leavenworth first housed inmates twenty-four years before Charlie's confinement.

After being authorized by Congress, the construction of Leavenworth began in 1897 at a site near the Missouri River that was a little more than two miles from the army's historic Fort Leavenworth. The fort, the oldest military post in the country west of the Mississippi River, was founded in 1827 on bluffs overlooking the western bank of the Missouri.

Serving as a gateway to the western frontier, the fort's troops were responsible for keeping peace among the Indians, protecting the fur trade and safeguarding commerce as well as settlers heading west on the Santa Fe and Oregon trails. The nearness of the Santa Fe Trail to the Leavenworth prison was a prelude to another interesting twist in Harris' life in that the trail also ran close to Bea Riley's property in Kansas, where Charlie spent his final years.

Inmates from the military prison at Fort Leavenworth comprised the initial crew for the construction of the new Leavenworth penitentiary. Under the watchful eye of the pen's first warden, James W. French, the inmates were marched the two or so miles each day from the fort to the construction site. There, they were provided materials from a sawmill, brick plant and stone quarry.

At first, the project proceeded slowly because many of the convicts were not skilled in building trades. Escapes and attempted escapes by the forced laborers also interrupted progress. Finally, in 1903, enough of the prison was completed for the movement of the first inmates into what later would serve as the institution's laundry building.

All of the federal prisoners who had been at Fort Leavenworth were housed in the new penitentiary by 1906. Although the first full-fledged cell house had opened in 1904, it wasn't until 1919 that all of the cell blocks in the initial building plan were completed.

As for arrivals to Leavenworth in 1927, Harris still was among those in the small-timer club at that point in his life. That was hardly the case, though, for three other new inmates with Illinois roots: Carl, Earl and Bernie Shelton.

Early in 1927, the widely known trio had been convicted in a federal court trial in Quincy, Illinois, of pulling off a mail robbery in Collinsville, Illinois. Consequently, each was sentenced to serve twenty-five years in Leavenworth. But, on May 4, a little under three months after the brothers entered the prison, a federal judge ordered their release after it was discovered that perjured testimony had helped convict them.

Ironically, Harris entered the prison only nine days later. By then, the Sheltons were gone, eliminating the possibility of a tense reunion between Harris and the men whose shipment of counterfeit money to Detroit had landed him in Leavenworth.

While fate would have it that the paths of Harris and the Sheltons did not cross in Leavenworth, Charlie had opportunities to rub shoulders with plenty of other big-name criminals. Besides Frank Nash and George Kelly, some other notable Leavenworth residents included Harvey Bailey, Lloyd (Red) Barker and Thomas (Tommy) Holden. He might have seen Julius (Nicky) Arnstein, too. A pair of inmates with whom Harris definitely became acquainted were Frank (Buster) Wortman and Frank (Cotton) Eppelsheimer, the latter a former Egan mob stalwart. Years after their time together in Leavenworth, Harris would have renewed contact with both, especially Wortman who became a major mob boss in the St. Louis area.

As for Arnstein, Harris may or may not have met him because he entered Leavenworth about the time Arnstein was finishing three years of imprisonment for a conviction on a Wall Street bond theft charge. Arnstein, a professional gambler and con artist, stood out because he was married then to popular radio and film comedienne Fanny Brice.

Sticking up banks wasn't for Harris. If it had been, he might have learned a lot from Harvey Bailey, once regarded as the "dean" of American bank robbers. During the 1920s alone, Bailey was thought to have walked off with more than $1 million from bank heists.

Lloyd Barker was one of the four notorious sons of Ma Barker, a name evoking memories of the so-called public enemy era—years mainly in the early 1930s when the exploits of primarily Midwestern criminal gangs, led by the infamous John Dillinger and others, gripped the press and populace. Barker had landed in Leavenworth in 1922 after his arrest for a mail robbery at Baxter Springs, Kansas. Actually, his rap sheet was relatively short in comparison to those of his bandit brothers Herman, Arthur and Fred, especially the latter two. Bank robberies, murders and kidnappings were specialties of a gang led by Fred and Arthur and Alvin (Creepy) Karpis, who'd be formally tagged as Public Enemy Number One before his downfall.

After Lloyd Barker was paroled from Leavenworth in 1938, he went straight, serving as an army cook during World War II and then running a market in Denver. Nevertheless, when his wife murdered him in 1949, he died just as violently as his mother and brothers. Herman committed suicide after being stopped at a police roadblock; Arthur was killed while attempting to escape from the federal prison Alcatraz; and Fred was fatally wounded along with Ma in a gun battle with the FBI in Florida.

Thomas Holden, reputedly the first man named to the FBI's Ten Most Wanted list, entered Leavenworth a year after Harris. Two years later, in 1930, Holden and his mail train holdup partner, Francis Keating, escaped from the prison. Before being recaptured in 1932, they had joined Fred Barker, Karpis, Frank Nash (another Leavenworth escapee in 1930) and others in a series of spectacular bank robberies in the Midwest.

It was the recapture of Nash on June 16, 1933, at Hot Springs, Arkansas, that led to an epochal event in American crime fighting.

The day after his arrest, Nash was being returned to Leavenworth by a contingent of police officers and agents of the Bureau of Investigation (the name Federal Bureau of Investigation was not approved until a year later). As Nash and the others were climbing into two cars in the parking lot of Kansas City's Union Station, they were ambushed by three men with pistols and submachine guns. By the time the firing stopped, three of the officers and one of the agents, Raymond Caffery, were dead. Two of the other lawmen were wounded. Also killed was Nash, the person the attackers assumably were trying to free.

The shooters in the slaughter, dubbed the Kansas City Massacre, were identified by Bureau Director J. Edgar Hoover as onetime sheriff turned trigger-happy bad guy Verne Miller, bank robber Adam Richetti and his more famous partner in crime, Charles Arthur (Pretty Boy) Floyd. The event prompted passage by Congress of major crime legislation that, in granting the bureau a greatly expanded mandate and the authority to enforce it, gave its agents the right to carry firearms. Moreover, the murder or assault of a government agent was made a federal offense.

Understandably, the bloodbath at Union Station topped the country's sensational crime list in 1933. Another encounter that same year back in Illinois near Collinsville, although little publicized, would have long-term meaning for Harris. In that incident, Buster Wortman and Monroe (Blackie) Armes, then young thugs aligned with the Shelton gang, beat up federal agents raiding a Shelton still. As a result, each was convicted of assault and sentenced to ten years in Leavenworth.

Wortman proved to be a troublesome inmate, and, like the equally unruly Armes, would be transferred to the tougher penal atmosphere of Alcatraz, which sat on an island in San Francisco Bay. But, during his time at Leavenworth, Wortman and Harris hit it off. Certainly, to some degree, this was an outgrowth of the belief by both that each was taking a fall for the Sheltons. Sadly for the Sheltons, the day did arrive when the brothers sorely regretted the bonding of Harris and Wortman at Leavenworth.

As opposed to the recalcitrant Wortman, Harris appeared to pose few problems for the screws (guards) in his first years at Leavenworth. He wasn't a model prisoner—few were—but his rule violations were sporadic and mainly minor. Records on Leavenworth inmates filed at the National Archives' Central Plains Region office in Kansas City cite only two noteworthy infractions by Harris during his first three years behind bars.

He was written up March 14, 1928, for "shirking work and loafing" when guards caught him playing dominoes in a room where he was sent to install a sash cord. For this, he was docked four weeks of yard and amusement privileges. In November of that year, he was found fighting another inmate in the carpenter shop. This landed him in isolation and on a "restricted diet" for a few days.

However, for the most part, he kept his cool, apparently not wanting any negativity on his prison dossier in the early years that might reflect poorly on his chances of securing a new trial in Detroit. His pursuit of redemption in court was that of a man on a mission; a person preoccupied with a single goal. Although he did not succeed, his intensity and concentration in the undertaking seemed to impress prison officials.

His prospects took a turn for the better when his relatively good behavior was taken into account. He was assigned to a job in the office of the prison's chief clerk. Landing in such a spot was reserved for inmates in pretty good standing. If there was any doubt of that, it was erased in August 1930, when Harris was moved farther west to the federal road camp at Fort Riley, a storied army cavalry post on the Kansas River. Only inmates earning a degree of trust from prison officers made it to the work camp.

Fort Riley had been established in 1853 to buttress Fort Leavenworth in providing security for traffickers on the Santa Fe and Oregon trails. The fort was named in honor of Major Bennett Riley, who led the first military escort along the Santa Fe. So, here again, a phase of Charlie's life journey was occurring near the old trail to Santa Fe. After the Civil War, soldiers stationed at Fort Riley included a very aggressive and flamboyant cavalry commander named George Armstrong Custer.

Harris may have heard talk at the work camp about the killing of Custer and his troops by Sioux and Cheyenne warriors at the Little Bighorn battle in 1876. Conversant about history, he might have discussed the Custer annihilation with William Niederluecke, a work camp inmate whom Charlie had befriended back in the Leavenworth clerk's office—an individual destined to have an impact on Charlie's future.

As anticipated when Harris was switched to the camp, he carefully toed the line in discharging his duties. He soon felt sufficiently comfortable to launch a bid for parole, and he succeeded.

Harris was released from the camp December 15, 1930. As a parolee, his movements and activities were to be closely supervised. But, he could resume life in the outside world. He was able to breathe the air of freedom after more than three and a half years of incarceration and in spite of his failure to win a new trial.

At long last.

Back in the Can

He blew it. His freedom lasted exactly 407 days. After that, as a parole violator, he was back in Leavenworth.

Harris undoubtedly personified the old adage that some people simply cannot stand prosperity. His early period as a parolee had gone okay; he'd spent time in Kentucky and Mount Carmel, Illinois. They were places where he kept his nose clean and made a favorable impression on those he encountered.

Things went out the window, though, when he went to Chicago in September 1931 without the approval, or even knowledge, of his parole adviser. He was only in the Windy City a few days before he landed in hot water, thanks primarily to William Niederluecke, the inmate with whom he'd shared a tent back at the Fort Riley work camp.

Harris admitted going to Chicago at the request of Niederluecke, but insisted his goal in doing so was to get a job with one of the construction crews engaged in preparation work for the Century of Progress World's Fair, which was set to open in the metropolis in 1933.

When Niederluecke met Harris upon his arrival by train in Chicago, Harris later said he thought his friend also was out on parole. He did not know, he maintained, that Niederluecke actually had run away from the work camp six months after Charlie's parole, making him a prison escapee sought by the law.

Harris bunked with Niederluecke for three days in a room he was renting and then accompanied his friend to a new apartment at 4127 Ellis Avenue. There, after only a day or so, federal agents and Chicago police raided the apartment and arrested Harris along with Niederluecke. In searching the apartment, the cops found a briefcase belonging to Niederluecke that contained two revolvers and red bandannas. In a bit of an understatement, William A. McGrath, a federal probation officer, later reported that arresting officers had an "impression that the handkerchiefs were to be used to cover faces during a holdup."

McGrath related that in addition to insisting that he didn't know Niederluecke was a fugitive, Harris offered an explanation for the handguns. Harris maintained that "he was told by Niederluecke that he had secured them from a man to whom he made a loan."

Predictably, Harris' contention of innocence in the situation fell on deaf ears. Fred A. Howard, a federal probation officer for eastern Illinois who served as Harris' parole adviser, made it clear that Harris had not been granted permission to go to Chicago. And, Ray L. Huff, a parole supervisor in the Federal Bureau of Prisons, laid groundwork for the revocation of Harris' parole when writing to the United States Board of Parole in Washington that Harris, besides moving "without the knowledge of his parole adviser," was "found in company with a person of bad reputation...under suspicious circumstances."

Added McGrath, "It strikes me that Harris has seriously violated his parole. While he presents an alibi, it is serious conduct for any parolee."

The upshot? On January 26, 1932, Harris reentered Leavenworth.

Just as he did in appealing his conviction in Detroit, Harris argued that he was again a victim of railroading even before his cell door slammed shut. But, this time around, Harris was aided by a number of relatives and others as he lobbied for another parole or release from prison. Eventually, even the federal judge who'd sentenced him to Leavenworth put in plugs for executive clemency for Harris—an action considered not once but twice by the administration of President Franklin Delano Roosevelt.

Prison documents reveal that, shortly after his return to Leavenworth, one of the first relatives to seek a renewed parole for Harris was a half sister, Mrs. J. E. Inskeep, of Mount Carmel, a Wabash River town east of Wayne County. During much of his time out on parole, Harris had lived with her and worked on her properties.

He told Leavenworth authorities, in a written statement, that he did the following work on a house that belonged to her:

"Put on complete new roof. Put two coats of paint on outside and two on border. Painted two rooms inside with two coats. Repaired plaster of ceiling and walls of one room. Also papered this room and painted the woodwork with two coats. Tore away one chimney and repaired two more. Raised two rooms and put new sills and new foundation under them. Tore away porch and built new one. Rebuilt and painted an outhouse."

Harris, a veritable jack-of-all-trades, handy at more than carpentry, said he performed similar tasks at numerous other places in or around Mount Carmel. If released again, he noted, he would tend to more construction jobs or farming opportunities at Mount Carmel, some offered by Mrs. Inskeep.

In a follow-up, his half sister went to bat for him in a letter dated February 16, 1932, to N. R. Timmons, a parole officer at Leavenworth. If Harris "could be directly paroled to me," Mrs. Inskeep wrote, "I guarantee I will do my best to see that he keeps his parole to the letter."

Besides her own contact with Leavenworth authorities, Mrs. Inskeep persuaded others to follow suit. One was Kate J. Adams, the relief administrator of Wabash County, of which Mount Carmel was the seat of government. She alerted penal officers to a report regarding an interview with Mrs. Inskeep by Lucile Andrus, one of Adams' caseworkers.

In the opinion of Mrs. Inskeep, Andrus related, Harris "was a harmless, lovable boy and was merely made the 'goat' for a lot of bootleggers when sent up." The fall guy assertion showed that Harris' relatives were not hesitant to share his unending contention that the Sheltons bore the blame for his predicament.

Mrs. Inskeep also exhorted Emma Sloan to add her voice to the appeal for their half brother's release. By this time, Emma had left Detroit and moved to Newport, Kentucky, where Harris had spent the first three months of his parole helping Emma's husband Henry in his trucking business. Emma made a pitch to Timmons for the freeing of Charlie after she was told in a letter from Mrs. Inskeep that he had been "trying to do right."

According to what Mrs. Inskeep told Emma, Harris had been living the straight and narrow in Mount Carmel. As a result of his newfound virtuosity, Mrs. Inskeep wrote, he had "cut out all the girls but one" and, furthermore, had "never missed out one Sunday going to Sunday school."

His sudden interest in religious education also was mentioned in a letter to Timmons from Robert H. Cowling, a Mount Carmel furniture dealer. While Harris was in town, noted Cowling, he was "a more or less regular attendant" at "the Christian Sunday school here, of which I am the teacher."

Another Mount Carmel businessman, Cecil A. Canedy, urged a second parole for Harris, saying that Mrs. Inskeep needed him "so badly" because of her sickliness. He vouched for Harris' work ethic, noting that "I am (in) the paint and paper business, and I personally helped him select paper and paint suitable for…property that he repaired for her."

Even the Mount Carmel night police chief, M. E. Hastings, wanted Harris paroled again, telling Timmons that "during my time on the police force I have never had any trouble with this young man."

Still, notwithstanding the numerous testimonials in support of a renewed parole for Harris, the United States Board of Parole in the Department of Justice steadfastly refused to give him another shot at freedom. On one occasion, Irvin B. Tucker, a board member, reiterated in a letter February 3, 1933, to Leavenworth Warden F. G. Zerbst that the panel "felt that he (Harris) was unquestionably a parole violator and that his reparole for some time, at least, is incompatible with public interests."

Undeterred, Harris continued to press for another release, and it appeared, at one point, that the Leavenworth hierarchy was on his side. No question, F. L. Morrison, the deputy warden, and other officers seemed favorably impressed with Harris when they convened May 24, 1934, to evaluate his fitness for another chance at freedom.

After underscoring Charlie's good conduct since his return to Leavenworth, Morrison said on the record that "in an effort to determine Harris' attitude towards his present circumstances and future possibilities, I have had a rather lengthy talk with him. I am pleased to state…that I find this man to have a very splendid attitude…."

In a report at the conference, Timmons offered that Harris "has a rather likeable personality and expresses a proper attitude toward society." To Timmons, Harris was "of average intelligence and…mentally competent."

All agreed that Harris' work record was outstanding. Since returning to the prison, he had been assigned to the boiler room, the shoe factory and furniture shop. He received good marks in each. In the boiler room, H. C. Burgess, the chief engineer, characterized Harris as "an excellent worker…trustworthy, friendly, pleasant, energetic and faithful."

A few days before the May meeting to determine his future, Harris suffered painful burns on both hands when he came in contact with an electrical wire in the furniture workplace. When Harris himself was interviewed during the conference, the burns were noticeable.

"A short circuit, wasn't it?" Dr. D. E. Singleton, a prison psychiatrist, asked Harris.

"Yes, sir," Harris replied. "Insulation was bad, shorted out with conduit."

"Any permanent injuries?" queried Dr. Singleton.

Harris answered: "Dr. Nelson did not think so. It is brown on the back. There are some skin burns." (Dr. K. R. Nelson was the prison's chief medical officer.)

Subsequently, Dr. Singleton declared that he saw "no medical reason why he (Harris) would not be able to carry out the provisions of his parole." He also had determined earlier that Harris revealed "no outstanding mental abnormalities, and no evidence of any psychosis." Too, he said Harris had an intelligence quotient of 99, which as Timmons observed was average.

Dr. Singleton also suggested that Charlie's get-together with Niederluecke in Chicago might have been "accidental." This supposition followed the submission by Timmons of an affidavit by Niederluecke in which he contended that Harris had no knowledge that he, Niederluecke, was an escaped prisoner or that he had firearms.

The favorable impression of Harris was buttressed by prison librarian Oliver Isaac's impressive list of books, many fictional adventures, requested and read by Charlie. They included *The Three Musketeers* by Alexandre Dumas and *The Pathfinder* by frontier novelist James Fenimore Cooper. On the pragmatic side, he checked out a book about becoming an electrician.

All the good vibes generated by Harris went for naught, though. The federal parole board remained implacable in its denial of another release.

Nothing convinced the panel to change its mind, including a new plea for his parole in February 1935 by another of his half sisters, Viola Harris Johns of Pasadena, California.

She said a job awaited Charlie at a cafeteria run by her and a son, Robert. She stressed that they would be "pals" to Harris until "he makes good." The absence of reliable friends had been a bane for him, she argued, starting off with a father who was "too old to be bothered" when Charlie was born. She wrote to prison officials, in an obvious attempt to tug at their heartstrings, that John Michael Harris "must have been 80 or 85 years old" at the time of Charlie's birth. This was a bit of an exaggeration in that the father actually was sixty-seven at the time.

Viola received a reply from Timmons in which he said that "new and material evidence" needed to be submitted to the board for a reconsideration of its turndown of Harris. Even then, he cautioned, "I would not advise overoptimism as to the results."

Timmons' admonition was on target, judging by a letter to Harris in June 1935 from Arthur D. Wood, the parole board chairman. Wood declared in no uncertain words that "you have no one to blame for your present predicament except your own dear self." Apparently in response to the cafeteria job for Harris mentioned by Viola Johns, Wood stated that "offers of…employment do not constitute grounds for re-parole."

Moreover, perhaps prompted by annoyance at Harris' refusal to accept the board's stance against another parole, Wood had some unvarnished advice for Charlie.

"May I suggest," Wood wrote, "that you settle down and do your time in the same manner as others who have contributed to placing the parole system in general in bad repute by flagrant misconduct…."

Giving up was not in Harris' makeup.

Denied a renewed parole, he launched a second bid to the White House for the granting of executive clemency, a finding or show of mercy for Harris that would trigger his release. This undertaking was aided by yet another relative taking up his cause, Ellen Merritt Atkins of Decatur, Illinois. Ellen was a niece of Harris—only a few months younger than her uncle—who had written to the warden that "Charley is like a twin brother to me."

For a start, she enlisted support from Charles Simons, the federal jurist in Detroit who first dispatched Harris to Leavenworth. Earlier in 1933,

Simons had endorsed the initial but unsuccessful move by Harris for executive clemency. Now a federal appellate judge, Simons acquiesced to Ellen's plea for help by urging clemency in a letter to the Department of Justice November 19, 1935.

Since the return of Harris to prison after his parole violation, said Simons, "I understand...he has been a model prisoner, and (that) he and his friends and relatives give assurances that he will not again be found in company with the persons with whom he had been previously associated...."

"I think," Simons concluded, "the cause of justice has been fully satisfied."

The Simons communication was followed by similar recommendations for clemency from David A. Wolff, an assistant United States attorney in Detroit, and George F. Boos, the chief of the Treasury Department's Secret Service operation in the Motor City. Boos, whose office was familiar with the counterfeit money case against Harris, pointed out that he had received "letters of assurance from Mr. Harris that his conduct in the future will be exemplary...."

Ellen didn't stop with the honchos in Detroit. Leavenworth documents reveal that she appealed her uncle's continued incarceration to none other than President Roosevelt's wife, Eleanor. In turn, the First Lady forwarded a letter and petition in support of the Harris bid for freedom to the Department of Justice for evaluation. It was paperwork that had been sent to her by Ellen.

The reply wasn't what Charlie and his niece wanted.

Writing to Ellen on July 20, 1936, and to Mrs. Roosevelt two days later, a top department official said that, since it was not possible to restore the "good time" lost by Harris because of the parole violation, he most likely had to serve out his sentence.

Mrs. Roosevelt was informed that "the only recourse which Mrs. Atkins' uncle has is through executive clemency or reparole...." However, the letter to the First Lady added that both courses of action already had received "careful consideration."

Undaunted, Ellen decided to travel to Washington to plead in person for approval of clemency. To do so, she needed money. Harris wanted to finance her trip with $148 in funds earned by or credited to him in prison.

However, the Federal Bureau of Prisons ruled that a withdrawal from his kitty for that purpose was not permissible.

Furthermore, F. Lovell Bixby, the assistant director of the bureau, wrote to Leavenworth October 29, 1936, that "it is quite unlikely that anything at all would be accomplished by her (Ellen) coming to Washington, at least not until the pardon attorney had indicated that such a trip was desirable in order to clear up the case."

The air was cleared in a letter to Leavenworth June 5, 1937. In it, Daniel M. Lyons, a pardon attorney in the Department of Justice, stipulated that Harris' second application for executive clemency had been denied because "nothing has been presented which would warrant the department in resubmitting the case to the President."

In the end, Ellen Atkins was as stonewalled as the other relatives and friends of Harris in trying to get him out of Leavenworth before the end of his sentence. Her endeavor was even more complicated because she was refused permission to visit Harris in August 1936 to lay further strategy for the second bid for clemency. Charlie was in the prison doghouse—off limits to visitors.

She received this discouraging news in a letter from E. H. Eckholdt, the warden's secretary. He explained that Harris was "now under certain restrictions for disciplinary reasons, and will not be entitled to any visit for a period of three or four months."

Harris' splendid behavior since reentering Leavenworth—good enough to make him an almost model inmate—went down the drain April 29, 1936. He broke the rules that day by loafing at a hospital annex for the purpose of surreptitiously soliciting bets for a baseball gambling pool. Three months later, he stole a heavy cake of ice from the hospital and took it to his cell, another infraction. A month after that he landed in segregation after the discovery in his possession of a pocketknife from the shoe factory.

Before the end of that year, he was placed in isolation for mouthing off to Fred Scott, a guard. The screw caught Harris talking to three other inmates at the prison coal pile. Scott ordered Harris to break up the huddle, but Charlie refused and yelled "bullshit." Then, in further defiance, he shouted: "I not dummy up!"

His bent for running gaming on baseball got him in hot water again. On August 21, 1937, guard W. C. Rohman reported finding Harris with "a complete book layout" that included "odds on various games" and a "re-cord of amounts of bets made per day." Charlie argued that the stuff was left over from the previous year, but it covered the current season.

Macaroni, of all things, was an issue when guard Scott again got on Charlie's back in an incident October 19, 1937. Contending that Harris had become an agitator, Scott charged him with "trying to cause trouble" by summoning a waiter to fetch him a second helping of macaroni. Scott held that Harris knew this was a no-no, but that he wanted to disrupt meal-time decorum.

The desire for more macaroni was the final rule breaking by Harris. Two months and eight days later, on December 27, 1937, he said good-bye to Leavenworth. He was discharged more than seven months after his original ten-year sentence would have ended. The extra time was tacked on because of his parole violation.

He exited Leavenworth with only a few dollars in his pocket; his certificate of discharge identified him as a poor convict. In the document, signed by a United States commissioner, it was noted that Harris was unable to pay the $5,000 fine levied against him at his Detroit sentencing. Consequently, the certificate waived the payment as a condition for his release. In other respects, the certificate added, Harris had "complied with the requirements of the law" during his imprisonment.

He may have been destitute, but at least he was free. At forty-one years of age, he had a new chance to put his life together. People like Niederluecke were part of a past that would not be repeated, he assured Leavenworth officials and anyone else who'd listen. He was confident that sympathetic friends and relatives would aid in his resurrection.

True, his future would include a number of these persons, along with others who went from being friends to being enemies. And then there were those who were born during his years in Leavenworth.

One was Bea Riley, his dependable niece, who was born May 30, 1927, a daughter of Charlie's sister, Mabel.

Another was Betty Lou Shockley, born March 4, 1932, in Centralia, Illinois. She was a pretty daughter of John Shockley, an industrial worker and carpenter who'd served in the infantry in World War I, and his wife, Mattie.

There was Richard Cochran, born January 17, 1930, in Carmi, Illinois. He became a successful and highly respected attorney in Fairfield.

James Arthur Lawder Jr. of Murphysboro, Illinois, was another attorney who surfaced in Harris' future. He was born September 25, 1937, a son of a Jackson County treasurer.

And the list went on and on. Not all would regret meeting Charlie, but some surely did.

9

Return of the Wayward Son

She was ten years old on that very cold night shortly after Christmas 1937. She had begged to go ice skating not far from her Pond Creek neighborhood home, but her mother Mabel had said no. Ignoring her mom, she jumped from an upper story window of the house and made it undetected to the pond. After getting a delightful fill of gliding over the ice with her young friends, she returned home—to face the music.

Beatrice Bell knew that her strict mother would be hopping mad and that a whipping was likely. She was the youngest of Mabel's kids and the one always subject to more discipline than her older siblings.

But the rod was spared that evening. Beatrice could tell that Mabel was predictably angry when she came back to the house. However, her mother not only tried to hide the displeasure, but surprisingly remarked that she was not upset by Beatrice sneaking out to skate.

Beatrice soon recognized that her unexpected pardon was thanks to the presence of a man who'd arrived at the home while she was at the pond. Her instincts told her that the man did not want her to be punished. She sensed too that her mother had gotten the message that a licking for Beatrice would upset him.

The night signaled the start of a long and eventful relationship between Beatrice and the person who'd become her favorite uncle, Charlie

Harris. For her part, she'd grow to idolize him. He'd be much more than a safety buffer between her and the punishment her mother seemed eager to dispense.

Charlie became her protector against all comers. He insisted in years to come that she make something of herself, and he helped her do it. She was his favorite niece, and she honored their tie with loyalty to him through some very perilous days.

The virtual adoption of Beatrice by Harris was in no way a slap in the face for Mabel, his only full sister. People in the know recognized a loving trust between Charlie and Mabel, going back to her girlhood when she lavished attention on her cute younger brother who sometimes went out in Little Lord Fauntleroy garb.

There was no better sign of their closeness than the appearance of Charlie at Mabel's house the night of Beatrice's skate outing. He just had been released from Leavenworth, and Mabel's home was the place where he felt most welcome—the spot from which to once again pick up the pieces of his shattered life.

His return had a fortuitous side for Mabel. Part of her home was an old log house that needed renovation. Charlie wasted no time employing his carpentry skills to rebuild that section of the house. He'd gained a lot of construction know-how when he did property repairs for Mrs. Inskeep, his half sister in Mount Carmel, during his abbreviated parole from Leavenworth.

Everybody assented to the wish of Cora Harris to be called by her middle name, Mabel. Second only to Charlie, she was the child of Talitha and John Michael Harris who'd remain most familiar to Wayne countians. Born in Leech Township in 1891, she stayed in the county until her death in 1964. Cleve, Jim and Oliver, her other brothers, lived their lives away from southern Illinois.

Asked to describe Mabel when the author sat down with Beatrice in Elkhart in 2008, she recalled, first and foremost, that for many years her mother endured a hardscrabble life as she strove relentlessly to provide for her daughters and sons.

Beatrice, long known by then as Bea Riley, recollected that Mabel "would wear her (black) hair in long braids folded up over her head. In thinking back, I would describe her as nice looking and somewhat quiet.

She loved to square dance and, yes, would drink beer. But, I never saw my mother drunk."

The sharpest memory, though, was poverty. Mabel scraped to make money, working for the federal employment program called Works Progress Administration during the Depression and then spending years taking care of ailing people. She barely kept her family's head above water.

"Undeniably," related Beatrice, "we were poor as church mice. I wore hand-me-down clothes."

Bringing in dollars was complicated by the fact that Mabel didn't drive a car. Often, to reach the home of a person under her care, she hitched a ride with Beatrice on the back of Old Baldy, an over-the-hill mare that she rode around Pond Creek. (Horses would be an important part of Beatrice's life for decades. At least one, a little mare named Chicata, was bought later on for her by Charlie.)

During her early years in Pond Creek, Beatrice answered to the nickname "Jakie." To her classmates at the Windland School, which she attended for eight years, she was Beatrice (Jakie) Bell. This misled some folks because highway worker Virney Bell, the first husband of Mabel and father of Beatrice's older brothers and sisters, died in 1925, two years before Beatrice was born. Mabel gave birth to Beatrice by her second husband, farmer Ross Suddarth. When Beatrice was one year old, Mabel and Ross divorced. Mabel, who never married again, raised Beatrice for all practical purposes with the surname Bell.

Beatrice's childhood in Pond Creek was not unlike that of other kids in rural downstate Illinois. She was baptized in the Little Wabash River, which was not far from her home. The ritual may have been like a scene in a Norman Rockwell painting, but Beatrice never forgot thinking that "the preacher was going to drown me."

Youngsters in the country, Beatrice included, seldom ignored watermelon patches. One near Windland School was too inviting for Beatrice and a few friends to resist. It was on the farm of William Smith, whose daughter Lelah had been the first wife of Charlie Harris, and who by then was getting up in years. When Beatrice and cohorts raided the patch during a school day, an angry Smith appeared at Windland a short time later and complained loudly about the intrusion.

Beatrice recalled, "Prompted by old Mr. Smith, our teacher, Mr. Xanders, lined each of us up and gave us a whacking with a little switch. I didn't dare tell Mabel about it that night because that would have meant another whipping."

Another highlight of life in those years was the carnivals that came to Fairfield. These occasions are what spurred Beatrice's early awareness of the Shelton family. She and Little Carl, a son of Dalta Shelton, a brother of the gangsters, happily rode together on merry-go-rounds and other rides. To Beatrice, Little Carl was "such a cute little guy."

Mabel and Beatrice sometimes would forgo Old Baldy and walk to Fairfield. On the way, they might pass the house of Ma and Pa Shelton and see them moving around. Greetings seldom were exchanged, but that didn't cause Beatrice to think that problems existed between her family and the Sheltons. "To me," she said, "they were just neighbors."

One day she sensed something was wrong after accepting an offer by Dalta for a ride to her home in his car. In spite of the seemingly innocent lift, Beatrice was warned by her mother and Charlie to never again get into a vehicle with a Shelton.

As a teenager in the early 1940s, Beatrice became much more aware of budding hostility between the Sheltons and Harris, who finally was getting back on his feet economically. Those were years when she frequently was a passenger in automobiles driven by Charlie. Beatrice later suspected that seeing her youngest daughter tooling around with Charlie must have made Mabel very uneasy. Yet, her mother kept her anxiety to herself.

In truth, Beatrice could hardly suppress her own fear during the moments she and Charlie encountered Carl Shelton in the company of one or more of his brothers and his bodyguards.

"I knew, of course, they had machine guns in their cars." she said, "And, Charlie had his."

Nevertheless, she made it clear that "Carl Shelton was a real gentleman around me, just like Uncle Charlie was. Honestly speaking, Carl was a nice guy to talk to." But, she added, "you didn't want to do either one (Charlie or Carl) wrong."

Charlie enjoyed telling Beatrice, in a joking manner, that he felt safe with her in his car because "they (the Sheltons) wouldn't kill a kid." However, Beatrice never quite convinced herself that her uncle was saying this only in jest.

During the World War II years in the first half of the 1940s, Carl and Bernie Shelton spent much of the time up north in Peoria, Illinois. They had a tight grip on the unfettered gambling and other vices in the city; it also was the headquarters for their still vibrant network of largely unlawful enterprises in some other parts of downstate Illinois.

Yet, Carl and Bernie, especially Carl, had not abandoned Wayne County. Consequently, when Carl was back home checking on his considerable holdings of land and herds, Harris more than once dispatched Beatrice on horseback to "trot down to Shelton territory to see what Carl and his boys were doing."

"It was one way to check up on the Sheltons," she said, "and I guess it worked because, like Charlie told me, nobody would suspect anything about a young gal riding around on a horse."

The antipathy between Harris and the Sheltons was not evident in the first few years following Charlie's return from Leavenworth. More than one person sympathetic to the Sheltons insisted that the brothers, contrary to later denials by Harris, took steps to help him bounce back. For instance, these individuals asserted, the Sheltons played a positive role in helping him get his hands on some Pond Creek land. They also provided opportunities for him to make some bucks, including one job he held at the time of a fatal clash.

It happened in 1940. The episode propelled Harris' name into newspapers around the state for the first time. This was mainly because Carl Shelton, a longtime front-page figure, also was involved.

Carl had a passion for roller skating, so much so that he bought a portable rink that he'd circulate around towns in southern Illinois. His sister Lula operated it, and Harris was hired to help her. One had to keep in mind that, at this stage, Charlie still was regarded—at least by outside observers—as a Shelton follower.

Violence erupted on a day the rink was set up at Fairfield. The combatants were Harris and J. C. (Blackie) Anderson, an oil-field worker who had slapped around a niece of Harris. Charlie cornered Anderson at the rink, intending to give him a dose of his own medicine, but Anderson beat him to the punch by whipping out a knife and stabbing Harris. Carl, who was present, quickly tossed a gun to Harris to give him a better chance to defend himself.

Charlie, reeling from his injury, wildly fired more than one shot. Anderson was fatally wounded, and another bullet struck Carl Shelton in his chest. However, before striking Shelton, the bullet hit a steel spectacle case in his breast pocket, causing it to lose much of its force. To say Carl was incredibly lucky was an understatement.

While Anderson lay dead at the rink, Harris managed to reach Mabel's house even though he'd lost a lot of blood. Part of the blade from Anderson's knife had broken off and remained in his hip. Mabel undressed her brother, wrapped him in a sheet and had him stand in a tub. As she was washing blood off his body, a doctor and the law arrived.

The sawbones realized that the blade had to be removed from Harris without delay. He asked Beatrice to assist in the extraction, and she complied. As the blade was being pulled out, Charlie—who'd been given nothing to blunt the pain—fainted.

Afterward, Beatrice recalled the doctor telling her she should become a nurse. She took the admonition to heart. Nursing would be her calling, a course encouraged by Harris and initially inspired, she said, "by what I experienced that unforgettable day in helping to remove that broken blade."

Law officers at first moved to pin Anderson's killing on Harris, but he escaped prosecution after they remembered the clumps of blood at Mabel's house and agreed that Harris fired at Anderson in self-defense. In the meantime, Carl was ready to post bond for Harris—just in case he might be jailed while the law decided what to do with him.

The rink encounter, three years after Charlie's departure from prison, occurred during a period when a degree of amiability still seemed to exist, outwardly at least, between Harris and the Sheltons.

By many accounts, Harris nurtured a grudge against the brothers born out of his Detroit conviction and imprisonment. There'd never be complete forgiveness of the Sheltons, he had confided to Mabel and others close to him, for the decade of his life that he fervently believed they had cost him. However, his resentment was held in check as he waited to see the extent to which the Sheltons supported him after his return from Leavenworth. His biding of the time was interpreted by some as a mellowing of his indignation toward the Sheltons, a willingness to let bygones be bygones.

As noted earlier, there were individuals who felt the Sheltons did what they could for Harris. He never came to see it that way, believing instead that their penny-ante jobs were far short of what they owed him. Some predicted it would be only a matter of time before Charlie, tempestuous as he was, no longer could restrain the ill will he bore.

Then came the so-called final straw.

Harris' smoldering grudge passed a point of no return when he concluded that Carl had tried to swindle or undercut him on the ownership of some Wayne County farmland.

At issue was a tract in Pond Creek adjoining Shelton property and also along farm acreage that Harris already had acquired and begun to work. Charlie desired the tract, which was obtainable because of back taxes owed. According to Harris partisans, he agreed to let Carl help facilitate the transaction. However, based on their version, Carl was deceitful in offering to cooperate with Harris because he really wanted to keep Charlie at bay while taking steps to add the ground to his own large domain.

Details of what exactly transpired remained murky, but the incident brought to an abrupt end a fragile truce between Harris and Carl. Charlie's enmity toward Carl and the other Sheltons now was out in the open, and it would become a feud that would color—if not totally dominate—the worlds of the Sheltons and Harris. People would be forced to take a side, and middle grounders would be hard to find.

Harris pursued his end of the animus in several directions. One involved the emergence of Charlie—no longer a pauper and with farming interests of his own—as an accepted member of the Pond Creek community. The other took him away from his home territory. The mid-1940s saw the end of World War II and a big change in Harris' associations. It was suddenly not uncommon to see Charlie in the presence of gangster Buster Wortman and his henchmen in their East St. Louis hangouts. After the conclusion of his penal years, Wortman quickly had turned away from his old bosses, the Sheltons, and taken up with St. Louis and Chicago mobsters increasingly at odds with the Sheltons.

Back on the Wayne County front of the feud, Harris found fertile ground for taking out his hostility toward the Sheltons.

Carl, to a great extent, and Big Earl, to at least some degree, had used dough reaped from both their criminal and lawful enterprises to amass considerable land holdings. Especially with Carl, the acreage went beyond Wayne (for example, he also had acquired land in neighboring Hamilton County). But, it was in the Pond Creek area that the extensive Shelton properties garnered the most attention.

Hardly any Pond creeker was oblivious to the impact of the Sheltons. On the one hand, Carl and Big Earl were known to share their gains with a number of the poorer families in Pond Creek and other parts of Wayne County by picking up bills for funerals, groceries, medical care, restaurant meals and so on. Carl, most notably, was regarded in some quarters as a twentieth century Robin Hood.

There was another side to the coin, though. The bullishness displayed by the Shelton boys as poor teenagers still was in play as Carl, Big Earl and Bernie attained prominence. Bernie became more of a no-show in Wayne County during the 1940s, but Earl remained there for the most part, and Carl still spent plenty of time in the county even though he had a home in Peoria. In fact, as World War II was winding down in 1945, Carl started to gradually ease out of the rackets and appear even more frequently in his home area.

One reason was the election of a reform mayor in Peoria. Another was that Carl was increasingly drawn to the tending of his prosperous farming, cattle and other business interests, including his Basin Oil Well Service Company in oil-rich Wayne County. But, that's where a rub occurred.

Carl may have been accorded celebrity status by some, but not by a number of his Pond Creek neighbors. They found Carl to be overbearing in squabble after squabble over allegations that Carl allowed his cattle to roam at large while continuing to engage in land-grabbing schemes. The Sheltons also were accused, among other things, of trying to impose a levy of a few cents per bushel on loads of soybeans and other crops carted past their places.

The scenario was ripe for a needed counterbalance to the fear fostered by Shelton potency. Shelton hegemony had to be breached; its bubble had to be pricked. A remedy was at hand. The setting couldn't be more ready-made for Harris, a person no longer shaking in his boots at the specter of challenging the family. Besides, Charlie was close to an extended family of Pond creekers known as the Harris-Vaughan clan.

His open hostility to the Sheltons had been mounting. His track record also suggested to some that he might have an underside as sinister as that of the gangster brothers. For that reason, he too made some uneasy. But, the Shelton problem was paramount, and none but loyal Shelton followers objected when Harris seized the opportunity to project himself as a protector of Pond Creek farmers at odds with the Sheltons.

Standing up to the brothers—which primarily meant confronting Carl, the principal target of Charlie's ire—cast him in a role comparable to that of a tough western hero galloping into town to save the good folks from entrenched bad guys.

Carl might not have taken Harris' comeuppance as fully as he should have, a serious miscalculation. Still, it was evident that Charlie had made himself a burr under the Shelton saddle. It had to be galling for Carl to realize that Harris was making headway in the intimidation game.

After all, the quarrel was unfolding at a time when Carl still was recognized as the best known gangster in Illinois south of the Chicago area. True, he'd acceded to the request of the new Peoria mayor to leave the city, but Bernie had refused to do so and was attempting to run the gang's stake in downstate racketeering from his tavern on the outskirts of Peoria.

With Carl apparently having retreated from active leadership of the brothers' string of illicit and legitimate businesses, organized crime figures in Chicago and St. Louis reasoned that the time finally had arrived to take over Shelton territory. One entrusted to lead the way was Buster Wortman.

Carl obviously detected the intended encroachment by the big city guys. Being Carl Shelton, he also had to know that Harris was palling around with Wortman. Putting two and two together was not difficult. Wortman had befriended Charlie at Leavenworth and, like Harris, had become an enemy of the Sheltons in the years after prison.

Carl seldom was caught off guard in his heyday. Spotting enemies like Charlie and Buster together in the old days would have spurred him to eliminate any threat. That was then. The Carl Shelton entering the late 1940s was coasting on his reputation, perhaps not caring much at all about a perception that he was going soft.

He still had the luxury of bodyguards, a protection Charlie Harris didn't have. He also had laid the groundwork for living like a wealthy country gentleman in the Pond Creek neighborhood, one place where he always felt safe.

10

Buster

He looked a lot like the movie actor Lee Marvin, who portrayed a slew of rough characters on the screen. But, Frank (Buster) Wortman was a real-life tough guy. Running the underworld in downstate Illinois required brains, cunning, scorn for authorities and, above all, two-fisted swagger. Wortman was fully qualified.

Buster was among the last of Illinois' dying breed of big-time mobsters south of Chicago. The heavily populated Illinois counties of St. Clair and Madison, across the Mississippi from St. Louis, were organized crime strongholds. Called the East Side, they were the heart of the fiefdom of Wortman, an undisputed gangland boss by the late 1940s.

Wortman also was part of a broader picture in which he served as the principal representative or agent in the greater St. Louis area for the almighty crime syndicate in Chicago nurtured by Al Capone.

Supposedly, Wortman had met Capone years before Buster was riding high. By the time Wortman was king of the hill in his part of the world, Capone was incapacitated and near death. The syndicate figure who dealt with Wortman was Jake (Greasy Thumb) Guzik, a Capone loyalist and accounting genius who filled Capone's shoes in the latter part of the 1940s and early 1950s. That period included the best years of Wortman's rule.

Wortman's passage from the scene in the 1960s left Harris—long known by then as Black Charlie or sometimes Blackie—as the only remaining big name in southern Illinois gangland.

School kids in the lower reaches of Illinois may not have been able to identify the governor or their congressman, but the name of Buster Wortman was another matter. Just as they grew up hearing about the Shelton brothers and Black Charlie, talk of Wortman was commonplace.

Author Bill Nunes recorded in his books memories of persons, like himself, who lived in East St. Louis in the middle of the twentieth century. Few recalled life in the hard-as-nails city without mentioning—besides the Democratic machine denizens who ran the town—the ominously hovering shadow of Wortman. A chill actually ran through Nunes when as a youngster he spied Wortman turning a corner in a dark sedan.

As with many gang lords, Wortman had an inauspicious start. He was born in St. Louis, but also got acquainted with the Illinois side of the Mississippi while growing up. This was because his father got a job at a steel casting plant in East St. Louis and went on to become a politically connected fire captain in the city. However, his dad's stature didn't dissuade Frank from bad behavior. Before he was twenty-five, he was a confirmed petty criminal with a rap sheet a mile long. Oddly though, hardly any of his arrests—mainly on suspicion of robbery—resulted in jail time.

Wortman's career progressed when he became a hanger-on with the Shelton gang in the 1920s. His aggressiveness with his fists and guns eventually caught the eye of Carl Shelton, who feared that he might be too reckless. When Wortman and fellow young Sheltonite Monroe (Blackie) Armes were imprisoned for assaulting federal agents raiding a Shelton still in 1933, Carl was described as indifferent to their plight. Both were led to believe that Shelton could have used his clout to prevent their incarceration.

After Buster started his imprisonment at Leavenworth, he met Charlie Harris, who shared his dissatisfaction with the Sheltons—primarily Carl.

For decades to follow, Harris testily sloughed off the widespread belief that he had hooked up with Wortman in his post-prison days in the 1940s to accelerate the Shelton fall from control of downstate Illinois racketeering. To hear Charlie tell it, he had little or no contact with Wortman after their time together at Leavenworth in the 1930s.

Eyewitness accounts and police and newspaper files suggested differently. After his fallout with Carl, Harris was observed with Wortman frequently enough for law officers and others to question whether he'd become a member of Buster's mob. Harris also was seen making the rounds with Blackie Armes, who by the early 1940s had abandoned the Sheltons to join Wortman.

Carl R. Baldwin, a widely respected reporter for the *St. Louis Post-Dispatch* who kept close tabs on the Illinois underworld, certainly felt that Harris had allied himself with Wortman. Tracing the ascendancy of Wortman to a mob bigwig, Baldwin wrote in a memorandum to his editors:

"Buster Wortman took a page from Carl Shelton's book on 'how to be a successful gangster'...by splitting asunder Shelton's organization... (which had) grown fat and middle-aged. He talked Monroe (Blackie) Armes of Herrin and Charles (Black Charlie) Harris of Fairfield into quitting the Sheltons. That was easy because both had been let down by Shelton promises after serving long prison terms."

Blackie Armes was shot and killed in 1944, prior to the dethroning of the Sheltons. But Wortman, not to be deterred, attracted other onetime Shelton adherents into his fold. They included southern Illinois hoodlum Roy (Tony) Armes, Blackie's brother.

Then there was Cotton Eppelsheimer, another Harris acquaintance from Leavenworth. Harris and Cotton were seen together during the span when Eppelsheimer and David (Chippy) Robinson, an old Egan gang mainstay like Cotton, were helping Wortman muscle his way to the top of the hugely profitable East Side gambling business.

One common thread ran through the relationship of Harris, Wortman and Blackie Armes. After getting out of prison, all hated the Sheltons, largely as a result of feeling shortchanged by Carl before and after their prison years.

Note of this was made by the special United States Senate committee on organized crime headed by Tennessee's Estes Kefauver. In a report printed in 1951, the panel said: "Following Frank Wortman's release from Alcatraz in the early 1940s (a few years shy of the ten years in federal prison to which he was sentenced), he again became associated with his former pals, the Sheltons. He and Blackie Armes, however, are stated to have been peeved because of the small automobiles given them...." Thus, it was added, "Wortman turned against the Sheltons...together with the Armes brothers...."

Kefauver's committee apparently had no doubt whatsoever that Harris was part and parcel of the Wortman-led revolt against the Sheltons.

Calling attention to the 1943 deadly machine gunning of two Shelton-aligned burglars near Caseyville, Illinois, the panel declared that the killings were "believed to be an outgrowth of a split from the Shelton gang led by Frank (Buster) Wortman and Charles (Black Charlie) Harris."

Continuing, the report pointed out that "Monroe (Blackie) Armes, who sided with Wortman and Harris, surrendered after the shooting for questioning." Another suspect in the double-murder was Wyncil Urban, cited in the report as a "muscle man" for the "new Wortman gang." Urban, a gunman and bank robber, was another of those in Wortman's circle to die violently. In 1945, he was found strangled with his lips taped and body bound in baling wire in a ditch near Kankakee, Illinois.

Harris, of course, was not among the Wortman associates who met untimely deaths. After the perceived interaction between Buster and Harris reached its peak in the late 1940s, simultaneous mention of their names tapered off.

An exception occurred in 1957. News articles in May of that year revealed that Wortman's outfit was seeking to expand or extend its tentacles into parts of southern Illinois, including Wayne County. There, one story noted, the goal was to open the county for slot machines while taking over liquor supply operations. To bring this about, it was related, Harris and a Wortman relative "made overtures to private club operators." However, the move was dropped, it was said, after its disclosure by the press.

The attempted incursion into Wayne, where Wortman never had been a factor, came during a period when Buster's empire was past its peak. Wortman experienced his headiest days in the late 1940s when the Sheltons finally were out of the way, and the East Side and some southern Illinois counties were a mecca for wide open but illegal gambling under Buster's iron hand.

Things changed convincingly in 1950 after Governor Adlai E. Stevenson reorganized the Illinois State Police and ordered the suddenly less corruptible troopers to shut down flagship gaming parlors, including high-flying casinos ran by Wortman.

Unrestrained wagering was the cash cow for Wortman, as it had been for the Sheltons. When that particular bonanza was crushed, Wortman had to look elsewhere for dollars.

"For Wortman was a gambling man, primarily," wrote Baldwin of the *Post-Dispatch*, "and when gambling had to go underground in 1950, it put a crimp in his wallet and in his aspirations. He dabbled in other fields, such as labor racketeering, trucking, jukeboxes, pinball machines, race horses, real estate developments, restaurants, nightclubs and loan companies. But income from these ventures was a trickle compared with the big money that comes from gambling with the wraps off."

This didn't mean that Wortman failed to rake in dough, because he did with some of the new enterprises. Profits were more or less assured because Buster had the tools to discourage or eliminate competition through strong-arming or, if necessary, more severe means.

A number of infamous gangsters, such as Shelton rival Charlie Birger in the 1920s, had wallowed in their newspaper publicity. An equal number—including the Sheltons and, for that matter, Harris—tried to duck reporters. However, few hated the press with the passion of Wortman. Fisticuffs were not out of the question when scribes were on his trail.

No way could Buster be ignored; he was, in journalistic lingo, great copy. His gang automatically was suspect in any illegal undertaking or unsolved murder of a shady character in Wortman territory. It was true, since Buster did not condone narcotics, prostitution or kidnapping, that hoods attempting to engage in these activities in his terrain might not reach old age.

Wortman couldn't escape attention in other areas either. His need for security prompted him to have a home built that may have been the most talked-about residence in the St. Louis region. The spacious, two-story house was constructed on a then secluded tract near Collinsville and, in a throwback to the Middle Ages, a deep moat was dug around the home. Curious people ventured out to see the house, but dared not cross the moat's bridge because of always visible sentries.

As expected, bodyguards routinely shadowed Wortman when he was out and about. A man in his position could take no chances in even innocuous situations. When he visited The Toggery, a men's clothing store in Belleville, Illinois, its entrance was locked temporarily as Leslie Pensoneau, the establishment's owner and the author's father, measured Buster for new suits. Furthermore, one or two muscle men stood inside the store's front door to further discourage any possible funny business.

Henchmen also mingled with patrons at the lounge-restaurant in East St. Louis operated by Wortman and a brother, Ted, a sometimes business partner. The Paddock was a popular night spot for years. On any given evening, a reporter if able to sneak into the place may have seen public officials, show business celebrities, gangsters from outside Illinois and even cops among the customers.

Two negatives—a hot temper and booze—plagued Wortman in his later years. Incidents occurred when he was drunk. Some were simply embarrassing and without repercussions, but not all. His mistreatment of an internal revenue agent when on a bender helped spur an investigation that led to his conviction and that of several associates in a federal district court in 1962. Buster was sentenced to five years in prison for conspiracy to evade income taxes, but never had to serve the time because the guilty verdict was reversed in a higher court. Afterward, he was freed at a subsequent trial.

His legal expenses, however, reportedly drained him financially. He also was burdened by numerous ailments that were aggravated by heavy smoking. He died in 1968 at age sixty-three.

Ten years after Wortman's death, Charles O. Stewart, a top-notch investigative reporter for the old *Metro-East Journal*, watched a headache ball level Buster's nightclub, The Paddock. Stewart had been hard hitting in his coverage of Wortman, but he couldn't avoid a little nostalgia in his story regarding the restaurant's reduction to rubble.

"The Paddock…became nearly as well known as Wortman," wrote Stewart. "For more than 20 years, it served as his hangout.…"

Stewart threw in a sort of backhanded kudo to Wortman in the article, noting that he "outlived Prohibition, gang wars and post-World War II gangland power struggles."

The single most important struggle faced by Wortman involved Carl Shelton in the 1940s. It ended brutally and without complete closure because of threads left dangling.

Black Charlie Harris was among the loose ends.

11

Murder in the Morning

C hicago had its St. Valentine's Day Massacre in 1929. Downstate Illinois' paramount gangster assassination occurred on the resplendent morning of October 23, 1947.

The life of Carl Shelton, the most celebrated gang leader in the state south of Chicago, ended that morning in a hail of bullets on the Pond Creek Road a few miles east of Fairfield.

Overnight, the killing set in motion a bloody transfer of power in the control of downstate racketeering. Less evident was the identity of Shelton's assassins. Their names remained shrouded in mystery, much like the fog that surrounded the role that Charlie Harris may have played in the fateful event.

For a time, Harris was on a hot seat in the investigation that followed the killing. He was, and would remain, the only suspect ever identified publicly. Wayne County authorities tried to pin the murder on him, but the fact that the rubout went unsolved was hardly surprising to crime buffs. Convictions for the shooting of gangsters—whether they were two-bit hoods or big-name fellows like Shelton—were rare. Very rare.

Naturally, conjecture about the slaying was on a front burner for decades. It was the headline event of the year in southern Illinois in 1947, second only to the death of 111 men in a blast at Mine No. 5 of the Centralia Coal Company at the south edge of Centralia.

The most logical supposition was that the elimination of Shelton was a predictable outcome of the pressure exerted on Buster Wortman by organized crime leaders in Chicago and St. Louis to wrest control of the downstate gambling terrain dominated for so long by the Sheltons.

If anything, the wide openness of many Illinois communities during World War II accelerated in the late 1940s. Illegal gaming, in particular, continued to get a pass from many state and local officials whose palms were greased by payoffs from gambling interests. Rewarding officialdom for looking the other way was a practice that had been perfected in the lower part of Illinois by none other than Carl Shelton.

Illinois was a golden goose for gambling, second to few states with the exception of Nevada, where it was legal. The continual rolling of dice and spinning of roulette wheels hardly was confined to the glamorous casinos in the bigger cities. The action in cheap sawdust joints in smaller towns also was lucrative—and these operations almost always were found in downstate locales still paying allegiance to the Sheltons.

When Carl Shelton seemingly bid adieu to Peoria in 1945 at the request of the newly elected reform mayor, the Chicago and St. Louis crime lords figured that the time had arrived at long last to annex Shelton territory. They formed a combine to cover the takeover and started off with peaceful overtures toward the Sheltons. Surely, the brothers could see that their day had passed and could be convinced to cede, or at least share, their territory. But, the combine was rebuffed.

Carl may have retreated to the trappings of his ill-gotten gains in Wayne County, but he gave no sign of going along with any approach by the Chicago-St. Louis combine. Hotheaded Bernie Shelton, still operating out of the Peoria area, was clearly adamant. He told the emissaries from the combine to go to hell. But, it was Carl, smoother and smarter than Bernie, who worried the big city guys.

Gamblers long subservient to the Sheltons were reluctant to listen to offers to leave the fold without a word or sign from Carl. It had been ingrained in them that Shelton approval was necessary before profiting from a racing wire service or a Western Union racing news ticker.

Long-standing loyalty to the Sheltons was the governing factor for many downstate gaming practitioners. But, a sizable number also still feared or suspected that Carl, semi-retired or not, might not look kindly on defections from the racketeering network that he—its godfather—had fashioned.

Some Shelton followers suspected that talk of Carl going soft reflected wishful thinking by some, including brazen members of the gang on the East Side under emerging strongman Wortman. In fact, true-blue Sheltonites still were willing to bet that the day would arrive when former allies like Charlie Harris would regret joining Wortman.

The refusal of the Sheltons to voluntarily give up their domain cemented the enmity of the Chicago-St. Louis alliance and triggered the next alternative—bloodshed. The Sheltons themselves were old veterans of a resort to violence after the failure of a velvet glove approach. There was no argument. As long as Carl Shelton remained alive, his aura was a stumbling block for those hungrily eyeing his world.

So it was that word went out well before 1947 that bounties of thousands of dollars would be paid for the bumping off of Carl, Bernie and Big Earl. Some believed the offer also extended to Ray Walker, the Shelton chief lieutenant and one who'd spurned a request to desert the brothers and throw in with Wortman.

Common sense pointed to the Wortman mob as being first in line to collect the rewards for Shelton heads. Buster and those he represented obviously stood to gain the most by dethroning the Sheltons. Too, the patience of Chicago crime bosses waiting for Wortman to unseat the Sheltons could wear thin even though the Chicagoans themselves knew first-hand the difficulties in combating the Sheltons.

Gunmen from Chicago had come up short more than once in trying to trap the brothers. On one occasion, a crew from the Windy City was set to ambush Carl and Bernie at the latter's headquarters in the Parkway Tavern on the edge of Peoria. But, Carl's legendary sixth sense for smelling a rat was as keen as ever, and several carloads of Shelton henchmen showed up at the bar instead of Carl and Bernie. The Chicagoans beat it back up north.

A new sense of urgency may have permeated the anti-Shelton drive with indications in 1947 that Carl was considering a return to a hands-on role in the burgeoning gambling scene. It may not have been coincidental that, as this rumor circulated, the fraternizing of Harris with the Wortman crowd noticeably increased. None of Buster's soldiers had the insight of Harris into the byways of the Sheltons' home lair.

Then, as if anything more was needed to further energize the antipathy of Harris for the Sheltons, a sudden flare-up on the home front could not have happened at a more crucial juncture.

Sheriff Hal Bradshaw of Wayne County was told by Carl that some of his blooded Black Angus cattle had been rustled. During a search by the Sheltons for alleged culprits, a man named Virgil Vaughan—said to be close to Harris either through family or friendship—was pummeled in a roadhouse by Little Earl Shelton, a nephew of the brothers, and two other Shelton followers, one of whom was Ray Walker. Vaughan refused to file charges, declaring instead that "they will be taken care of." Subsequently, Vaughan barely escaped death when occupants of an automobile fired shots into a car in which he was riding. Wounds suffered by Vaughan in the ambush between Fairfield and Albion were serious enough to leave him crippled.

The shooting enraged Harris. Bradshaw, who liked Charlie, shared his anger. Without fanfare, he appointed Harris as a "special deputy" so he could guard Vaughan from further attacks.

Carl Shelton was no less furious. According to his partisans, he'd had his fill of Harris either siding with Pond creekers critical of the Sheltons or, in some instances, purportedly goading Shelton neighbors into confrontations with him or Big Earl.

Had Carl finally tagged Harris a marked man? Some thought so, including—as he later claimed—Charlie himself.

Something had to give. And it did, on that unforgettable October day not long after the wounding of Vaughan.

Ironically, it was the same day that Carl had made an appointment to meet Frank Borah, a Fairfield acquaintance, to discuss the drafting of a will. Before seeing Borah, Shelton wanted to tend to some farm business.

For that reason, he was driving one of his favorite vehicles, an army surplus jeep, on Pond Creek Road around eight o'clock in the morning. He was being followed by Walker and Little Earl in a truck. When the convoy reached a small bridge not far from the Wagner School, gunfire exploded from thick brush and trees on the west side of the road. Carl toppled out of the jeep, while Walker and Little Earl leaped from the truck and scurried into a ditch near the bridge. They then scrambled along the bottom of the depression to make their way under the bridge, doing nothing to assist Carl because neither one was armed. (Persons later found that hard to believe—especially in the case of the normally gun-toting Walker.)

Little Earl and Walker were the only individuals present during the assassination who'd be available for questioning. They first talked to lawmen and subsequently repeated what they'd said transpired at an inquest by a Wayne County coroner's jury five days after the death of Shelton.

Based on accounts by Walker and Little Earl and on follow-up newspaper articles, the killing reminded some folks of the slaying of a young murderous couple, Clyde Barrow and Bonnie Parker, in Louisiana in 1934. For example, both wipeouts were sensationalized by the press. Like Carl, Clyde and Bonnie were ambushed on a rural road by attackers firing from behind underbrush or trees. The shooters were in a posse of peace officers led by Frank Hamer of Texas Ranger fame, who'd been hired to hunt down the pair.

Carl Shelton also was picked off by more than one assailant, but they were not carrying badges. While their identities never were determined, sources in both the law enforcement community and the underworld assumed Shelton was hit by at least four shooters tied to Chicago's Capone mob and its St. Louis-area allies. Other theories were voiced, but given little or no credence.

According to Little Earl and Walker, moments after jumping into the ditch and crouching under the bridge, they heard the voice of Carl beseeching the ambushers to stop firing. Walker peered up and saw Carl still on the road, walking or stumbling around. While screaming at Carl to retreat into the ditch, Walker said he got a glimpse of a man standing across the road from Carl—an individual of medium weight wearing a gray suit, hat and dress shirt, but no tie. Walker was sure the man, whom he did not recognize, was clutching either a shotgun or a rifle. A new hail of bullets sprayed every which way, sending Walker back under the bridge.

At one point during the gunfire, both Walker and Little Earl claimed to hear Carl utter, "Don't shoot me any more, Charlie. It's me, Carl Shelton. You've killed me already."

It was a plea that would echo through criminal lore for years.

Little Earl elaborated on the Harris factor in his testimony at the coroner's inquest. Carl's nephew said he emerged slightly from under the bridge and saw Harris standing at a corner of it. Charlie "had a gun," Little Earl said, "and he fired it while I was looking out from under the bridge." Without hesitation, he tacked on, "I ducked back down...."

When the shooting finally ended, Little Earl and Walker had a clear view of a car occupied by more than one person spinning onto the road and heading south. They described the auto as a black, 1946 model Ford sedan with a sun visor over the windshield.

After the car barreled away, the pair cautiously came out from under the bridge just in time to see a man turning to run north on the road. Both swore it was Harris.

Walker told the coroner's jury that he asked Little Earl to start the truck so they could drive north to summon help in the unlikely chance that Carl was not dead. But, the truck barely had moved when Harris stopped running, turned around and pointed what Walker said was "either a shotgun or rifle" at the vehicle.

"I couldn't say whether he shot or not, (but) something knocked the tire down and wrecked the truck," Walker stated.

Little Earl added, "Something happened to one of the tires...it was either shot, or something. It went flat all at once and caused us to run off in the ditch."

After Harris resumed his flight, Little Earl said he and Walker got into Carl's jeep and drove through back roads to Fairfield. At least two hours passed after the killing of Carl before the two men could notify law officers and return to the scene of the shooting. They were accompanied by Bradshaw, Lieutenant Ben Blades of the Illinois State Police and Big Earl. They found Carl's body in the ditch by the east side of the road. His feet were about a foot from the top of the ditch and his head and face were turned downward. Blades and the sheriff felt the body should be left there until pictures could be taken. But Big Earl protested, insisting that he did not want his brother lying there "like that."

In picking up the body, the trio saw it had been shielding a gun that Big Earl identified as Carl's revolver. Blades opened the weapon and noted that five of six shells had been fired. Searching the ground on the west side of the bridge, Blades and Bradshaw found many empty cartridges and shells, some of which that had been spent by an automatic pistol or submachine gun. Later, at the Nale Funeral Home in Fairfield, it was determined that at least seventeen rifle, handgun and machine-gun bullets had entered Carl's body, causing twenty-five bullet holes in his head, body, arms and legs. Those who compared Carl's death to the killing of Bonnie and Clyde noted that Barrow was hit twenty-five times and Bonnie twenty-three by Hamer's posse (armed with powerful Browning automatic rifles and other weapons).

The murder of Carl was the talk of towns far and wide. In Wayne and neighboring counties, much discussion revolved around the possible extent of Harris' culpability in the matter. His presence at or near the site of the ambush was not doubted. However, according to statements of persons other than Walker and Little Earl, Charlie was not on hand when the shooting started. One who attested to that was Beatrice (Jakie) Suddarth Bell, the name used in newspapers to identify the then twenty-year-old Bea Riley.

She was in the company of Charlie that day and would experience nothing more traumatic in her young life. She did not relish being shoved into the spotlight as a result.

More than sixty years later, Beatrice recalled the day she would rather have done without. She told the author that her uncle had picked her up in the morning to drive her to St. Louis to board a bus for the start of a trip to Phoenix, Arizona. Bea, who had graduated from high school earlier in the year at Phoenix, was back in Wayne County for a brief visit.

"We were on that gravel road not far from the place where Carl was murdered," she said. "We suddenly heard a lot of gunfire. It couldn't have come from very far away, but we weren't close enough to see what was going on. Charlie had always told me to get out of the car and run if shots were fired when we were riding together.

"So, he yelled to me, 'Remember what I told you. Get out of here and run.'"

She obeyed instinctively. After quickly sliding out of the car, she watched her uncle drive off in the direction of the shots. Then she ran toward a nearby farmhouse.

"Whatever was going on with all the shooting, and what Charlie did or didn't do when he got to where it was happening...I didn't know," she said.

Individuals testifying at the coroner's inquest put Harris near the site of the ambush, but none substantiated the contention of Little Earl and

Walker that Charlie joined in the gunfire aimed at Carl. Two questioned extensively were Marjorie Keen and her husband Gladstone, who lived about three-quarters of a mile north of the bridge. They asserted that, in their opinion, Harris was too near their home just prior to the shooting to have participated in the gunfire.

About a minute or two before the shots erupted, Marjorie related, she was on the porch of her house and saw Harris and Beatrice driving south toward the bridge. Either right before or just after the firing stopped, she and her husband got into their car and drove toward the area of the gunfire. Reaching the Wagner School, she said they saw Harris' auto parked about halfway between the schoolhouse and the bridge.

"I could see through the back window he (Harris) was sitting under the wheel," she said, "and as we drove up he opened the door and got out of the car...." Looking toward the bridge, she said, "I saw this truck and the jeep." Later, she went on, she watched the jeep turn around and head south.

Marjorie did not see Beatrice and asked Harris where she had gone. He replied that "when they drove down there...she jumped out of the car" and ran into a bean field. However, Marjorie said she suspected that Beatrice had gone to a nearby Wagner family farmhouse. Driving there in her car, she exited and started to walk to the house. Before reaching it, she saw Beatrice advancing toward her. Moments after they met, Marjorie said she "noticed that Mr. Harris and my husband were coming down the road in his car." When Harris pulled up, she said, her husband joined her, and Beatrice ran to get into Charlie's auto. Harris then departed, driving south, she said.

Minutes afterward, and long before Bradshaw, Blades and Big Earl arrived, she said she and her husband drove across the bridge, but "didn't see Carl's body." They did notice the truck "run off in the edge of the ditch," she noted, but "didn't know anyone had been killed or anything."

Gladstone Keen's testimony mirrored that of his wife, except that he was asked if he saw any firearms in Harris' possession when they were together after the shooting.

"I never noticed any," Keen replied.

His answer prompted a laugh of sarcasm from Bernie Shelton, who had come from Peoria to attend the inquest.

Nevertheless, Lem Harl, another person questioned at the inquest, said the same thing. Harl drove in his truck with a friend, John Tondini, toward the area of the shooting shortly after it was over. Like the Keens, he saw Harris at his car between the school and the bridge.

When asked if Harris was armed, Harl answered, "No, I didn't see no gun."

Despite the observations of Harl and the Keens, the coroner's jury felt it heard enough to not let Harris off the hook. Although the jury concluded that Carl Shelton "came to his death by gunshot fired by persons unknown to the jury," the panel recommended that Harris be arrested and held for a Wayne County grand jury investigation into the murder.

To put it mildly, this was a coroner's jury under extraordinary pressure. The inquest was held in the midst of an explosive atmosphere in the county, and there were rumors that violence might break out at the proceeding itself. The panel's finding that Harris should be detained for further scrutiny pleased the Shelton partisans, including Big Earl. He quickly opined, "That's the way it should be." Harris sympathizers felt otherwise, claiming that Walker and Little Earl were lying to make Charlie a fall guy.

No question, jury service in this instance took courage because the side not pleased with the panel's conclusion—whether it be the Shelton or Harris camp—had men with itchy trigger fingers. It was a catch-22 situation for members of the jury, who were identified in the transcript of the inquest as Olen Baker, O. E. Brock, Delbert Morris, F. C. Scott, Lawrence Owen and Ora Hubble, who later became mayor of Fairfield.

Acting on the jury's recommendation, Walter Young, the Wayne coroner, delivered to Bradshaw a warrant for the arrest of Harris.

There was a problem. In the five days since the murder, the whereabouts of Harris had become a mystery—at least to most folks. Bradshaw expressed confidence that the issuance of the warrant would convince his friend Harris to surrender without delay.

Maybe. Maybe not.

12

A County on the Edge

T he warrant for his arrest did not propel Harris to surrender.
He disappeared in short order after the murder of Carl Shelton, fearing that his life might not be worth more than a proverbial "plug nickel" if it fell into the hands of Carl's brothers or followers. By continuing to remain out of sight after the issuance of the warrant, Harris became a person on the lam.

Sheriff Bradshaw ordered a manhunt to corral him, but visits to Harris' farm as well as sweeps through the Pond Creek bottoms proved to be fruitless. However, the search did reveal that Wayne County was ripe for an outbreak of violence; it was a tinderbox waiting to explode.

The anger of Shelton partisans gave credence to the fear by Harris that he might not have survived if his fate had been left up to them. They were of the same mind as Ray Walker, who remarked portentously at the coroner's inquest that Harris was lucky on the day of Carl's slaughter that he, Walker, was not carrying a weapon.

"If I had been armed, Charlie Harris would have been there with Carl Shelton, and there would have been no dispute about who did it," said Walker.

A *St. Louis Globe-Democrat* reporter endeavored to further dramatize Walker's declaration by noting that it caused a "stir" at the inquest as "spectators weighed the words and studied Walker's lean face with its scimitar-shaped scar, such as an old knife wound would leave under his right eye." As Walker spoke, the reporter added, "his thin lips grew tighter, and his pale blue eyes were icy."

Harris sympathizers were just as threatening, and there appeared to be more of them. To begin with, word circulated that Buster Wortman's hoods were prepared to invade Wayne County if Harris seemed likely to fall victim to a Shelton-inspired lynch party. The thugs never showed up, though, because Harris appeared to have more than ample protection from home-grown guardians. They included Pond Creek farmers who were appreciative of Harris standing up to the Sheltons and also those simply tired of the Shelton impact on the county's image.

The staunchest backers of Harris cared little that he may have been one of the triggermen in Carl's murder. And they assuredly didn't give a hoot if Harris—while maybe not among those pumping bullets into Shelton—had somehow orchestrated the killing. Most agreed that gangsters outside of Wayne County could not have selected, on their own, such a perfect place for an ambush. Too, outsiders were not privy to the movements of Carl Shelton inside his little kingdom.

If not guilty of murder, newspapermen were quick to write, Harris at least seemed to be a finger man in the slaying.

No matter what, Sheriff Bradshaw was far from wrong in saying that "with the whole community as his friends, Charlie Harris could hide for a year and we'd never find him."

Virgil W. Mills, the state's attorney of Wayne County, suggested that Harris might surrender if he realized he could be released under bail. But, Charlie did not take the bait offered by Mills even though he considered Mills at the time to be a friend and one who was fair in the conduct of his office.

Information coming to light afterward revealed that Harris constantly was on the move after the ambush, never staying in one place very long, whether in Pond Creek or elsewhere.

After leaving the vicinity of the shooting on October 23, Harris and Beatrice drove to St. Louis. Based on reports published later, he left her at the Lafayette Avenue home of Russell Slattery, a pipe fitter married to Laverne Bell, a half sister of Beatrice. He felt she was safer there than in

Wayne County until, as he phrased it, "things quiet down." Beatrice also spent part of her time in St. Louis at the home of Slattery's father, Carl, on Connecticut Street.

At one point in the days following the ambush, St. Louis police were informed that Beatrice accompanied Russell Slattery to Wayne County in an attempt to get Harris' car. However, a farmer close to Charlie warned the pair that they might be shot if seen in the auto. Consequently, the farmer drove Slattery and Beatrice to Carmi, Illinois, where they boarded a train to return to St. Louis.

Beatrice remained in St. Louis for several more days before she received a telephone call and left the home of Carl Slattery in a taxicab at night. She exited by the Maplewood loop at Manchester and Yale avenues, a point from which bus lines made frequent departures. Beatrice entered a Greyhound station and waited a while before being joined by Harris. He then bought two tickets to Tulsa, Oklahoma.

Not long after the bus carrying Charlie and his niece departed, Martin Cliffe, a St. Louis police detective captain, followed a lead that brought him to the Greyhound depot.

Cliffe was able to pick up Beatrice's trail by following up on a report by fellow detective captain, Otto Selle. Before going off duty, Selle had noted that Beatrice had been observed leaving the house on Connecticut Street in a cab. When Cliffe reported for duty, he quickly decided to pursue that angle. He contacted the taxi firm's dispatcher and was told that Beatrice was driven to the Maplewood loop. Cliffe and his crew hurried to the site and began questioning persons working and living in the area. None had seen Beatrice.

However, a later newspaper article detailing what it labeled as "painstaking detective work" said that Cliffe was "seized with a hunch" when he noticed the Greyhound station as "he methodically worked his way along the street."

"He wondered," continued the story, "if Harris, unable to get possession of his own automobile at Fairfield, Illinois, had been forced to resort to flight by bus."

The hunch paid off, the article concluded, when a woman clerk at the depot recalled a girl fitting the description of Beatrice being joined by an older man and engaged in "earnest conversation." That was followed by the purchase of the tickets to Tulsa.

The St. Louis cops immediately notified the Illinois State Police of their finding. An alert was relayed to Tulsa, where detectives responded by speeding to the Greyhound station in the city. They got there thirteen minutes after the arrival of the bus from St. Louis. Suspecting that Harris would continue his flight on the next west-bound bus, the officers went to the All-American Bus Terminal. Harris and Beatrice were there, waiting with tickets for Phoenix.

Years later, Beatrice had no problem remembering the arrest, which occurred a week after the Shelton killing.

"Charlie and I saw these well dressed men coming toward us," she said. "He told me, 'Chucklehead, we are going to get picked up.' When they came up to us, they asked him if he was Charlie Harris. He said he was, and they said, 'You are wanted for questioning.'"

Beatrice, who was arrested along with Charlie but released shortly afterward, did not recall a version of the apprehension given to reporters by W. V. Caffey, one of the detectives. He said that Harris, when confronted, "went to pieces and started shaking." However, by the time Harris and Beatrice were at Tulsa police headquarters, Caffey said Charlie had regained his composure. Harris was even quoted as telling J. D. Bills, a police captain, to "turn us loose and we'll go back by ourselves."

That idea was nixed by Bills, who informed Harris and Beatrice that they were being held pending the arrival of lawmen from Illinois. Neither Charlie nor Beatrice commented on Shelton's murder. When arrested, Harris was not armed and had $506 in currency.

Three days after the arrest of Harris, Bradshaw and several special deputies arrived in Tulsa. Before Charlie was taken from the Tulsa city jail, officers put handcuffs and leg shackles on him. The constraints did not last long.

Beatrice, who accompanied her uncle and the lawmen, recalled that the cuffs and shackles "came off once we were out of sight of Tulsa. The ride was not unpleasant because it was obvious the sheriff and Charlie liked each other." Bradshaw himself said that Harris was amiable on the trip. The Shelton ambush was not discussed, the sheriff said, but "we talked about everything else in creation."

Still, getting Harris back to Illinois was a tense undertaking. Finding men to accompany him to Tulsa had not been easy for Bradshaw because of worry that riding in a vehicle with Harris exposed one to danger. Bradshaw recognized the chance of ambush by certain St. Louis area gunmen not wanting Harris to go to a possible trial. And there always were old Shelton gangsters thirsty for revenge.

Harris was aware of the risk. When informed by Tulsa police that Bradshaw was coming for him, he reportedly suggested that the sheriff be urged "to have plenty of reinforcements as soon as we get east of St. Louis."

Motoring back to Illinois proved to be uneventful. In an attempt to avoid any planned assault, Bradshaw drove on secondary or out-of-the-way roads. Once within the state, Harris was jailed at an undisclosed location.

Bradshaw likely exercised sound judgment in taking this step because tempers of many folks were at a boiling point. Aware that Harris was back in Illinois, the Shelton brothers struggled to keep their anger under control. Additional Illinois State Police troopers on the scene in Fairfield brushed shoulders with the surviving Shelton brothers and the ever dangerous Walker. Big Earl demanded a meeting with Harris, but Bradshaw refused to oblige.

This infuriated Big Earl, prompting him to tell a *St. Louis Post-Dispatch* reporter that "my brother was killed. Who has a better right to talk to Harris than I have?"

Harris himself wanted to be released from jail in order to melt once again into secluded parts of Pond Creek where his supporters remained ready to shield him. He stood to get his wish when Circuit Judge J. Caswell Crebs of Robinson ruled in a habeas corpus proceeding, backed by Harris lawyers, that Charlie was eligible for release on a $7,500 bond. Bradshaw voiced concern about "getting Harris out of jail without anything happening," but Crebs ruled that Charlie's bid for release was legitimate since he had not been charged with a specific offense.

In anticipation of Harris' release, Bradshaw quietly moved him to the Wayne County jail in Fairfield. He was bailed out on November 7, fifteen days after the Shelton murder. Harris ducked out of the rear door of the jail at noon, slipped into a slow moving auto and was driven to Pond Creek.

Just as Charlie exited, Big Earl was in a car on the town square, a few steps from the jail. He and others had been led by authorities to believe Harris would be released at night. Instead, his departure came when downtown traffic was heavy and sidewalks crowded, a situation thought by officials to discourage a clash between Shelton followers and friends of Harris.

A contingent of Pond Creek men in the city at the time of Harris' release did draw attention. They only were on hand, asserted John Burgess, a Harris attorney, to help other friends of Charlie post the $7,500 bond needed to ensure his appearance in the event of a grand jury indictment. Three of the bondsmen were Brose Vaughan, Courtney Meritt and Howard S. Taylor. Vaughan, an oil-field pumper, was married to Margaret Bell, a niece of Harris. Meritt and Taylor were Pond Creek farmers and close friends of Charlie at that time. In the case of each man, though, the friendship eventually would be shattered. Brutally shattered.

Harris walked out of jail five days before a special grand jury was convened in the county to consider the recommendation of the coroner's jury that Charlie be investigated in connection with the Shelton killing. The interval passed without incident as increasing numbers of persons appeared to be falling into the camp of Harris supporters.

State's Attorney Mills, the official in charge of the grand jury deliberation, already had echoed the prevailing view when he went on record to say that available information made it appear the "actual trigger work" in the murder was done by St. Louis area gangsters. Underworld sources continued to call it a "no brainer." Shelton was hit, they insisted, in traditional gangland fashion by men from the old Egan gang linked to the Wortman-led mob controlling East Side rackets at the behest of the Capone organization.

Nevertheless, on the eve of the grand jury inquiry, Mills said his thinking still did not rule out a connection by Harris to the murder.

Pond creekers who had taken the side of either Harris or the Sheltons were on opposite ends of the courtroom near the grand jury room in the Wayne County Courthouse as the inquiry commenced. Two troopers were stationed there to preclude a confrontation, but the two groups ignored each other.

Walker and Little Earl repeated to the grand jury the eyewitness testimony they gave to the coroner's jury. They again asserted that Harris took part in the shooting. However, their contention was countered by a surprise witness at the inquiry: Beatrice.

Her whereabouts since the arrest of Harris in Tulsa had not been revealed. Hardly anyone outside of her family knew whether she had returned to Illinois with her uncle or gone elsewhere.

Residents of Fairfield did not learn of Beatrice's presence until she appeared before the grand jury. Deputy Sheriff Elmer Brown revealed that she had been ensconced in the quarters occupied by himself and his wife in the county jail building while awaiting her call before the panel. After a roughly fifteen-minute appearance before the jury, she was escorted back to the jail building. Bradshaw refused to answer questions about her next destination or future plans.

There was no uncertainty, though, about her testimony. Beatrice corroborated the accounts of witnesses at the coroner's inquest who said they believed that she and Harris were too far away from the scene of the killing for him to have been part of it. Her words must have carried weight with the grand jurors.

Unlike the crowd that had been present in the courtroom when the inquiry started, only four spectators were on hand—plus reporters and lawyers—when the decision of the grand jury was revealed November 14. The panel returned a no true bill, clearing Harris of any complicity in the murder.

Two of the spectators were Big Earl and one of his sisters, Lula Pennington. When he was informed by a reporter of the exoneration of Harris, his face was impassive as he nodded his head. Then he quietly left the courtroom. The manner of his departure was fitting in that it would symbolize a new order in Wayne County.

Harris had argued that he fled the county not as a result of guilt, but because of fear of vengeful Shelton followers. With the grand jury decision leaving Charlie free to go where he pleased, some expected retribution by the Sheltons to come anytime. That it didn't happen spoke volumes. Especially so in that even many Harris partisans assumed that he indeed was a finger man in Carl's killing. Whether he was or not, Harris paid no price. The Sheltons of old, whose gang had stood up to the Ku Klux Klan and rolled over rival outfits, apparently no longer existed.

The impact of Carl's demise was under way before the ground had settled over his grave in Maple Hill Cemetery at Fairfield following a funeral service that was the biggest event Wayne County ever had seen. Some

Shelton associates were shutting down their gaming houses while others agreed to cede control of their operations to the Chicago-St. Louis mob combine represented by Wortman.

The mystique of Shelton impenetrability in Wayne County had gone up in smoke. There was a new guy on the block to be feared, and his name was Harris.

13

A Split Personality

*T*he Strange Case of Dr. Jekyll and Mr. Hyde, the widely acclaimed novella written by Scottish author Robert Louis Stevenson and published in 1886, was a vivid portrayal of a man with a split personality.

The story tracked a London lawyer as he investigated the behavior of the title character, a person with two conflicting sides. On one hand, there was the lawyer's kindly friend, Dr. Henry Jekyll. But the good doctor also had a mean and secretive side that surfaced in Edward Hyde.

Harris, born ten years after the novella was released, emerged in his own life as an individual encompassing the duality of human nature.

His disposition embodied an irrational patchwork, a temperamental makeup in which a genial bearing became unhinged at the slightest provocation. Many people never saw anything but a proper gentleman in Harris. All were aware, though, of a dark side that could lead to dire consequences if triggered. Anyone who wasn't a fool gave him a wide berth.

The Federal Bureau of Investigation compiled a thick dossier on Harris, and it addressed what agents perceived to be a man with a complicated, dangerous demeanor.

According to its files, the FBI categorized Harris as one who "speaks in a very soft voice and has good manners, giving the impression of being very polite. However, when angered, he has a violent, uncontrollable temper." At the same time, Harris was said to be capable of remaining "calm under pressure, never displaying any temper until he has the advantage, whereupon he will…go into a rage."

The FBI concluded in the 1960s that Harris had "lived a life of violence for (which) he makes no attempt to hide." Yet, he was credited as a person wanting "to be known for paying his legitimate debts." But, it was added, "He also wants it known that he will not stand for anyone fleecing him in a business deal."

Carl Shelton surely found that out in the years following his imbroglio with Charlie in the early 1940s over the tract of land in Pond Creek that both coveted. The confrontation, in which Harris felt betrayed by Carl, cemented Charlie's hatred for the gang leader and other members of his family.

Several decades passed before Harris again had reason to feel undercut by a friend or neighbor. During that period, Harris got along well with his fellow Pond Creek farmers as his holdings increased and he appeared to prosper. He was not hesitant to lend a helping hand to those in need, so much so that many hailed him as a good fellow to have around.

Beatrice Bell was not the only individual encouraged by Harris to lead a better life, but she was an obvious example.

Her uncle was a motivating factor in her move to Arizona in her teenage years. He pushed her to attend Phoenix Union High School, where she graduated in 1947. Then, at the instigation of Charlie, she enrolled in nursing school at Good Samaritan Hospital in Phoenix. Money was tight, but he aided her in the training program with financial assistance, and she graduated in 1950.

Beatrice enjoyed some of her best days with Charlie in Arizona. They hiked up mountains, went to rodeos and rode horses together through the streets of Phoenix. They sometimes didn't dismount until they reached the hotel run by Charlie's brother, Jim.

Chicata, the horse she rode, was purchased for her by Harris. He originally had intended for her to ride Thunder, a small white stallion. However, because Thunder was rambunctious, he decided it was best if he kept the horse, which he eventually took to Illinois.

Looking back, one might wonder if Thunder was the horse involved in an incident that illustrated the side of Harris that folks did not care to see.

Jack Newton, a construction worker living near Fairfield in 2008, recalled witnessing the episode as a young boy. Newton was in the presence of Harris on Charlie's farm when a white horse refused to leave a pond.

"The horse was laying in the water," Jack said, "and wouldn't budge when he (Harris) wanted it to come out. So he waded in, hitched a long chain to the horse, linked it to a tractor and drug the horse from the pond."

"He was doing that out of anger," contended Newton. "He wasn't concerned at all about the horse's health." Little did young Newton realize that the man he was observing would greatly affect his own life in the future.

Unlike Newton, many never witnessed an eruption of Harris' temper. He labored, often masterfully, to present a façade that masked his untoward side. He was different from a number of lawbreakers, including some of his contemporaries who actually relished the public spotlight. He refused to own up to his reputation—except for reported slips a time or two.

When he was imprisoned late in his life after being found guilty of a 1964 double murder, Harris still maintained with a smile that he was "the most overrated gangster and gunslinger in the world." He offered the self-assessment in an interview with the *Evansville Courier*, a question and answer session that left reporter Maria Pojeta as challenged as others in trying to define Harris.

The best she could conclude was that the "passage of time builds upon the lives of the notorious until only the skeleton of fact remains, and the rest is fashioned into legend."

"So it was," she wrote, "with the outlaws who stalked the prairies of the old West. And so it has become with Charles Bryan Harris...." His story, she conjectured, "is shrouded in mystery or loaded with hearsay, but most often is wrought from contradiction."

How contradictory? Taken to the extreme, Harris may have been a twentieth century Jekyll and Hyde. Pojeta, the reporter, found persons who praised Charlie as "the nicest man they...ever met." The FBI saw a lot more of Edward Hyde in Harris.

Researchers understood that information in the bureau's files was not infallible. However, if the agency was on target in what it gleaned in the

1960s from full-blown digging into past and current activities of Harris, the picture drawn of him was astounding.

The profilers under FBI Director J. Edgar Hoover labeled Harris a "veteran and vicious criminal...allegedly responsible for killing 20 to 25 people." The assertion—made in the absence of detailed proof or supporting evidence in the files—was based largely on the tapping of the bureau's legendary network of informants in the underworld.

For Harris to have knocked off that many persons, he almost certainly would have had to be a hit man—the nomenclature for a professional assassin normally in the employ of organized crime figures. If so, he was very adept at leading a double life.

Harris scoffed at the FBI depiction of him. He dismissed it as totally ridiculous. Harris was known to have acknowledged responsibility for only one killing. That was his shooting in self-defense of Blackie Anderson, the oil-field worker with whom he clashed at Carl Shelton's skating rink at Fairfield in 1940.

Yet, there were folks in his life who heard him utter curious statements in rare moments when he may have let down his guard. One was to the effect that he never killed a person "who didn't deserve to be killed." Another was a sinister insight. As he put it, "There is a difference between putting a bullet into an animal and into a human body."

After the slaughter of Carl Shelton in 1947, other well-known members of his family were either murdered or wounded in succeeding years. In several cases, Harris was tagged as the main suspect. He denied pulling any of the triggers and never once was prosecuted.

In view of his insistence of his innocence in the attacks on the Sheltons, the eyebrows of crime historians were raised by a purported 2008 revelation by an ex-convict to Phil Luciano, a well-regarded columnist for the *Peoria Journal Star*.

Luciano wrote that John (Peck) Smith heard a startling admission from Harris when both were inmates at the Menard State Prison at Chester, Illinois. Harris told Smith, according to the Luciano column, that "he was behind every one of the Shelton shootings...until the (Shelton) family cleared out of Illinois." Most importantly, Smith contended that Harris specifically fessed up to killing Carl and Bernie.

When Harris arrived at Menard late in 1965 after his conviction for a 1964 double murder, Smith already was there serving time for a failed robbery. Smith told Luciano that he had been aware of Harris from his teen years when he, Smith, worked for a Shelton gang member who ran a roadhouse outside Peoria. Even though Harris was sixty-nine years old when he entered Menard, the columnist wrote that Charlie "still commanded fearful respect."

Smith related to Luciano that Harris—although not a "real talkative person" in the pen—struck up a conversation with him one day. The column noted that Smith was not sure "why Harris decided to open up," but guessed it may have been "because of their common bond of Peoria." The two started chatting about the city, and the conversation veered toward the Sheltons.

Harris was quoted as telling Smith—after Harris vented the reasons for his contempt for the Sheltons—that he had murdered Carl and Bernie. The confession, if true, broke new ground.

Taking credit for the murder of Bernie was one thing. However, saying he killed Carl was problematic. Little Earl Shelton and Ray Walker did place Harris at the scene of Carl's murder. But, little or no doubt existed that a number of shooters assailed Carl. Too, more than one person testified that Harris was not at the site of the ambush when the firing commenced. So, perhaps this was Harris' way of ending years of denial by finally acknowledging that he did indeed finger or set up Carl for his murder.

Charlie's claim that he himself bumped off Bernie Shelton in 1948, the year after the death of Carl, was more easy to accept. The killing of Bernie was of primary interest to *Journal Star* readers since it occurred at his bar headquarters just outside Peoria. In addition, it remained one of the major unsolved murders in downstate Illinois.

Detectives wrung their hands over the mysterious culprit in Bernie's death just as much as they did in the following decade on the enigmatic disappearance of Joliet, Illinois, journalist Molly Zelko. She had used *Spectator*, a weekly newspaper, to harass powerful racketeers in Will County. When she disappeared in 1957, reporters from Chicago, St. Louis, Washington and New York descended on Joliet to aid in the search for her. The dragnet became a cause celebre, but Molly was not found.

The shooting of Bernie was captivating because it had a big impact on Illinois politics as well as on the criminal world. Law enforcement officials had a strong hunch that the killing was another murder ordained by the Chicago or St. Louis syndicates to hasten the downfall of the Shelton gang. The murder also sparked widespread disclosures about unethical financial dealings between crooked gambling lords and Illinois public officials, beginning with then Governor Dwight Herbert Green.

Bernie, the Shelton mob's brawny enforcer, was on the parking lot of his Parkway Tavern at the edge of Peoria when he was wounded fatally by one shot from a man who crouched or lay in thick undergrowth near the base of the steep, wooded hill behind the bar. After firing, the assassin scrambled up the slope to St. Joseph's cemetery, where he jumped into a waiting Chevrolet sedan being driven by another man.

Harris related all of this in detail to Smith, even down to the dark green color of the getaway car—the same description of the Chevy provided by several workmen in the cemetery. Harris told Smith that he and the other fellow, who was not identified, proceeded to drive back to Fairfield.

Luciano's column stipulated that this was the only time Harris talked to Smith about the Sheltons. Smith naturally wanted to hear more, but Luciano wrote that "Smith didn't dare get pushy with a man as scary as Harris." Smith also waited years after Harris' death before revealing the alleged conversation, explaining to Luciano that he "would never say anything about him (Harris), unless I knew he was dead."

If Harris had been considered a suspect in the killing of Bernie, it received scant notice. Charlie did make the newspapers in 1948, but not in connection with Bernie's death. Still, the publicity was not exactly flattering.

Harris and two other men, all described by the St. Louis press as hoodlums and former Shelton gang members, were arrested in March of that year by East St. Louis police for questioning in connection with a $31,400 holdup at the Bussmann Manufacturing Company's plant in St. Louis.

The *Globe-Democrat* reported that the cops suspected Harris was in "a trio of masked bandits, who, in a professional manner, calmly looted the place of a payroll shipment and made their escape in a stolen auto." The others arrested were Roy Armes and Dale Stamper.

Harris and Armes were picked up while they were riding in a black 1947 sedan bearing Missouri license plates. Charlie, who was carrying $296 and a .38-caliber revolver, was identified by the *Globe-Democrat* as the "reputed finger man" in Carl Shelton's murder—an assignation he hotly denied at that point. The paper reminded readers that Armes, who went by the name of Tony, was a brother of the late Blackie Armes, an infamous gangster who had been a friend of Charlie's. Tony Armes often was one of the first persons mentioned in speculation about the identities of the shooters in the Carl Shelton ambush (although he never was charged in the unsolved slaying). Stamper, the third suspect in the Bussmann heist, was an East St. Louis resident, a tavern operator and, according to the *Globe-Democrat*, a convicted murderer.

All three men were released shortly after their arrests when employees of Bussmann could not identify any of them as being among the masked robbers.

Several weeks later, Charlie and Tony Armes were in the news again. Each was fined $100 by W. W. Hindenberger, a justice of the peace in East St. Louis, for carrying concealed weapons. He had initially fined each man $300, but reduced the amount on a promise by Harris and Armes that they would stay out of East St. Louis. Here again, the press called Charlie "a hoodlum."

Harris was not named a suspect, at least openly, in the next assault on a Shelton. The target this time, Big Earl, was wounded May 24, 1949, by one of three bullets fired through a window of his Farmers' Club, a second-floor gambling establishment on Fairfield's courthouse square. The assailant, who was never identified, got a clear view of Shelton by climbing a ladder to the roof of an auto dealership next door to the club. Big Earl suffered blood loss in the shooting, but recovered.

Another Shelton, Little Earl, was attacked in the early morning hours of September 9, 1949. Hit by a barrage of shots, it was a miracle that he did not die from his multiple wounds. The attempted assassination was part of what would be an eventful day in criminal history.

Canadian Edwin Alonzo Boyd, a World War II veteran who led a gang that became as notorious in his country as the Shelton outfit was in America, committed the first of his numerous bank robberies that same day in his hometown of Toronto. Also that day in Canada, all twenty-three persons on board a Canadian Pacific Airlines DC-3 died when a bomb exploded following takeoff from a suburb of Quebec City. The bomb, comprised of dynamite and an alarm clock, was stashed on the plane by Albert Guay, the husband of one of the victims. The marriage of Guay and his wife Rita had become quite stormy, and on the day of the flight he took out a sizable insurance policy on her life.

Guay was executed for his crime, but nobody paid a price for the shooting of Little Earl. At least several assailants were involved, and Little Earl declared that one was Harris. Although Charlie denied any involvement, he was arrested and formally charged with assault in an attempt to commit murder. The charge was dismissed when Little Earl failed to aid in the prosecution of Harris. Nevertheless, if Harris was on the level in what he professed to "Peck" Smith years later at Menard, Little Earl was right in seeking to implicate him.

A storm of bullets had riddled Little Earl's Buick as he stopped outside his Elm Street home in Fairfield. Although wounded, he threw himself on the floor of his car, a move that probably saved his life. As the shooters drove away, Little Earl managed to draw his gun from a shoulder holster and get off several shots. Afterward, at Deaconess Hospital in Evansville, Indiana, doctors saw that he had been hit by eight shots. The bullet holes in his car came from two types of weapons, one apparently a machine gun.

Shelton later told Sheriff Bradshaw and Gerald Mayberry, the new state's attorney of Wayne County, that in the light of the headlights from his car he could see Harris along with one or more other gunmen in what appeared to be a black sedan. Furthermore, Little Earl claimed to have noticed the license number of the attackers' vehicle, a number that was issued to Harris.

Even though Harris was charged with attempting to kill Little Earl, local lawmen were inclined to believe Charlie's denial of any knowledge of the crime. They doubted that Little Earl saw much of anything because of the early morning darkness. Officers also noted that Harris' car had no bullet holes, even though Little Earl was fairly positive that the shots he'd fired hit the assailants' auto.

The charge against Harris was dismissed by Magistrate Arch Hill on a motion by Fairfield attorney Kelley Loy, who represented Harris. The motion followed an announcement by Mayberry that Little Earl had declined to appear in prosecution of the case for several reasons. Mayberry said that Shelton told him he had no witnesses to substantiate his identification of Harris. And, Mayberry said, Little Earl concluded that prosecution of Harris most likely would be a waste of time because his testimony against Harris in the murder of Carl Shelton was not believed.

In May of 1950, Big Earl was hit in the right arm, but not seriously wounded, when he and Little Earl were driving through the Pond Creek area, inspecting oil drilling operations on property owned by Big Earl. Little Earl, who was not injured, said the gunfire came from one or more individuals hidden on a bank overlooking the road.

Two weeks later, on June 5, Little Earl and an associate, Dellos Wylie, were targets of a rifle and shotgun fusillade as they sat in Shelton's car in front of a garage outside Fairfield. Wylie and Shelton—who had been slightly nicked by the shots coming from undergrowth across the road from the garage—managed to get out of the auto and run into the building. When the hidden gunmen continued to fire, Wylie moved to escape from the garage. He immediately was cut down by bullets, leaving him seriously wounded.

Two days later, Roy Shelton, the oldest of the sons of Ben and Agnes, was shot and killed by a lone gunman as he drove a tractor on farmland owned by Big Earl near Pond Creek Road, only a mile or so from the spot where Carl was slain.

Blaming Roy's death on the Chicago or St. Louis mobs seemed a stretch. Although he was in trouble throughout much of his life and had spent more time behind bars than his celebrated brothers Carl, Bernie and Big Earl, Roy never was considered to be part of the Shelton gang. The primary assumption was that his killing was at the hand of a person in the local community.

Obviously, Harris came to mind. However, by that juncture folks were very cautious about attributing anything to Charlie. The man always appeared to have an alibi, or to have people willing to provide him with one. He was known to take particular note of persons crossing his path the wrong way. It was alarming the way talk about him always seemed to reach his ears.

If Harris in fact was the ultimate demon stalking the Sheltons, he may have been behind the homemade bomb that wrecked Big Earl's home at his Hill Top Farm before 1950 ended. The incident proved to be the last straw in Wayne County for Big Earl. Early in 1951, he and his wife Earline, along with Little Earl and his family, left southern Illinois. As Big Earl's brother Dalta had done earlier, they ended up in Florida—specifically the Jacksonville area, a neck of the woods Big Earl knew well from his liquor-running days.

Very few members of the family of Agnes and Ben Shelton remained in Wayne County (Ben had died in the early 1940s). The small number still on hand included Agnes herself and Lula, her youngest daughter.

Assuming Harris' goal truly was to drive Ben and Agnes Shelton's family out of Illinois, which he belatedly contended to fellow convict "Peck" Smith at Menard, he had great success.

The Edward Hyde side of his personality was quite effective.

14

June 28, 1951

Another bloody day in Wayne County. Another wounding of a Shelton by gunfire, this time the youngest sister of the late gang leader Carl Shelton. Another round of finger-pointing at Charlie Harris as the alleged trigger-man. Another mysterious shooting the same day, leaving a man dead in a bootlegging joint. Another day for newspaper reporters from far and wide to flock to Fairfield and join the Wayne County Press in covering the repetitious violence that appeared to have no end.

The machine-gunning of Lula Shelton and her husband Guy Pennington was a particularly brazen assault. The attack was launched in broad daylight in a residential neighborhood not far from Fairfield Memorial Hospital.

Lula and Guy flatly identified Harris as the shooter, and most of the initial press coverage openly assumed that Harris was the assailant.

Take the *St. Louis Globe-Democrat* for example. Its second-day story on the assault under a heading, "Sister of Mob Chief and Her Husband Shot," was accompanied by a front-page picture of Harris. The photo surely came from the paper's files because Charlie wore a broad smile.

A second picture accompanying the article would turn out to be highly ironic. It showed a pretty, nineteen-year-old married woman looking at bullet holes in the windshield of the automobile in which the Penningtons were riding when attacked. The curious bystander was identified as Betty Newton of Fairfield. She would, of course, be a prominent figure in Charlie's life in later years.

Some sought to link the shooting of Lula and Guy with the enigmatic murder, a few hours later, of laborer Louis Sons at a bootleg hangout near Fairfield operated by Ogie Pennington, a brother of Lula's husband. One theory was that Sons might have witnessed the ambush of Lula and Guy. Members of Sons' family did say later that he was to have been painting a house near the scene of the crime and may have been looking or working at the home when the shooting occurred.

Another guess was that Sons, not known to have any enemies, was mistaken by his slayer or killers for Ogie Pennington, who did see the machine-gunning since he was following Lula and Guy in another auto.

Authorities wasted no time charging Harris with the attempted murder of Lula and Guy, and Harris was just as quick to deny responsibility. A familiar scenario working to Charlie's advantage then unfolded. His guilt appeared more and more in doubt as a service station attendant provided an alibi for him, and several folks in the neighborhood of the shooting asserted that the attacker didn't look like Charlie.

It would be one more case in which a Shelton's claim of being assaulted by Harris would end up going nowhere. (Who at the time could have foreseen the future prison conversation in which Harris reportedly claimed to be behind the shootings of all the Sheltons?)

Whether or not Harris was the assailant of Lula and Guy, reason dictated that the culprit was not an outside hit man sent to Fairfield by organized crime bosses. The Shelton racketeering network was a thing of the past by 1951; its remnants had been absorbed by the big city mobs. And another factor could not be ignored. Crime syndicates adhered to certain strictures, one of which was that women and children were supposed to be off limits to violence.

As one old-timer at the Wayne County Courthouse put it, "Shooting a woman in cold blood is bad business." Between spits of tobacco juice, he added, "Men shooting each other is bad enough. But, this has got the town mighty upset."

The ambusher of the Penningtons, it was widely felt, most likely was a Wayne countian with a personal score to settle. More people than Harris held a grudge against the dwindling Shelton family, but Lula and Guy— backed up by Ogie Pennington—never wavered in insisting their attacker was Harris.

The machine-gunning occurred as Lula and Guy's car reached an intersection near the hospital. Their car as well as Ogie Pennington's suddenly was blocked by a black Mercury sedan occupied by a man and possibly one or two women.

When the Pennington vehicles stopped, machine-gun fire perforated the windshield of Guy and Lula's auto, striking both of them. She and Guy jumped out of the car, only to be confronted immediately by a man with a machine gun who'd exited the Mercury. Guy, who had a wound in his side, took off running toward his brother's auto. Lula, more seriously wounded, did not run. One version of what ensued was related vividly in a story by *Globe-Democrat* writer Edwin Krell.

"The machine-gun gangster, identified as 'Black Charlie' Harris in the attack on the Guy Penningtons, was a leering, laughing crazy man who told Mrs. Pennington, 'I'm going to kill all of the Sheltons, just like I did your brothers,'" wrote Krell.

Lula was said to plead for her life, screaming: "I never did anything to you."

According to Krell's article, the assailant only replied, "Now you are going to get some of the same stuff your brothers got." The *Wayne County Press*, in its reporting of this exchange, noted that Lula also claimed Harris added an additional threat.

It was, she alleged, that he intended "to cut your mother up in little pieces and throw her around the county."

During the issuance of the threats, Lula struggled to back away from her attacker by slumping into a patch of weeds on a vacant lot beside the street. The assailant again opened fire. At the sound of renewed gunshots, Guy Pennington, still on the road near his brother's car, dove into a ditch.

The man continued to shoot until the machine gun jammed. Then he ran back to his auto and sped away.

The contention that Harris was the gunman was not bolstered by the accounts of several individuals living near the site of the ambush. Sam Mercer, identified as a retiree living on nearby Maple Street, observed part of the encounter from a back porch of his home. He told authorities that he saw "a man shooting at the woman first, then shooting at the man running west." To Mercer, "It sounded like firecrackers."

Mercer related that he did hear "the woman holler." Her words, according to him, were: "Don't shoot me. I've never done nothing to you." She then yelled for help, he said. He said he did not hear the attacker say anything.

The woman "stumbled and grabbed her side and her leg, and set down in the grass," Mercer said. "He (had) shot (at her) a couple of times at about the time she hollered. I don't think he shot at her any after she stumbled down."

Mercer thought the man might have had handguns, not a machine gun. He said the shooter was a little under six feet tall with hair that "didn't look very dark, (but) looked kinda light." The description didn't fit Harris.

After noting that "someone said...the man was Charlie Harris," Mercer had this to say:

"If that was Charlie Harris, he has grown a lot since I saw him. I knew Charlie since he was a kid." But, Mercer added, "The last time I saw him was in 1925."

A person who witnessed the final moments of the episode was Mary Crickman, whose home on Northwest Ninth Street was only a few steps away from the outburst.

"I was cleaning a chicken, and I heard the shots and thought it was firecrackers," Mary told a *Wayne County Press* reporter. "Then, I heard a woman scream. I ran outside just in time to see the gunman get in his car and drive away. I was so excited. I didn't know what he looked like."

Charles William (Bill) Crickman, a grandson of Mary Crickman, was a young boy living with his grandmother at the time of the incident. He recalled aspects of it when he was interviewed by telephone September 23, 2008, from his home near Spokane, Washington. At the time, he was a retired school administrator.

While playing a small marble pinball machine with his older brother Joseph in the living room of Mary's house, Bill heard the shots and, like others, said "they sounded like a string of firecrackers going off." He and his brother followed their grandmother outside. While standing on the front porch, he recalled hearing Lula loudly beseeching the shooter to not fire again.

"I never saw the man actually fire," Crickman said. "I only retained a vague image in my head of seeing him very briefly. I remember thinking he had on a dark suit. I know his car was a very solid black."

Not long after the attacker had driven away, Bill ventured to the lot where Lula had sought refuge. He found her sitting in weeds "about knee high." A picture of her embedded in his mind was of "a woman slender or thin, certainly not heavy, with dark brown hair that was not short."

Two other persons living close to the shooting site, Carl and Mattie Orth, were attempting to comfort Lula, he said. He added that his grandmother, who was a nurse's aide at the hospital, also was assisting.

After an ambulance arrived, Crickman said he never erased the memory of watching Carl Orth as he helped load Lula into it. Orth "had on a kind of white T-shirt that was covered in blood," Bill said. Too, he recalled spotting blood in the weeds "where she had been."

He also remembered that "while Lula was being put in the ambulance, her husband had come back and seemed to want to get in the ambulance with her. But, he was told to go on to the hospital on his own."

As for the shooting, Crickman said his grandmother "explained later that she didn't know what the man looked like because she only saw his back, not his face. However, she didn't believe the man was Harris because he was too tall to be Charlie."

The "whole thing" was difficult for Mary Crickman, her grandson said, because "she knew Lula, and she (Lula) had been to our house." At the same time, she also knew Harris "prior to the incident," he said. "But as to how she knew Charlie…well, I didn't know."

The observations of Mercer and Mary Crickman were not helpful to those trying to build a case against Harris. More damaging to the effort, though, was the statement of an employee at a gas station on Highway 15 about six miles from the ambush site. This person was quoted as saying that Harris—although driving a black Mercury sedan—was at the station buying gasoline at the time of the shooting. Harris himself argued that he did not even learn of the ambush until he was back home listening to a radio broadcast of a baseball game.

Within hours of the incident, Willard Pearce, then an assistant state's attorney of Wayne County, issued a warrant charging Harris with attempted murder as a result of statements by Lula and the Pennington brothers.

Harris was quick to surrender on the warrant the following day—doing so in a calm, deliberate manner that was observed closely by a sizable number of persons who had congregated in downtown Fairfield.

He seemed to savor the attention as he flashed confident smiles to acquaintances among the folks milling around. His reception seemed too friendly to an Evansville reporter, who remarked that Charlie's "surrender looked more like the return of the town's leading celebrity."

Globe-Democrat writer John Costello picked up on the celebrity angle too, reporting that Harris was followed around by an "admiring procession" of "starry-eyed youths and smiling elders."

"Children gaped at him as if he were the Cisco Kid," wrote Costello. "One boy of eight or nine ran hurriedly back to the car, parked along the curb, where his mother was putting a coin in the parking meter. 'Mom, I saw Charlie Harris,' the youngster informed her, excitedly."

True enough, some came out to see if there was anything to rumors that Big Earl Shelton and a few of his old followers intended to appear and confront Harris. Nothing of the sort happened. In the event it had, Charlie's favorite half brother, Lem Harris, was standing by with a number of Harris' friends from Pond Creek.

Harris appeared first in the city square before proceeding to the office of his attorney, Kelley Loy, across the street from the courthouse. After a conference there, Harris and Loy began a walk that would end in the court of Magistrate Arch Hill.

Charlie was his typical dapper self, clad in a gray sports shirt, slacks of the same color, a fawn colored fedora and highly polished brown shoes. One newsman remarked that Harris looked more like a professional golfer than a farmer.

No question, he had the look of a cool customer during his stroll in downtown Fairfield. His composure did not waver as reporters shot questions at him about the shooting of the Penningtons. All they got back was a grin revealing his gold teeth and a comment that it "looks like the fleet's in."

Harris made certain in his walkabout to pass the window of the *Wayne County Press* on East Main Street. A long-standing tradition was in play as a number of individuals stood there reading the news bulletins that were stuck on the window each day. As Harris went by, the window watchers turned around to gaze at him. One who did not, however, was a daughter of the murdered Louis Sons. She wept as she read news items mentioning her father's death.

Harris was not detained very long after appearing before Hill. A bond was set at $10,000 to ensure his appearance at a July 27 hearing on the attempted murder charge. Four of his neighbors signed the bond, posting as security farm and oil lands valued at $20,000. The signers included Courtney Meritt and Gladstone Keen. It was not the first time Meritt had helped Harris post a bond. Keen was among those asserting at the coroner's inquest into the killing of Carl Shelton that Charlie was too far away from the site of the murder when the gunfire started to have participated in it.

During the weeks leading up to the hearing for Harris, Fairfield remained enveloped in its latest tragic drama. Tension thick enough to cut with a knife hung in the air. A Mount Carmel radio station cautioned its listeners, in the wake of the shooting, that "unless it's absolutely necessary, we advise you not to visit Fairfield…more trouble is expected there…."

Two days after the ambush of the Penningtons and the death of Sons in the bootleg establishment, the place was torched and destroyed. The following day, more than 500 persons showed up for the funeral service for Sons in a local undertaking parlor. The cortege following his body to the cemetery was more than a mile long.

Public discourse over the goings-on was taking center stage. The Reverend Eugene Leckrone, a Methodist pastor and head of the Fairfield Ministerial Alliance, said that the ceaseless violence was abetted by the indifference of citizens refusing to assist law enforcement officials. "When good people laugh at the laws," declared Leckrone, "the bad people disobey them."

Few were on a hotter seat than State's Attorney Gerald Mayberry.

Long after his days in public office in Wayne County, Mayberry spent time at Springfield working in Illinois state government. As deputy clerk of the Court of Claims, he was lauded for his efforts to modernize the court's operation. Now and then, he joined in a short but daily afternoon coffee break at the Capitol during which reporters and lobbyists would mingle with appointed and elected officials near the third floor's renowned brass rail.

Those aware of downstate history sometimes would quietly point to Mayberry as one, if willing, who could provide the inside scoop on the legendary violence in Wayne County involving the Sheltons, Black Charlie and other notorious characters. When this was mentioned to his face, Mayberry usually replied that the day might come when he'd consider talking. Then, he'd smile wryly and add, "Maybe."

During his stint as state's attorney, Mayberry was not hesitant to express his frustration in trying to deal with the rampant hostility. It didn't help that principals in law enforcement were viewed unevenly by the combatants. The Sheltons, still in the county when Mayberry took office, suspected that Mayberry had it in for them; Harris let it be known that he had a favorable opinion of him.

Personal feelings aside, Mayberry was hamstrung in seeking to prosecute Harris for the shooting of the Penningtons because nobody stepped forward to substantiate Lula and Guy's version of the incident. People with knowledge that might have implicated Harris in this case and other acts of violence "just don't want to talk," Mayberry told newspapers.

"It seems a little unusual that no one sees anything."

Days later, the *Wayne County Press* chimed in on the issue with the following tidbit.

"Did you know that some of the residents who live next to the scene of the Pennington shooting received telephone calls from 'friends' advising of the need for 'a poor memory' on their part?" While that may have had some validity, one who did not receive such a call was Mary Crickman.

Reverend Leckrone stated publicly that individuals apparently were afraid to tell what they knew, but Mayberry countered that it was more likely that most persons regarded the onslaught against the Sheltons as an outgrowth of a feud that was none of their business.

If feud was the right word for the situation, the Sheltons were the losers.

Three weeks after they were ambushed, Lula and Guy quietly left the hospital—even though neither had recovered from their wounds. James Shelton Zuber, Lula's son, drove them, along with Agnes Shelton, to Mount Vernon. They were joined there by Little Earl, who'd come up from Florida.

With Little Earl driving Lula and Guy, and Zuber his Grandma Agnes, they departed for Henderson, Kentucky. There, the party met Big Earl and his wife Earline, who also had journeyed up from Florida. From that point, they all traveled to Florida. No members of the family of Ben and Agnes who'd been in the public eye were left in the Fairfield area.

To the surprise of no one, neither Lula nor Guy returned to Fairfield for the hearing on the charge that Harris tried to murder them. Mayberry had predicted, in view of the fact that Lula and Guy were the complainants against Harris, that failure by them to show up would result in dropping of the charge. When this prediction materialized, the charge was dismissed for want of prosecution, and Harris walked out of Hill's court a free man.

The same resolution had occurred when Harris was alleged to have ambushed Little Earl in Fairfield in 1949. Little Earl did not surface at the hearing, prompting approval of a motion to dismiss the charge against Harris for lack of evidence.

After surviving the latest accusation of attempting to murder a Shelton, Harris also may have had Little Earl in mind when he talked to a *Wayne County Press* reporter.

"I don't know why they keep digging at me every time something comes up," Harris contended. "I don't know anything about it. It may be like Joe Louis. They may get in a lucky punch." Harris, who followed sporting events, apparently was referring to boxer Ezzard Charles' upset of hard-punching Joe (Brown Bomber) Louis, a former heavyweight champion, in 1950.

His emergence once again unscathed from an assault charge on a member of the once-feared Shelton family had left Harris a major news maker. Only Buster Wortman and Paul Powell may have had more name recognition among those living in southern Illinois. However, Buster wasn't viewed by many as a real southern Illinoisan since East St. Louis was regarded widely as a world of its own. Powell, a Democratic state representative from Vienna in Johnson County, had matured by this time into a downstate political powerhouse.

Harris' name rang a bell with readers all over the landscape, even though he avoided reporters outside of Wayne County. Because of such elusiveness, writers from big town dailies found him a quarry worth stalking. Here was an evasive, mysterious individual gaining a bigger-than-life reputation through reputed misdeeds. By nailing down an interview with Harris, hard as it was to get, a reporter was assured of scoring a "beat" on the competition.

With few exceptions, out-of-town reporters wanting direct quotes from Harris had to settle for reprinting his comments that appeared in the *Wayne County Press*, where there were staffers who knew him personally. The *Globe-Democrat's* Costello obviously could not get Charlie to talk for his extensive feature on the world of Harris that ran July 8, 1951. The piece did not contain one word from Charlie himself.

This was more than a little strange because Costello apparently gained access to Harris' house in Pond Creek for the story. Otherwise, he could not have written that "in the narrow living room, which extends across the front of the white, asbestos-shingled house, are gimcracks with a western motif, a miniature brass sombrero and an ashtray fashioned from a spur."

Costello also made an interesting discovery while walking outside the house, which he said formerly belonged to Carl Shelton.

"Whether he (Harris) got much...book 'larnin' is doubtful," the reporter wrote. "His family name, hand-lettered on the rural mailbox in front of the house, is misspelled 'Harriss.'" Upon further investigation, Costello noticed that Carl Shelton's name was "scratched in the brick and concrete foundation of the front porch."

Costello also wanted readers to be aware that the house sat on a small hill surrounded by empty fields, giving its occupant "what the army calls a clear field of fire."

Unlike the *Globe-Democrat*, the *Chicago Tribune* did have a rare sit-down interview with Harris. The lucky reporter was George Woltman. His article ran five days before Costello's.

Woltman's face-to-face meeting with Charlie in a clandestine setting actually was encouraged and arranged by Harris, according to the resulting story. In fact, an interesting part of the article was Woltman's recitation of the interview's cloak-and-dagger touch.

The reporter related that he "rode out of town (Fairfield) to the clay bottom road leading past the house of Big Earl Shelton, which was leveled by a dynamite bomb last fall...." That was the first step in following instructions that led Woltman to a rendezvous with Harris in his neighborhood.

Although "an occasional light in a farmhouse blinked," Woltman mainly navigated in "pitch dark" to reach the destination—a "rutted road" under overhanging trees. Once on this lane, the following occurred in the *Tribune* scribe's words:

"Suddenly the lights of two oncoming cars appeared. I slowed down and the motorist (in the first car), a teenaged boy, called out, 'Blackie's right behind me.' Harris left his car and got into mine and asked me to drive up the road. He left his car and the other one behind. We pulled into a drive, and he asked me to turn out my headlights. He objected even to the soft glow of the parking lights.

"'I've got to be careful,' he apologized.

"And then in pitch darkness I sat, unable to take notes as he related his story."

Charlie detailed his grievances with the Sheltons, starting with his arrest in Detroit. Newspapers also came under fire for unfairly making him, in his words, "a central figure in these parts."

He credited the years in Leavenworth with giving him time to think straight and, in the end, inspiring him to "make something of himself" when he was released.

Woltman quoted Harris as saying he decided to acquire property, not in a city but farmland. "On a farm you can plant a potato, and it grows and you can eat it. You won't starve on a farm, and you're less likely to get in trouble."

Harris pointed out that some of the money he needed to acquire acreage in Pond Creek came from his employment as a carpenter in "war plants" in the early 1940s. (Harris worked, or at least applied for a job, at a powder plant of E. I. du Pont de Nemours & Co. at Charlestown, Indiana, in 1941. Later, he did the same at an ordnance plant by Marion, Illinois.)

As Charlie discussed his buying of farm tracts, Woltman asked him about the land transaction dispute with Carl Shelton a decade earlier that cemented their mutual enmity. Harris gave his version of it in what may have been his first comments on the subject to a reporter.

Saying he "heard of a 220-acre farm in Pond Creek owned by an East Chicago woman upon which the mortgage had been foreclosed," Harris said he "went to Carl Shelton seeking information on how to go about acquiring it, knowing Carl had picked up many such parcels of land."

The reporter then wrote, "He (Harris) said Carl promised to look into the matter for him, but later discovered Carl had taken steps to procure it for himself." With that, Harris "then consulted a lawyer, and upon advice paid the owner directly for rights to the farm."

When Shelton learned of Charlie's action, the *Tribune* article stated, Carl did "a quick burn, saying 'that little devil, I'd give a thousand dollars to have my hands on him right now.'"

Harris went on to explain his opposition to what he termed the bullying of many Pond Creek farmers by Carl and Big Earl. Consequently, Harris said, "Ever since then, I've been blamed for whatever shootings occurred.

"You ask me who is killing them off? Why it's like running through a briar patch and turning around to look for the one that stuck you."

Keep in mind, Harris averred to Woltman, that the Sheltons had made many enemies as they brought bootlegging, vice and corruption to Wayne County and much of southern Illinois—and with all that the "killings, pistol whippings and hell raising that bring you reporters down here."

Harris apparently didn't share his thoughts with any more newspersons in the days preceding his hearing on the Pennington assault. After the shooting charge was dropped, he assiduously sought to avoid the press as he moved to escape the limelight and, as much as was discernible, lead the life of a normal farmer.

With the Sheltons gone, the bullets stopped. The fires didn't. Shelton antagonists obviously had an irresistible impulse to destroy visible reminders of the family.

A month before the end of 1951, the abandoned Shelton homestead at the Merriam crossroads, last lived in by Agnes, was burned to the ground. In March 1952, the last remaining structures at Big Earl's farm, one a vacant house that Ray Walker had occupied, were destroyed by one or more arsonists. The location of what had been Big Earl's Farmers' Club was the site of the windup of the campaign to eliminate vestiges of the Sheltons.

Early on the morning of July 15, 1952, Fairfield was awakened rudely by an explosion that greatly damaged the building on the city square that had housed the upstairs gambling establishment. Law officers attributed the blast to a nitroglycerin bomb placed at the front door of a recently opened restaurant on the first floor of the building, believed to be the last one in town owned by Big Earl. No injuries were reported, but the explosion heavily damaged adjoining garages and shattered windows in structures around the square.

Neither Harris nor anyone else was charged in the fires and explosion. Some folks had ideas about likely suspects, but nobody talked. If anything, a feeling of relief drifted through the air after the Farmers' Club bombing because it was the last Shelton-related target of any significance to be struck.

Suspicious fires in Wayne County hardly were a thing of the past, though. Harris himself found this out late in 1954 when his farm home was destroyed by a blaze. The cause never was determined, but almost everybody assumed it was intentionally set. Shelton loyalists still resided in the county, and a number were capable of arson.

However, some guessed that the fire may have been tied to the reputed but hushed-up involvement by Harris in the contest for sheriff of Wayne County in 1954. The election was close, with Democrat Bob Wilson barely losing to his Republican opponent. Wilson demanded a recount. It could not be done, though, because the ballots were stolen from the county courthouse.

Although the matter remained shrouded in mystery at the time, a knowledgeable Fairfield attorney was told years later by Emily Hodges, a housekeeper for Harris, that Charlie had stolen the ballots and burned them in her presence in the furnace at his house. The attorney also was told that Harris surreptitiously was let into the courthouse to pick up the ballots by someone who did not want Wilson to win.

However, that person was not Republican Elmo Mugrage, the new sheriff of Wayne County. No aspersion was cast on Mugrage's reputation because he was not linked to the incident. His good standing in the community remained intact.

After the alleged meddling by Harris in the local political scene, the remaining years of the 1950s were relatively calm for him and, more importantly, for Fairfield and Wayne County. Perhaps the sensational criminal activity finally was part of the past. At least, there was hope.

Fairfield needed a vacation from the spotlight.

15

Almost a Regular Guy

T he 1950s seemed like a long-awaited decade in which the ebb and flow of life were slow enough for Americans to catch their breath. Looking back, the fifties came across as an orderly period, a far cry from the upheaval in following years that restructured society.

If a steadfast state of affairs ever had existed in America, the 1950s may have come closest to setting the stage. It was a decade minus surprises at every turn; call it an era for something approaching regularity in everyday life.

Many historians labeled the fifties as a time-out from the gripping tension of World War II in the 1940s and the civil rights revolution that tore apart the country in the 1960s. Routine was a watchword of the 1950s that suited a lot of persons who welcomed a chance to let the dust settle for a while in their lives.

Black Charlie certainly needed a breather. Or at least it would have seemed.

Following the hubbub over the shooting of Lula and Guy Pennington early in the 1950s, Harris was quite successful in avoiding more sensationalism in his life during the rest of the decade. Instead, he seemed to realize his oft-stated intent to live a peaceful existence as a typical farmer.

Later, the FBI would mince no words in asserting that Harris had led a double life in the 1950s. The implication—not clothed with supportive evidence—was that Charlie was available for dirty work ordained by crime bosses far from southern Illinois. If so, any person in Harris' home territory who might have suspected anything of the sort kept it to himself or herself. Most people quaked at the mere thought of ticking off Harris.

Fairfield was pretty much in tune with the tone for the fifties set by Dwight Eisenhower, who hammered Illinois Governor Stevenson in the 1952 presidential election. Eisenhower's plan was designed to steer the country down the middle, where left and right extremists were shut out by middle Americans—the quintessential folks who paid most of the taxes, cast the majority of the votes and clung most closely to the time-cherished values of home, church and community.

Fear of nuclear weapons may have hovered overhead like a sword of Damocles, but the 1950s were colored mainly by conservative politics, social conformity and economic prosperity for a large number of Americans. Challenges to traditional cultural standards came later. Images of the fifties portrayed people living tidy lives with wives staying home to bear children at soaring numbers and businessmen primly attired in suits and ties. Material success increasingly became a top priority.

Harris looked to be a good fit for the decade. His head seemed to be well above water with his farming, financially speaking, and his sartorial splendor hardly went unnoticed. In the words of one of those hanging out at Otis Brach's service station in the fifties, "Charlie always had on a white shirt with a tie, and he usually was in a suit too. He was one spiffy guy."

Dressing smartly was a high priority of Harris. The penchant often led him to Lex B. Tickner's Men's Clothiers on Fairfield's Main Street. One of the haberdashery's best customers, he insisted on top-of-the-line apparel, such as Seinsheimer suits and Florsheim shoes. In addition, few patrons of the Tickner store were more affable in getting fitted.

A toned-down albeit well-dressed Harris was visible in the early 1950s when he'd show up nearly every Saturday afternoon to hash over things at Brach's DX service at the corner of First and Main streets in Fairfield

There, he was conversant on Communist North Korea's invasion of South Korea in 1950, and on the dispatch of United States ground forces to combat the incursion. He was up on the cold war with Russia, intensified at the time by the Communist power's securing of its own atomic bomb and by President Harry Truman revealing that his country was developing an even more destructive nuclear weapon, the H-bomb. Public anxiety in the early 1950s also was fueled by Wisconsin Senator Joseph McCarthy's claims of heavy Communist infiltration of the State Department. Charlie had an opinion about that, but was notably silent on another hot subject— the Kefauver Committee's exposure of widespread underworld activities.

Bringing up the past when talking to Harris was verboten. An exception might occur if the man himself broached it, but that was indeed rare.

As a regular Saturday congregant put it, Harris seemed "like one of us...loafing and shooting the bull. The way he was then, he would kid around and, really, hardly ever stop smiling. Besides the farming and the weather, it was true that he could talk about all the stuff going on in the world. But, of course, we never got into the gangster thing."

Charlie never scrimped on the maintenance of his cars, and the servicing at Brach's establishment usually was time consuming. Charlie always insisted that his vehicle be washed. This was not always an easy chore in view of the dirt from the dusty roads of Pond Creek. For a while, Harris pulled into the station in a 1949 red Pontiac convertible. Then he turned up in a maroon 1952 Super Buick convertible with a white top.

The later model convertible was one of the cars that Charlie purchased from the Buick-Pontiac dealership owned and operated by Emmitt Hoffee on the Fairfield square. He was a member of an old Wayne County family raised on a Pond Creek farm, and he did not hesitate to call Harris a friend. For that matter, Shelton family members also purchased vehicles from Hoffee. However, Carl Otis Hoffee, a son of Emmitt, did not recall seeing Harris and any Shelton at the dealership simultaneously.

Carl Hoffee, a Springfield attorney who also still practiced law in Fairfield when interviewed in 2008 at the Sangamo Club in the Illinois State Capital, emphasized that "neither my father nor my Uncle John ever were afraid of these guys. There was never any hostility in my family's relationship with any of them. You had to remember that this was a situation where everybody knew everybody else because it was a small town, a small county.

"And as far as it went with Charlie Harris, my dad and Uncle John grew up in the same Pond Creek neighborhood as he did."

The uncle to whom Carl referred was John Hoffee. He sold Studebakers in Fairfield before opening the Farmer's Store in the city in the 1940s, a retail business that became known throughout southern Illinois.

Carl Hoffee, who was born in 1934, recalled occasions when he was in the presence of Harris at his dad's dealership, but cautioned that "those things about his reputation never were discussed when I was around." Nevertheless, Carl remarked, "good friends in Springfield asked me through the years if I was dangerous because of being from Fairfield."

"Of course," he added, "they were just joking."

Not surprisingly, persons from Wayne County who later resided elsewhere, like Carl Hoffee, became accustomed to questions about the Sheltons and Harris. The same was true for individuals who moved to Fairfield after living in other places. William (Bill) Schmitz called Springfield home before moving to Fairfield in 1989. From that point on, Schmitz, a state employee, faced inquiries about the Wayne County headliners when on the road.

"When I'd go back to Springfield or somewhere else," Schmitz said, "people would ask me about the Sheltons or maybe Harris. I discovered this great interest in these guys. It made me want to try to learn more myself about them so I could answer some of the questions."

However, Schmitz found many in Wayne County "rather hesitant" to discuss the personalities or activities of the gangsters. He soon recognized that "people here looked on them differently than (those) in the rest of the world." After all, he noted, "if you consider the Sheltons, for example, you have to acknowledge that most of the stuff for which they were known happened far from Wayne County."

On the other hand, the traumatic events that shaped the final legacy of Harris did occur in the county. Human nature being human nature, people who knew Harris, or were aware of him, noticeably shied away from open reflection on the violence that landed him in prison for a third and final time. They were more comfortable in recalling memories of Harris in his relatively trouble-free years after the elimination of the Sheltons.

For some, it was simply the exciting realization of setting eyes on a person so well known.

Larry Bunting was a grade school pupil in Albion on the day that his father, dairy farmer Nile Judge Bunting, stopped at a service station east of

Fairfield with Larry in the car. Larry noticed two persons playing checkers on an oil barrel in the station. One was an older man in a short-sleeved white shirt and tie. To hear the man talk, Bunting said, "I would have thought he was a preacher." After leaving the place, Nile Bunting told his son that he had just seen Black Charlie Harris.

"Naturally, I knew right away who my dad was talking about," Larry said nearly a half century later, when he was an insurance agent living in New Berlin, Illinois. "Everybody growing up down there had heard the stories."

David Lynn Musgrave was an employee of the Illinois secretary of state in Springfield when he remembered the time, five decades earlier, that he first saw Harris. Twilight had descended on the farm of his father, William Vernon Musgrave, three miles north of Burnt Prairie, when young David saw the silhouette of a man chatting with his dad. The visitor wanted Musgrave, who went by Vernon, to help with the cutting of corn.

"I was aware that the man was named Charlie Harris," said David, "but I was pretty young at the time and really knew nothing about him." But, he added, "That would change as I got older and listened to the men talk."

Not long afterward, David's brother Ray related an observation that gave David a little insight into the mind-set of Harris. Ray accompanied his father when he went to Harris' place in the evening to settle up on the corn cutting. There was no response when Vernon knocked on Charlie's door.

"But then, pretty soon, Ray told me that Charlie came walking around the corner of his place, twirling a hat on his finger or something," recounted David. "When he (Harris) saw it was my dad, he put the hat on his head. And then dad and Ray could see that he'd been twirling the hat on a pistol, which he proceeded to stick under his belt."

Weapons often came to mind when thinking of Harris.

The nature of the beast was recalled in a 2008 telephone interview with Charles Edward Rountree, a robotic systems designer then living in Island Lake, Illinois. As a young lad, Rountree—whose mother, Mary Ann, was a daughter of Charlie's niece Laverne Slattery—insisted that he'd once gotten a close-up view of Harris' marksmanship. While sitting in Charlie's lap in the early 1960s, Rountree watched him pull out an old revolver from his clothing and take aim at a paper cup blowing across the yard.

"He fired three or four times," said Rountree, "and he never missed the cup. That's the kind of thing you don't forget."

Also worth remembering, Rountree said, were days when Harris drove him and other little kids into Fairfield for ice cream. "Persons yelled and waved at Charlie," recollected Rountree, "and he sometimes stopped and talked to them in their front yards."

The man "could be a true gentleman," Rountree asserted. Yet, he acknowledged that Harris also "could be ruthless," and that "yes, everybody was afraid of him." Rountree, who lived several years in Pond Creek with his great-grandmother Mabel Bell, Charlie's sister, said that she dubbed him "Little Blackie" because "she said I had the same mean streak that he did."

In addition to remembering Harris' prowess with a revolver, Rountree never forgot one very painful spanking from Mabel. Playing with matches, he accidentally set fire to straw by her chicken shed. Soon it also was ablaze.

"She did not spare the rod on me because I couldn't have done much worse to her," he said. "The chickens were like her babies, her pets. She meticulously cleaned their coop every day."

During some of the nights spent by Rountree at Mabel's house, no inside lighting was allowed after dark. He explained that this was because Mabel herself was not divorced from bootlegging, thus necessitating precautions against cutthroat competitors in the moonshine business.

But, as long as Harris was on the scene, anyone seriously intending harm to Mabel would have been putting his life on the line, Rountree maintained. In the end, he concluded, Charlie was "like a paradox. You certainly did not want to do him wrong, but he normally was so polite that people loved him to death. He could be pretty much of a sweetheart."

Rountree spoke figuratively in calling Harris a sweetheart, but rumors suggested strongly that he truly was a paramour of numerous women in the 1950s. He apparently was not deterred from such red-blooded fellow pursuits by his marriage in the middle of the decade to Rena Damon, a telephone operator in New Harmony, Indiana. Harris was the first husband of Rena, a tiny and courteous woman who was introduced to Charlie by a friend of Rena's who lived near Mabel Bell.

Rena, the third and last wife of Harris, owned property in New Harmony and also a farm in the Pond Creek area that was worked by Charlie. During the time in their marriage when Harris was not imprisoned, the two usually lived together only on weekends, partly because Rena preferred to remain in New Harmony.

For a person who took pride in being labeled a ladies' man, Harris undoubtedly would have approved of a tribute to him in the August 1990 issue of *Springhouse* magazine. The author of the piece was La Donna Harrell Martin, a musician and singer at dances attended by Charlie. She was lavish in her praise of him, but there was not the slightest indication of anything in her relationship with Harris beyond admiration.

Her literary effort was noteworthy, not only for her heartfelt impression of Harris, but also for its depiction of down-home social gatherings in rural America.

Martin wrote that she met Harris when playing in "a little hillbilly band" at Saturday night parties. She was about thirteen years old when Harris "was the first man to kiss my hand," she noted.

"Charlie lifted my hand off the accordion keyboard, looked at me with those eyes, kissed my fingertips, and softly said, 'You are a lovely, talented little girl.' Then he turned, walked back to his square dance set, ready for our fiddler to start the next break-down."

Time and again at the dances, she observed Harris "whirling and swinging in his dark, pin-striped suit, starched white shirt and satin tie" as women "delightedly" joined him in an allemande. To Martin, he was "our best spirit of grace in elegance and good manners."

When Charlie showed up on those nights when La Donna was performing, she wrote that she "played and sang more carefully. I knew he would catch those special key changes, the extra clean, high yodel ending…the special tenderness I tried to give the low tones for a sweet ballad."

Harris easily stood out on those occasions, related Martin, when "country women" were permitted to escape "from a week of hoeing in hard, dry gardens; from canning green beans on hot wood cook stoves; (and) from carrying gallons of water from wells or creeks…."

Parties at times were held in homes, where "people would dance all over the house except for the kitchen," the article noted.

In the kitchen, it went on, "every flat surface was crowded with plat-ters of hams and chicken, dishes of potato salad and bean salads, (and) compotes of fresh fruit salads. Twenty or thirty pies and tall, luscious cakes of every color covered...makeshift plank tables."

However, Martin said she never saw Charlie eat. Instead, she ob-served, he "sat in a quiet corner, drank lemonade and talked with everyone who ambled over." She also found it impressive that he "sat up straight... (with) suit pants creased to a knife edge, (and) black high-polished shoes glistening on the worn linoleum floors."

She had to be flattered on those occasional times when music resumed after eating and Harris didn't hotfoot it to the dance floor. Instead, she wrote, he often just "watched me if I sang...just sat with his lemonade, didn't talk...watched."

For her, Charlie was "my first really sincere gentleman."

Harris did not rate highly with all women, though. Charles Ralph March witnessed this firsthand.

March was the longtime mayor of Palmyra, Illinois, in 2008 when he looked back on his visit to Fairfield at the start of the 1960s to offer free chest X rays as part of a statewide program to detect tuberculosis or signs of another pulmonary disease. Then a young technician for the Illinois Department of Public Health, March operated out of a white bus used by the agency to house a mobile X-ray unit.

On the day the unit was stationed near the Wayne County Courthouse, March was assisted by three or four volunteers, all local women, who sat at a desk in the back of the vehicle filling out registration cards and han-dling other clerical tasks.

Harris was among those entering the bus for an X ray. March knew nothing about him, but remembered that "on this particular day he looked kind of unkempt, not well manicured and needing a haircut. I didn't think much of it, though, because others sometimes came in looking like that too."

March quickly noticed that Harris was acquainted with the women workers. "He greeted them," March said, "and then started to actually kind of tease them.

"But, I could tell the ladies did not like him. They definitely were not comfortable with him being there."

Harris was cooperative as March shot an X ray of his chest, and then he wanted to know when the result would be available.

"I told him it normally took about ten days for results to be known," March related. "I had a feeling he felt he had some problems." March did not recall if the X-ray plates revealed anything negative. However, the earful he got from the women after Charlie departed was another matter.

"I remember them telling me he was a gangster and a womanizer. They brought up the Sheltons, fellows I had heard about, and all the stuff between him and them. Honestly, I couldn't hear enough about what they were saying because I always was interested in that sort of history."

Afterward, March drove the bus to other points in Wayne County. He was accompanied on those stops by Veda Hawkins, the county nurse, who supplied more background on Harris.

"After I found out just who he was," concluded March, "I never forgot the fact that I met him."

In retrospect, impressions of Harris varied greatly. One with a pleasant memory was Carmen Simpson, a daughter of Pond Creek farmer Edgar (Bud) Simpson and his wife Ida.

Carmen was a testament to the belief that all with connections to Pond Creek knew each other. Born in 1938, she was a pupil at the Windland Grade School when her father did farm work for Dalta Shelton. Her mother helped Mabel Bell can green beans and corn, and Carmen herself came to know Mabel as "a good person who, like everyone else, had faults." During her years at Fairfield High School, Carmen spent nights at the home of Leo Bell, a son of Mabel and nephew of Charlie. She was a close friend of a daughter of Leo.

Harris frequently was in Carmen's presence in the late 1950s when she and her then husband rented a farmhouse in the Pond Creek bottoms, only a half mile from Charlie's farm. Often a dinner guest at her place, Harris impressed Carmen as "a neatly dressed gentleman who ate lightly and did not smoke in my house." He always showed up alone.

When Harris "went to town (Fairfield)," Carmen said, "he'd often stop on the way and ask if I needed anything. I normally didn't take him up on it, but now and then I'd ask him to bring back milk for my babies. He acted as if he liked kids." Charlie also was helpful more than once in cutting down high grass and small trees by Carmen's home with a "bushhog" that he fitted on the back of a tractor.

Carmen was not alone as the 1950s gave way to the 1960s in considering Harris a good neighbor. But, cracks in this picture were starting to show up. A few persons were beginning to sense that the man who'd been a buffer against the aggressive Sheltons was himself getting out of bounds. One tiff in particular—with an old friend and ally at that—would lead to momentous trouble for Harris.

While an unusually placid period for Harris had evolved in the fifties, others with roles in his story were moving along in their own lives.

First, Beatrice Bell. A year after graduating from nursing school in Phoenix in 1950, she married Harold Riley, a Kansas farmer eighteen years her senior, in a wedding chapel in Wickenburg, Arizona. Beatrice, known after that as Bea Riley, spent the first year of her marriage breeding and running racehorses with her husband in the Southwest.

However, the birth of the first of their children convinced them that they needed a more stable home life. So, they moved to a wheat farm near Elkhart, Kansas, that was owned by Harold. Lightning struck their farmhouse in 1956, virtually destroying it, so they moved into Elkhart. Bea resided there for a spell before eventually returning to the countryside outside the city.

Next, Betty Lou Shockley. In the years after her birth in 1932 in Centralia, her parents, John and Mattie Shockley, moved to Fairfield, where Betty attended high school and was in a future homemakers' club.

At the age of fifteen, she married Charles Thomas Newton, a navy veteran from Wayne County. The ceremony was held at her parents' home, officiated by the Reverend Ruth Martin of Fairfield's Ellen Moore Methodist Church. Within a year, the couple gave birth to the first of their five children, daughter Carolyn Sue. Later, in the 1950s, Carolyn was joined by a sister, Kay Ellen, and brothers Kenneth Earl, Jack and Gary Ray.

Betty graduated from a beauty school in Mount Vernon, Illinois, but spent many of her working years as a waitress and barmaid. Her husband toiled as a laborer and car salesman, as well as spending several periods in the employment of Charlie Harris. Newton never overcame the lung injury suffered while serving on the USS *Clymer*, an attack transport, in the Second World War.

And then there was Richard Carr Cochran.

His life had taken interesting turns before he began his law practice in Fairfield in 1959 in the office of Kelley Loy. Harris had been among the clients of Loy, and Cochran himself would meet Charlie in due time.

In his pre-Fairfield years, Cochran had played a trumpet in dance bands in both his high school days at Carmi and undergraduate years at Vanderbilt University in Nashville, Tennessee. He may have known more about famed big-band leader Glenn Miller's arrangements than any other fellow his age. A year before Cochran graduated from Vanderbilt in 1952 with an economics degree, his father—who ran an abstract company—died.

Drafted into the army after Vanderbilt, Cochran served two years as an enlisted man and barely missed being sent to Korea. Following military duty, he returned to Vanderbilt and graduated from its law school in 1957. While there, he met and courted Anne Ogden, a nursing student at Vandy who eventually received an English degree from Peabody College in Nashville. They were married on St. Patrick's Day in 1957.

Other attorneys who did or would know Harris made headway of their own in the 1950s. By the end of the decade, Willard Pearce had been elected state's attorney of Wayne County. And James Lawder Jr. was on the path to getting a law degree at the University of Illinois.

Life seldom was static for people, including a good number whose past included Harris. As the 1960s progressed, Carmen Simpson, who'd shared her dinner table with Charlie numerous times, moved into another rented home in Pond Creek. It had been the residence of Howard S. Taylor, who was shot to death early in 1963.

She lived in the white, two-story frame home for three or four years. She was deadly serious in believing the house was haunted. She contended that "you could hear footsteps and water starting to run in the bathroom."

"It was a little eerie at first," Carmen admitted, but added that she "soon never really thought about it...about living in the home of a man who'd been murdered."

However, it was one house where Harris did not join Carmen for meals.

Some Charles Bryan Harris family members in the early 1900s. Standing (left to right): sister Cora Mabel; his father, John Michael Harris; young Charles; and his mother, Talitha Standerfer Harris. *Photograph courtesy of Beatrice Riley.*

Harris had his trademark dapper when he posed for a formal picture during his days as a young man in Arizona. *Photograph courtesy of Beatrice Riley.*

Cora Mabel Bell in the 1930s. The only full sister of Harris, she remained supportive of him during his leaner years in Wayne County. *Photograph courtesy of Beatrice Riley.*

Pond Creek, the sluggish stream in Wayne County that gave its name to a neighborhood identified far and wide with Harris and the Shelton brothers, his onetime friends who became his enemies. *Photograph by the author.*

Beatrice Riley in 1944 standing next to her first car, a 1936 Ford, in Arizona. Then seventeen years old, she still was known as Beatrice (Jakie) Bell. *Photograph courtesy of Beatrice Riley.*

Harris strolling with his favorite niece, Beatrice (Jakie) Bell, in Phoenix, Arizona, in the late 1940s. To her, he was a surrogate father and protector. *Photograph courtesy of Beatice Riley.*

Harris in the late 1940s, when his enmity with the Shelton brothers was making him a household name in downstate Illinois. *Photograph courtesy of Beatrice Riley.*

Betty Lou Shockley in 1947, shortly before she became the teenage bridge of Charles Thomas Newton in Fairfield. *Photograph courtesy of Carolyn Sue Bland.*

Betty Newton on familiar ground in Fairfield. She and her husband Charles returned to Fairfield from Arizona in 1963, a move that Betty reportedly was hesitant to make. *Photograph courtesy of Carolyn Sue Bland.*

Not long before she was murdered, Betty Newton was a waitress at The Grill, a popular Fairfield restaurant. *Photograph courtesy of Carolyn Sue Bland.*

Carolyn Sue Newton was a pretty six-teen-year-old when her mother Betty was murdered in 1964. *Photograph courtesy of Carolyn Sue Bland.*

Betty and Charles Newton were the parents of five children (left to right): Kay Ellen, Gary Ray, Jack, Kenneth Earl and Carolyn Sue. *Photograph courtesy of Carolyn Sue Bland.*

Harris requested that T. O. Mathews, editor of the *Wayne County Press*, take his picture in the Wayne County jail after Harris surrendered to authorities following his indictment for the 1963 murder of Pond Creek farmer Howard Taylor. *Photograph courtesy of the Wayne County Press.*

The Wayne County Courthouse in Fairfield, a building Harris came to know quite well as a result of his murder trials. *Photograph by the author.*

The bullet-riddled body of Howard Taylor was found in this automobile on a Pond Creek road January 5, 1963. *Photograph courtesy of the Wayne County Press.*

A jubilant Harris was all smiles after a jury acquitted him of murdering Howard Taylor. The tall man pictured next to Harris was Deneen Matthews, a Fairfield attorney who led Harris' defense against the murder charge. *Photograph courtesy of the Wayne County Press.*

Harris often was upbeat and conversant with everybody during his murder trials in the Wayne County Courthouse. *Photograph courtesy of the Wayne County Press.*

The smoldering ruins of the vacant Courtney Meritt farmhouse in which the bodies of Betty Newton and Jerry Meritt were discovered August 16, 1964. *Photograph courtesy of the Wayne County Press.*

Wayne County Sheriff Eugene Leathers spent considerable time in the 1960s keeping a watchful eye on Harris. *Photograph courtesy of the Wayne County Press.*

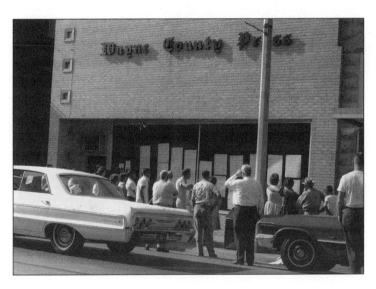

Folks frequently congregated at the window of the *Wayne County Press* to read the latest bulletins on Harris. The newspaper had a tradition of posting breaking news stories on its window. *Photograph courtesy of the Wayne County Press.*

Harris was popular with guards at the state prison near Vienna, Illinois, where he tended to flowers not long before his parole. *Photograph courtesy of Beatrice Riley.*

The downtown of Elkhart, Kansas, where Harris spent the last years of his life after his release from prison in Illinois. *Photograph by the author.*

As with many rural Kansas towns, grain elevators dominate the Elkhart skyline. *Photograph by the author.*

Harris lived in this trailer on Beatrice Riley's property until his death in 1988. He bought the unit for about $3,400. *Photograph by the author.*

A grandson of Beatrice Riley in the arms of Harris in the 1980s. *Photograph courtesy of Beatrice Riley.*

Harris was regarded as a pleasant, elderly gentleman in the final years of his life in Kansas. *Photograph courtesy of Beatrice Riley.*

The tombstone of Harris at Elkhart. He was buried next to his last wife, Rena Damon. *Photograph by the author.*

16

A Cold-Blooded Killing

Howard and Charlie were more than neighbors in Pond Creek. They had been close friends. Howard even had helped Harris post bond so he didn't have to sit in jail while a grand jury considered indicting him in the murder of Carl Shelton in 1947.

In his take on life, though, Harris said he had learned that "your best friend today may be your worse enemy tomorrow." Coming from Harris, this was a scary observation.

The words could have served as an epitaph for Howard S. Taylor—a person liked well enough by some of his fellow farmers to have been dubbed the unofficial mayor of Pond Creek.

The discovery of Taylor's bullet-riddled body on the rainy morning of January 5, 1963, returned Harris to the front burner of public scrutiny after years of successfully maintaining a low profile. Circumstantial evidence pointed to Charlie as Taylor's killer, and a special Wayne County grand jury soon agreed by indicting him for murder.

Although he professed his innocence, signs initially pointed to the likely conviction of Harris—a person who seemingly had nine lives in dodging past shooting allegations.

Individuals familiar with both Harris and Taylor said tracing the erosion of the pair's friendship was difficult. However, there was no doubt that animosity reached a boiling point in 1960 when Taylor complained that his crops were damaged by Harris' hogs roaming at will. Late that year, Taylor and his wife Marie engaged Fairfield attorney Lionel E. Clark to represent them in trying to make Harris pay for the damage.

Testifying later at Harris' trial on the murder charge, Clark said he had entered into negotiations with Charlie that led to his agreeing to try to settle a damage claim. Nothing was resolved, though, prompting the filing of a suit against Harris in February 1961 in Wayne County Circuit Court. Howard and Marie alleged in the petition that Harris "knowingly and willfully allowed swine to run at large on lands belonging to the plaintiffs." Trial on the suit was not set until October 1962.

At that point, Clark said, "Harris appeared without attorney, and we talked it over and entered into an agreement by stipulation in which Harris was to pay $550 by December 1." When Harris did not comply, Clark sought and obtained from Circuit Judge Randall S. Quindry a judgment for $1,000 against Charlie, the amount originally requested by the Taylors.

Subsequently, Clark forwarded to Sohio Pipeline Company a certified copy of court records detailing the judgment against Harris. This prompted Sohio to send Harris a letter from its Cleveland, Ohio, office on January 2, 1963, notifying him that his oil royalty payments were being withheld until the judgment was satisfied. The letter, according to later testimony, should have reached Harris on the morning of Taylor's murder.

Putting it mildly, the letter had to compound anger that Harris admittedly felt toward oilmen. Two years earlier, he issued a no-trespassing order to producers drilling a new well on his land. He said he was blocking completion of the well—even though he owned only surface and not mineral rights on the acreage south of Fairfield—because he was tired of unfair treatment from oil people. He decided not to interfere with other oil wells on his property at the time, but continued to complain that the receipt of little or no royalties increased his irritation at having to maneuver farm machinery around their pipes, tanks and other equipment.

As for the royalty-cessation letter from Sohio, prosecutors in Harris' murder trial argued it so incensed him that he immediately sought out Taylor for revenge. Harris maintained he never saw the letter before the murder and added that the matter was irrelevant because he did not kill Taylor.

Stark details of Taylor's death spread like wildfire.

His body was found slumped in his 1958 Chevrolet on the Pond Creek Road by Frank Keoughan, who with his brother Jack operated a company that serviced oil wells. Working that day on a well on Harris' farm, Jack later would testify that he had heard shots fired shortly after eleven o'clock in the morning, some twenty minutes or so before Frank, heading north on the road to Beulah's Café on Highway 15 for lunch, discovered Taylor's auto. It was resting on the west side of the road, facing south.

Pulling up beside the car, Frank noticed the windshield wipers were moving, but that the auto's motor was not running. Then he spotted bullet holes in the vehicle. Getting out of his truck, he peered into the car and saw the body of a man. Frank could not identify the person, noting only that he wore a heavy mackinaw and possibly a cap.

With little delay, Frank drove down the Pond Creek Road to fetch Jack, who accompanied Frank back to the Chevrolet. They counted thirteen bullet holes, but didn't touch the auto that had its windows rolled up. Jack would testify afterward that, like Frank, he did not recognize the man in the car, saying only that the person's "face was hanging down."

Jack recorded the license number of the car and headed for Fairfield to report its discovery to then Wayne County Sheriff Eugene Leathers. Keoughan reached the city's downtown just as the courthouse clock was striking twelve o'clock noon and found Leathers in short order.

The sheriff proceeded to the murder scene, as did Willard Pearce, the county state's attorney, and others. The car's windshield wipers still were operating when the officials arrived. They confirmed the Keoughan brothers' count of thirteen bullet holes in the auto. Leathers recalled afterward that the body, now determined to be that of Howard Taylor, was slumped to the right in the front seat. It contained multiple bullet wounds.

When the officers opened the car door and turned over Taylor's body, they saw that it had been shielding a .22-caliber pistol from which five shots were fired.

Word soon got around that Harris had showed up that same morning at the office of Dr. David Gershenson on the Fairfield square. Charlie had a wound in his left arm from a small caliber pistol shot. He told the doctor that he had been struck on his property by a bullet fired by an unknown person, possibly a hunter.

Gershenson ordered that Harris be transported by ambulance to Fairfield Memorial Hospital, where the doctor surgically removed the bullet.

Meanwhile, Taylor's car was towed to the garage of Brown Chevrolet in Fairfield, and his body was moved to the Nale Funeral Home, where an autopsy was performed by Dr. A. R. Marks and Wayne County Coroner Robert E. McNeill. It revealed holes in the corpse, McNeill told the *Chicago Tribune*, from three slugs "larger than .45-caliber" and from shotgun pellets. Two of the bullets were extracted.

Those bullets, along with shell casings, spent gun slugs and shotgun wadding found at the murder site, were sent to the state crime laboratory in Springfield for analysis. Taylor's pistol also was submitted for examination, as was the bullet removed from Harris' arm at the hospital. Subsequently, Pearce said tests showed that the bullet taken from Charlie came from Taylor's weapon.

Confident from the start that he could put together an ironclad case against Harris, Pearce wasted little time in calling for a meeting of a special grand jury to investigate the murder. The panel convened January 18, less than two weeks after the killing. Its foreman was Dominick Monge, the president of Airtex Products in Fairfield, and included a number of Wayne County's other leading citizens.

Before the jury began its deliberation behind closed doors, Judge Quindry addressed the panel publicly, not an everyday occurrence in the realm of grand juries.

"What you as a grand jury do here today will, I am sure, go a long way toward the restoration of dignity and self-respect to our county," Quindry told the jurors. "We do not have to live in a community bearing the stigma our community now bears. We bear this stigma because we lack the will to do anything about it."

The judge instructed the panel to fulfill its "duty to protect the innocent from unjust accusation of crimes, as well as the duty to return 'a true bill' against the accused where there is probable cause to believe he or she is guilty of the crime." He made no reference to any specific wrongdoing, but reminded the jury that it had the power to investigate all crimes. He added that the jurors would see every bit of evidence turned up in the Harris case.

Harris sympathizers later complained that Quindry's remarks were intended to bolster the will of the jury members to not shy away from an indictment of Charlie. It was widely understood that in the world of Harris, where each local official was given an up or down arrow, University of Kentucky law graduate Quindry was not in the favorable column.

The grand jury heard thirteen witnesses. Besides law officers who had investigated the murder, others brought before the panel by Pearce included: Dr. Gershenson; John Felix, a Pond Creek neighbor of Taylor and Harris not enamored with Charlie; Russell Wilson, who delivered mail in Pond Creek the morning of the shooting; and T. O. Mathews, the editor of the *Wayne County Press*.

Mathews' testimony encompassed a sober revelation that Howard Taylor, in leaving his picture with the editor some months before, had predicted that "someone was going to get him."

The jurors apparently heard enough to reach a decision before the day was over. An indictment returned late in the afternoon charged the sixty-six-year-old Harris with the slaying of Taylor. In a surprise move, the jury also charged a forty-year-old man named Willis O. Hutchcraft in the murder.

Pearce hesitated to discuss the reason for the indictment of Hutchcraft, a farm laborer and lumberjack who was said to live with his mother in nearby Golden Gate. Although Pearce had acknowledged that he could find no witnesses to the killing of Taylor, word leaked out that Hutchcraft—while under the influence of alcohol—may have stumbled on the murder scene in time to be aware of the shooter or shooters. Judging by the different kinds of shell casings found at the site, speculation was rife that more than one person may have fired at Taylor.

Within hours of the grand jury's adjournment, Hutchcraft was arrested by Harry Lee, a sheriff's deputy, and brought to the county jail. The *Press*, which ran a picture of Hutchcraft smiling broadly and clad in overalls in a cell, noted that he had been in trouble previously for check forgery and various minor offenses.

As for Harris, Police Chief Elmer Brown of Fairfield and Leathers quickly followed up on his indictment by searching for him in his Pond Creek neighborhood. However, they were told that he was in Indiana.

Early the next morning, Harris telephoned officers to say he would be in Fairfield a little later in the day to surrender.

Harris arrived at the jail in his own car. An unidentified woman was driving, and a big dog sat in the back seat. True to form, he was freshly shaven and neatly attired in a gray worsted suit, white silk shirt and a cravat with a white pearl tie tack. He wore a broad-brimmed hat, colored tan like the trench coat slung over an arm.

Before Harris entered the jail, onlookers watched him chat casually with Leathers, Brown and Pearce. One person hovering nearby with several out-of-town reporters told the *Press* that Charlie "seemed in the best of spirits." He still was upbeat a short time later when he was interviewed by Mathews as they sat together on a small bench in a bull pen on the first floor of the jail. When Harris went into the jail, he told Leathers that the editor of the *Press* was the only newsman to whom he'd talk.

Mathews, while making note of the fact that Charlie's black wavy hair was neatly trimmed, broke the ice by complimenting Harris on his suit. Tapping the ashes from a long black cigar he was smoking, Harris replied, "This is the first time I've worn it." Then, with a smile, he added, "It may be the last if I don't get out of here."

Harris predictably was cautious in the interview, except to contend that he would come out "clear" in the murder of Taylor "if the full story were told." Mathews pointed out that Harris did offer comments "off the record" about Taylor, but hesitated to discuss anything that might incriminate him in the killing. Harris also shied away from talking about the bullet he received in his arm on the morning of the shooting.

Instead, Mathews heard Harris expound on his personal outlook in the face of the murder charge.

About such, the editor wrote that "in his usual cool, calm, collected manner, he (Harris) observed that there have been cases where innocent men were convicted only to have evidence come out later—maybe after the person's death—that proved them innocent."

Telling Mathews that he was rejecting suggestions that he seek a change of venue for his trial, Harris declared: "I have cast my lot with my friends in Wayne County, and if they want to send me away (to prison), it will be alright." Whatever, Harris added, he felt no "ugliness or bitterness."

Before the interview ended, Harris requested that Mathews take his picture—something Charlie had refused to permit other newspeople to do. The photo, in which Harris posed with bars of the jail serving as a backdrop, became the classic shot that defined Harris pictorially for later generations.

As Mathews prepared to exit the jail, Charlie shook his hand and invited him to "come back and see me anytime." Harris' kindly feeling toward Mathews would not last, though. Not too far in the future, Harris would lump the editor with those who, in Charlie's mind, were out to get him.

The good mood portrayed by Harris in the Mathews interview may have diminished somewhat when he was informed the following evening that a vacant but well-known structure on his property had been burned to the ground. The latest, but not the last of Charlie's holdings to go up in flames, was situated a little south of his trailer home and was a onetime private home known as the Mansion on the Hill.

While the frame house was not exactly a mansion, it had operated as a roadhouse in which bootleg liquor flowed freely night and day. Law officers largely had turned a blind eye to the place, just as they had done with other drinking spots in Wayne County where alcohol was illegal. Periods of robust business at the "mansion" had forced Harris to sometimes employ help, such as Betty Newton's husband Charles.

Naturally, the fire was attributed to arson because of its timing. Instead of suspecting old Shelton cronies, though, the leading assumption was that the blaze was started by individuals incensed over the murder of Taylor. These folks thought Harris had murdered Taylor with an air of impunity that should not go unrequited.

Harris had little time to sulk over the fire because a hearing was scheduled in Quindry's courtroom for January 21, the day after the blaze, regarding his desire to get out of jail on bond. He sought and received help on this quest from attorney Richard Cochran. By that juncture, Cochran, thirty-three years old, had been practicing law in Fairfield for four years. He may have been viewed by Harris as a logical choice for legal assistance since Cochran's law partner, Kelley Loy, had represented Charlie during some of his troublesome times in the past.

When initially contacted by Harris in the wake of the Taylor murder charge, Cochran informed him that—since Charlie was accused, as Cochran understood it, of a capital offense—the court did not have to fix a bond. However, Cochran related in an analysis of Harris, written by the attorney and supplied to the author, that Charlie "let me know that I shouldn't worry about that...." Harris told Cochran to just prepare necessary paperwork, such as a motion for bond, and present it to the court.

Cochran endeavored at the hearing to make "the best argument I could" in asking for the fixing of a bond. Quindry responded by setting bond for Harris at $50,000 and at the same amount for Hutchcraft.

At that point, Cochran observed that a bond form for Harris already had been prepared and that certain individuals in the courtroom were prepared to sign it immediately, one being Courtney Meritt. To Cochran, the quick disposition of the day's business likely signaled that he (Cochran) "was the only man in the courtroom who didn't know the deal had already been made to get him (Harris) out on bond."

As Cochran was leaving the courthouse, he turned back to Harris and said, "Okay, I got you out on bond. Get yourself another lawyer because I'm not representing you any more in this matter."

Harris gave Cochran a hard look and replied, "I'm not through with you yet."

Cochran shot back, "Oh yes you are. I am not representing you in anything else, ever."

The attorney then began to walk away. After a few steps, he heard Harris snap, "I said I'm not through with you." Cochran ignored the comment and continued his departure.

Harris apparently was not convinced that Cochran would not help defend him on the murder charge. This quickly became evident when former Wayne County State's Attorney Gerald Mayberry, who then was living in Concord, California, surfaced in Fairfield and approached Cochran in his office.

Mayberry "started telling me how 'we' were going to handle Charlie's case," Cochran recalled. "I stopped him and said that 'we' were not going to do anything because I was not getting involved in defending Harris. I told him (Mayberry) he could do whatever he pleased, but that I was out of it."

It turned out that Mayberry himself did not stay around to defend Harris. But, he did serve as counsel for Harris when he pled not guilty to the Taylor murder at an arraignment January 30, 1963, before Quindry. Hutchcraft also entered a no guilty plea at the session, where he was represented by a court-appointed attorney, John Holland of Albion.

Up to that point, Hutchcraft, unlike Harris, had remained behind bars, unable to post the $50,000 bond set for him. However, on the day of the arraignment, Quindry accepted a motion by Holland to reduce Hutchcraft's bond to $10,000. He subsequently was released when John Jones of Golden Gate and three other individuals signed his bond.

The day of the arraignment also saw Quindry set the following May 14 as the opening day for the trial of both Harris and Hutchcraft. However, there'd be delays in the start of the trial, and by the time it eventually got under way, Hutchcraft no longer was a defendant.

The murder indictment against Hutchcraft was dropped in May at the request of Pearce. (The exact motivation for charging Hutchcraft in the killing never had been made clear. Pearce said only that the laborer, found walking on the Pond Creek Road on the morning of the Taylor shooting, had made statements that may have indicated knowledge of "certain facts" of the murder.)

However, Pearce noted in dismissing Hutchcraft from the case that his knowledge of these circumstances subsequently had been satisfactorily explained. Pearce also confirmed rumors that Hutchcraft had taken a lie detector test that completely cleared him of any connection to the crime. It seemed the Hutchcraft indictment had been treated as little more than a sideshow to the main event.

The interest in Harris' case was fueled not only by his own notoriety but by the addition and subtraction of attorneys.

Pearce realized he had his hands full in the prosecution of Harris. As a result, the state's attorney was authorized by other county officials to hire Ivan A. Elliott Jr., a Carmi attorney, as a special assistant prosecutor for the trial. Elliott, whose father was elected Illinois attorney general in1948 and served one term, was himself an assistant state attorney general in 1963. Well regarded for his legal skills, Elliott seemed to be a strong addition to the prosecution team.

Meanwhile, Harris stumbled around in his attempt to nail down his defense counsel. After Cochran rebuffed him, he fared no better with Mayberry. The onetime Wayne County state's attorney had stood at Harris' side during his arraignment, but returned to California not long afterward. Subsequently, Mayberry telephoned Quindry to say that he never intended to be anything more than a temporary adviser to Harris. This upset Charlie, who said he had been led to believe Mayberry would help defend him at the trial.

And then in May, Harris appeared to pull a rabbit out of the hat with a revelation that St. Louis attorney Lawrence Lee had agreed to represent him. Lee brought to Charlie's side a bit of the star power that Elliott gave the prosecution. Lee was associated with the St. Louis firm of big-time criminal defense attorney Morris A. Shenker. Besides representing mobsters, Shenker was an attorney for Jimmy Hoffa, the president of the International Brotherhood of Teamsters. Shenker also eventually would hold the controlling interest in the Dunes Hotel in Las Vegas.

However, Lee didn't pan out. He arrived in Fairfield only a few days before the scheduled start of Harris' trial. He asked Quindry to postpone the proceeding until the following September. When the judge agreed only to a continuance for one week, Lee said he had insufficient time to prepare an adequate defense and abruptly walked away from the case.

Harris was left with no lawyer and the trial looming on the horizon. But that soon changed.

The day before the trial was set to begin, the court held an unexpected hearing at which time Harris appeared with John Holland, the attorney who earlier had represented Hutchcraft. Holland told Quindry that he just had been hired by Harris.

Before the day was over, Holland argued successfully for Quindry to grant a motion to throw out a large panel of jurors who had been called for the trial—after Holland questioned the panel's validity. In addition, Quindry approved a thirty-day continuance for the opening of the trial. During that period, the sheriff or a special bailiff had responsibility for selecting a new panel of prospective jurors.

The appearance of Holland before Quindry exemplified the "small world" aspect of many downstate Illinois counties with small populations. Holland had moved to Albion after practicing law in Fairfield, where for a time he had been a law partner of Quindry before Quindry's election as a circuit court judge in the late 1950s.

Additionally, when Pearce began to practice law in Fairfield, he was associated with Mayberry and Virgil Mills, each of whom had or would serve as state's attorney of Wayne County. Harris had considered both of them, especially Mills, to be friends. In a taped interview in the late 1970s, Harris talked of a time when Mills kept "my books." Later, Harris said, the bookkeeping "reverted over to Pearce." The amiability with Pearce went out the window as he prepared to prosecute Harris for the Taylor killing.

As the reset trial date of June 20 approached, Pearce and Elliott were primed to present their case. However, only hours before the scheduled start, another surprising turn of events forced a further continuance.

Holland and C. Deneen Matthews, a newly hired lawyer for Harris' defense, filed a motion seeking the replacement of Quindry as trial judge. It was contended that Quindry, never known to be among the friends of Harris in the judicial system, was prejudiced against the defendant. The petition also asked that Roy O. Gulley of Benton, another judge in the Second Judicial Circuit covering Wayne and eleven other southern Illinois counties, not be permitted to hear the case. The problem with Gulley was not clear. As for Quindry, it was asserted that he showed bias toward Harris when he approved the $1,000 judgment against him in the Taylor lawsuit.

Although not agreeing with the contention that he would be unfair to Harris, Quindry granted the defense plea for a new presiding judge. He was replaced by Robert F. Cotton of Paris, the chief judge in the Fifth Judicial Circuit, which included Cotton's home county of Edgar in the eastern part of the state.

With the gavel now in his hand, Cotton immediately turned down a defense motion for another lengthy continuance. Instead, he set June 25 for the start of jury selection. Finally, a trial awaited with great anticipation by many persons throughout southern Illinois was about to get under way.

In a last-ditch effort to delay the start of the trial, the defense pointed out that Holland had taken ill and been advised by a doctor not to engage in trial work during the summer. Cotton didn't buy it. Matthews also argued that, as a new participant in the case, he needed more time to study it and interview witnesses.

However, Cotton held in ruling against a drawn-out continuance that "this isn't the usual case of a man being held in jail and hampered in efforts to get counsel. He has been free on bond. We cannot wholly disregard the state's right in this case. In justice, the defendant is not entitled to a continuance."

At one point in the sparring over the motion for a continuance, Cotton took notice of Harris' difficulties in securing counsel. He followed by asking Matthews and Holland: "How do we know you gentlemen will be here as his lawyers if a continuance is granted and the case comes up later?"

Answered Matthews: "I have been paid my fee and I will be here, and I will remain on this case unless they carry me out feet first."

Insistence by Matthews that he would not desert Harris was taken by knowledgeable judicial insiders as a positive omen for the defendant. Matthews, then fifty-nine years old, was a formidable figure in the community.

Charles Deneen Matthews, born in Wayne County in 1904, had been a youthful state's attorney of the county, serving from 1929 to 1933. He prosecuted some major criminal cases, including the sending of Elmer Gray to the electric chair and four others to prison for the murder of prominent Mount Erie area farmer Angus Moats.

Later, he lived for a time in Los Angeles, where he met and married Charlotte Lucille Holmes, a legal secretary and opera singer. Returning to Fairfield and the practice of law, he came to be regarded as an expert in probate and criminal proceedings. Several years after representing Harris in the Taylor case, Matthews was appointed a magistrate judge.

To most acquaintances, Matthews was a man with a mannerly, quiet demeanor, an individual who was very giving. (Before his death in 1982, Matthews and Lucille gifted a chapel to the First United Methodist Church in Fairfield.)

It was true that a few of Deneen's (he went by his middle name) fellow attorneys found him a tad aloof, and some did not always see him as the best presenter of evidence in the trying of a case. But in one key area, Matthews was virtually unparalleled. He was very skilled in picking juries with the potential to favor his clients, a capability of supreme importance in a trial.

Matthews and Holland wasted no time in testing Cotton with other pretrial motions. These filings sought suppression of certain evidence intended for use against Harris which, according to the defense lawyers, was seized illegally. Cotton denied the motions, but left open a door for the requests to be renewed during the trial.

One of these motions concerned the bullet removed from Charlie's arm. Matthews and Holland argued that it could not be used as evidence because, after its removal from the arm, it was given to law officers without Harris' consent and before he had been charged with a crime. Therefore, the defense argument was that the bullet was the property of Harris.

Harris' lawyers also objected on grounds of illegal search and seizure to the introduction into evidence of any of the at least eight pistols officers said they found in Harris' trailer home.

Holland argued that the guns, supposedly only "old souvenir style pistols" according to Sheriff Leathers, "should not be allowed to be dumped here on a courtroom table in front of any jury. They have no connection with the case, and would only serve to confuse the jury."

Responding, Leathers told the court that he and Pearce had visited Harris at the hospital when the bullet was removed from his arm. However, while saying that Harris then gave permission for a search of his trailer, Leathers acknowledged that it was done without a search warrant. Too, the search was conducted before Harris was charged. Holland and Matthews sought to make much of this matter, but were rebuffed by Cotton.

As the motions were debated, Harris roamed freely in and out of the courtroom. Often he chatted with friends among the spectators. When he sat with his attorneys to observe the proceedings, he cupped a hand around an ear to hear better. Holland had told the judge and other attorneys that Charlie was hard of hearing. He asked them to talk louder than usual when Harris was present, and all obliged.

The courtroom was not air conditioned, and folks sitting there noticed that electric fans were available for the judge, the attorneys and the section reserved for the jury. It was the outset of normally sweltering dog days in southern Illinois.

Sultry weather always seemed to be a given in so many courtroom dramas in southern settings, whether in real life or in books and movies. How appropriate that the murder of Taylor occurred in a region pictured by many as part of the South. And with the alleged involvement of Harris conjuring up memories of the Sheltons and their lawless heydays, great public interest in the sordid case easily was kindled.

During the months in 1963 preceding the trial of Harris, there was news elsewhere. The redoubtable federal pen on Alcatraz Island, where Harris had known a few of those incarcerated, was closed. The nation's nuclear submarine *Thresher* sank off Cape Cod, leaving 129 crewmen in a watery grave. More than a thousand African-Americans were arrested while protesting racial segregation in Birmingham, Alabama—some after

Eugene (Bull) Connor, who controlled the city's police and firemen, unleashed fire hoses and police dogs on them. On the lighter side, *Dr. No*, the first James Bond film, came to American theaters.

After the trial of Harris was over, the remainder of 1963 saw a meaningful nuclear test ban treaty go into effect, and Martin Luther King Jr. deliver his "I Have a Dream" speech from the steps of the Lincoln Memorial in Washington, D. C. Too, Beatlemania began in the United States with the release in this country of "I Want to Hold Your Hand" and "I Saw Her Standing There."

The epochal event of the year, though, was the assassination of President John F. Kennedy on November 22 in Dallas, Texas. It was seared into the memories of Americans.

For some in Illinois, the trial of Charlie Harris for the murder of Howard Taylor also would be remembered.

17

Beating the Rap

What better way to offset the summer doldrums than a good murder trial? One didn't have to venture into the Wayne County Courthouse, the redbrick building with the classic clock tower, to hear the buzz.

With the fate of the county's most widely known resident on the line, the topic of conversation was obvious. Frequently people looked around to see who might be listening before speculating about Charlie Harris and the Howard Taylor killing. Loose talk reaching the wrong ears could be dangerous.

Folks in downtown Fairfield flocked to the window of the *Wayne County Press* to read the posted bulletins on breaking news in the trial. More than once, their number included none other than Harris himself, an unnerving presence that certainly discouraged offhand remarks about his guilt or innocence.

Queasiness really surfaced among many of the more than 400 men and women called as prospective jurors for the trial. One after another was excused for various reasons. Some opposed capital punishment or said they already had an opinion as to whether Harris murdered Taylor. Others insisted they could not serve for business or health reasons. While not admitting it, few could disguise unease at the thought of facing Harris in the courtroom. It was bad enough that he was present and quite attentive as most of the prospective jurors were questioned.

A week passed before a jury of eight men and four women—individuals assumed to be acceptable to both the prosecution and defense—finally was seated. The women were identified as housewives, while the men included a school teacher, a factory worker, two farmers, an auto parts employee, an engineer, an insurance man and an oil-field worker.

Another week was required for the trying of the case. The prosecution called witnesses that it felt would convince the jury that Harris was guilty. One of the most imposing should have been Forrest R. Litterly of Springfield, a state crime laboratory technician.

He left no doubt that, in his view, the bullet in Harris' arm had come from Taylor's pistol. This corroborated what Pearce had been maintaining for weeks.

Litterly testified that lab results indicated the two bullets taken from Taylor's body, as well as three found in or under his car, were fired from the same .45-caliber weapon. This conclusion differed somewhat from the initial belief of Wayne County Coroner McNeill that the bullets extracted from Taylor were "larger than .45-caliber."

Two .401 rifle shell casings at the murder site were linked by Litterly to the same weapon. He also noted that pieces of wadding at the scene were from a .12-guage shotgun shell.

Litterly's examination also ascertained that three pieces of a plastic car hood emblem discovered by investigators at the shooting site matched up with the remains of a hood ornament removed by officers from Harris' auto the day of the killing. He contended further that slivers of metal taken from the hood emblem of the car, a white 1962 Chevrolet, could have been from a bullet.

"In my opinion," the crime technician testified, "these pieces are part of the same hood ornament—and were once originally a part of the Harris hood ornament."

Prosecutors hoped the findings by Litterly would be buttressed by the testimony of Jerry Meritt, a surprise witness against Harris. He was a son of Harris' friend, Courtney Meritt, who'd helped Charlie more than once by posting bond in criminal proceedings—including the current one. In order to take the stand, Jerry Meritt had to be released from the Wayne County jail where he was serving a short sentence for reckless driving.

Meritt said he was hauling hay and feed for Harris on January 5, the day of Taylor's murder. He related that, in the hours after the shooting, he saw Harris twice at the Fairfield hospital, both times in the company of Harris' housekeeper, Emily Hodges, whom Meritt identified as his aunt.

During one of the visits, Meritt testified, Harris asked him if law officers had taken a shotgun from his (Harris') garage. When he told Harris that they had not, Meritt said: "Charlie told me to take it away and get rid of it." He said he took it to his father, who in turn put it in a barn. Meritt added that his aunt later retrieved the weapon for Harris.

On cross-examination, Meritt was asked if he knew for certain that the shotgun belonged to Harris. He replied that, although he was not sure about its ownership, "Charlie asked me if they got it. So I figured it was his."

Meritt said he'd never seen Harris carry a .45-caliber weapon, but had noticed one in the glove compartment of the defendant's Chevrolet "one day last fall when we were picking corn."

On the day following the shooting, Meritt told the court, the damaged hood emblem came up in a conversation with Harris. The witness said Charlie asked if he and Emily had looked "down there" for the pieces broken off the emblem.

"Nobody said what 'down there' meant, but I took it to mean where the shooting occurred," Meritt said. He added that he and Emily subsequently searched without success for the fragments, apparently because the law already had found them.

On another matter, the prosecutors tried to show that Harris did receive, on the morning of the murder, the Sohio Pipeline Company letter informing him that his oil royalty payments were being suspended until he satisfied the $1,000 court judgment against him as a result of Taylor's suit. After reading the mailing, they contended, Harris was so enraged he immediately set out to confront Taylor.

To back up this belief, Pearce and Elliott brought to the witness stand two out-of-state Sohio executives. One, identified as A. Schmidt, a Sohio supervisor at its Cleveland office, confirmed that the letter was sent from there three days before the killing. The other, Raymond Rogers, the company's mail supervisor, asserted that the communication should have reached Harris by January 5.

The state also summoned two local postal personnel for input. Fairfield Postmaster Carson Stanley opined that a letter sent from Cleveland at the time cited by the Sohio officials should have been delivered to Harris' address the morning of January 5. And Russell Wilson, a carrier on the Pond Creek route, testified that he did indeed leave mail at both the Harris and Taylor homes that morning.

But, under cross-examination, Wilson backtracked to some degree, saying that he only "might possibly remember" delivering a newspaper to Harris' rural mailbox that day. He said that in retrospect he really could not recall whether he left any other "particular" mail there.

The defense took its best shot on Saturday, July 6, the day that Harris testified at length in his own behalf. However, two other defense witnesses that day were intended to illustrate that Harris had more to fear from Taylor than vice versa in their feud.

Harry Venable and Roy Burroughs, Wayne County loggers, swore that they heard Taylor threaten Harris in 1962, long after Howard and his wife had sued Charlie for compensation for damage to their crops from Harris hogs roaming freely.

Burroughs testified that, after clearing timber for Taylor the previous year, Harris asked them to clean out a right-of-way between his farm and Taylor's.

"On this particular day," Burroughs said, "we were working south of a tree-fence row, which Charlie told us to stay south of, when Taylor drove up in his truck. At the time, Charlie was blazing trees 150 yards away." According to Burroughs, Taylor asked, "Where in the hell is that black SOB?" Taylor then yelled to him and Venable to "get the hell out of here," Burroughs said.

At that point, Burroughs related that Charlie "came up" and told Howard, "Now, Mr. Taylor, leave the boys alone. They're working for me." Venable testified that Harris went on to say, "Mr. Taylor, we're neighbors, and we ought to get along."

To that, Taylor was quoted by Venable as replying: "Neighbors, hell! Fuzzy nuts, you black SOB, get out of here. If you didn't have these two witnesses here, I'd kill you in a minute!"

Both loggers testified that they noticed Taylor kept his right hand in his right pocket the whole time. However, both said they never saw a weapon.

The most anticipated testimony was that of Harris himself. It had earmarks of high drama for the overflow crowd jammed into the courtroom. Now and then, the audience displayed amusement at Harris' answers to lawyers' questions. Mostly, though, the spectators remained deathly silent as Harris endeavored in a calm manner to convince the jury that he was innocent.

Deneen Matthews, who conducted the direct questioning of Harris, began by getting into the record that Harris shared his trailer home at that juncture with his wife Rena, described by Charlie as an invalid, and Emily Hodges. Matthews also had Harris describe the locations of farm properties north and south of the trailer either owned or used by Harris.

Matthews then got down to business with a series of questions that opened doors for Harris to refute every assertion by the prosecution that linked him to Taylor's murder.

Nothing was more elemental in Harris' testimony than his flat denial of responsibility for the killing. According to a transcript of the testimony—which included all of the questions and Harris' replies—Matthews asked his client the following:

"Did you shoot H. S. Taylor?"

Harris: "No."

"Were you present at that spot where they say Mr. Taylor was shot the morning of January 5?"

"No," Harris replied, "I didn't see Mr. Taylor that day."

As for his whereabouts on the morning of the murder, Harris testified that he drove his truck to his "north feed lot" to tend to about thirty spring calves. When Matthews asked what transpired there, Charlie replied that he "got shot." The attorney then pressed Harris for details of the incident that, if true, explained the bullet in his arm.

Q. "What were you doing there at the time you got shot?"

A. "I had been carrying feed into the barn...."

Q. "In what direction were you walking when you got shot?"

A. "West. I was walking back to the granary to get more feed."

Q. "Tell what happened then."

A. "Something hit me in the arm. It felt like a bee sting at first. Having never been shot, I didn't know what a bullet would feel like. But I heard the gun report about the same time, and I decided I had been shot. I figured some hunters were in the area and had accidentally hit me. I ducked into the south end of the east shed, and I hollered out: 'Hey, there!' But nobody answered me."

Q. "Had you heard gunshots that morning before you were shot at?"

A. "Yes, I had heard gunshots. That's not unusual in that area. There's hunters there all the time. They use rifles, shotguns, what have you. It's a hunters' haven."

Q. "What did you do next?"

A. "I pulled up my sleeve and looked at the wound. It didn't look too serious, but it got more painful all the time. I got in my truck and drove back to my house, got into my car and came to town."

Harris contended that he did not even know of the Taylor shooting until after his visit to Dr. Gershenson's office and subsequent transportation by ambulance to Fairfield Memorial Hospital for the removal of the bullet from his arm.

Asked by Matthews how he found out about the murder, Harris said that Sheriff Leathers told him about it in his hospital room.

Harris also had an explanation for the damaged hood emblem on his Chevrolet. Prior to January 5, he testified, he had driven to Wayne City, west of Fairfield, to pay a traffic ticket fine to a justice of the peace. He said he stopped at a local service station to get directions to the justice's house. Before he returned to his parked car, he testified that a gasoline delivery truck backed into it, causing damage to the auto's front—including the emblem.

As for Harris' ties to the weapons believed to be used in the slaying, Matthews sought to illustrate that any connections were tenuous or nonexistent.

Questioned about the shotgun that Meritt seemed to link to Harris in his testimony, Charlie related the following:

"My nephew, James Woods, came by—it was sometime over the Christmas holidays—on his way back to Alabama, and he wanted to sell me the shotgun for $50. I told him I didn't need the gun, and didn't want it. But, if he needed $50, I'd let him have it. He said no, he just didn't want to take it to Alabama with him. I told him he could leave the gun if he wanted to. We were talking in the garage at that time. To this day, I don't know if he left that gun there or not. I don't recall seeing it."

In response to another Matthews question, Harris denied asking Jerry Meritt to get rid of any shotgun.

Matthews went further, asking Harris if he'd ever owned a shotgun.

"No, I didn't," the defendant replied.

He wound up his testimony by also denying ownership of a .401 rifle, a .45-caliber pistol "automatic" or a ".45 machine gun."

The issue of the guns was brought up in the prosecution's cross-examination that was handled by Elliott, the special assistant to Pearce. Harris was evasive in many of his answers, prompting looks of disbelief from spectators aware of his frequent depiction in newspapers as a former gun-toting gangster.

Besides denying again that he'd ever owned a shotgun, he added that he was not "too good" or "very accurate" in shooting one. Elliott then asked Harris about owning a .45-caliber pistol.

Harris quickly answered, "Never. I can't say I ever fired one, although I might have."

Elliott moved to undermine Harris' professed shortage of knowledge about weapons with the following exchange:

Q. "Do you know the difference between a pistol and an automatic?"

A. "I think a pistol is where you cock the gun and pull the trigger. Some you may not have to cock. And an automatic has a 'do-hickey' where the shells go up in the handle of the gun. I don't know if the gun keeps firing automatically."

Q. "Do you know the difference between an automatic pistol and revolver?"

A. "I always took it for granted a pistol and a revolver were the same. I'm not very familiar with hand weapons."

Sticking to the same subject, Elliott asked Harris how many guns were in his trailer January 5. Charlie responded that he "wouldn't know. People were always leaving guns there...hunters would leave one and take another."

Queried about the kinds of guns in the trailer that day, Harris said he "wouldn't know the types. They were probably scattered all over. I couldn't say where they were in the trailer."

Elliott specifically pressed Harris to explain eight older handguns that law officers discovered in his trailer the day of the killing. Harris said he didn't "have the least idea" about the weapons. With that, Elliott asked if Charlie was denying their existence.

"No, I'm not denying it," Harris retorted, and then added, "They were a bunch of antiques."

That same day, Joe Puckett, a defense witness, testified that he left those guns at Harris' place in 1961. Puckett, a familiar face in Fairfield prior to operating a car dealership in Evansville, Indiana, said the guns were old revolvers and pistols that included Belgian and German makes in addition to American ones.

During his testimony, Harris was quite equivocal on the subject of ammunition. Quite a few in the audience grinned derisively when he stated that he could not recollect where ammunition was kept in his home. Asked if there even was ammo in the trailer on January 5, he averred that he was "not sure if there was or not."

In one of the most unequivocal parts of his testimony, Harris depicted Meritt as a liar. He declared that Meritt was not with Emily Hodges during either of her visits to him at the hospital on the day of the murder.

Keeping with his pattern of denial, Harris insisted that he was not aware on January 5 of the Sohio letter curtailing royalty payments.

After handing Harris a copy of the letter, Elliott asked: "Did you receive this letter mailed to you...by A. Schmidt of Sohio?"

"I didn't receive it," Harris snapped. "Never got it."

Delving into another matter, Elliott asked Harris if someone else may have driven his Chevrolet the morning of the shooting. The prosecutor received the following response:

"I'm not sure. You don't need the keys to turn it off or on. I wouldn't say anyone else had driven it—but anybody out there knows if they're needing short transportation, they are welcome to my truck or car. They're always welcome to take it."

The absence of a clear-cut answer to the question typified the difficulties incurred by the prosecution in attempting to pin down Harris on any of the components of the case. Nevertheless, Pearce and Elliott remained confident that they had made the jury aware of sufficient evidence to justify a conviction—even if much of the evidence was circumstantial.

Elliott acknowledged the incidental nature of some of the evidence when he spoke first in the trial's closing arguments July 8. He did not ask for the death penalty, but told the jurors they had little choice but to find Harris guilty of murder.

He summed up what he believed occurred January 5 in spite of Harris' denials that any of it was true. In Elliott's scenario, Harris blew his stack after receiving and reading the Sohio letter halting his oil payments. Soon, he saw Taylor drive by, heading south. Charlie pursued him in his Chevrolet, but did not see Taylor pull off the road for a brief stop at the nearby home of John Felix. Thinking he'd lost track of Taylor, Harris eventually turned around and drove back north. Then he met Taylor, who'd returned to the road and resumed in a southerly direction. Both stopped, and an argument ensued. Elliott surmised that Taylor, acting out of "mortal fear," may have fired first, hitting Charlie in the arm. Harris quickly reacted by getting a shotgun from his car and firing into Taylor's auto. Then, Elliott concluded, Harris used the .401 rifle before finishing the job with his .45-caliber weapon. But, before he succumbed, Taylor got off more shots, one of which hit the emblem on Harris' car.

Elliott finished by beseeching the jury not to believe the obviously outright lies by Harris in his testimony.

In a rebuttal, Matthews pleaded with the jury to discount the state's version of what happened, contending that reasonable doubt permeated every point the prosecution tried to make. Instead, Matthews asked for acceptance of Harris' account of his activity on January 5.

After the final arguments, Judge Cotton read instructions to the jury detailing three possible verdicts: guilty with the death penalty; guilty with the leaving of sentencing to the court; or not guilty. In accord with proper jurisprudence, Cotton reminded the jurors that the defendant had to be proven guilty "beyond all reasonable doubt."

The jury filed out of the courtroom in late afternoon to begin its deliberation, leaving behind the nearly 400 men and women who'd come to hear the windup session. Some expected the jury to return a verdict in rapid fashion, but when it became apparent that it was not going to happen, the crowd gradually dispersed.

Not long after the jury began to weigh all it had heard from the witnesses and lawyers, the *Wayne County Press* was inundated with telephone calls from those wanting to know if the panel had reached a decision. People crowded outside the newspaper's window until midnight to read updated bulletins.

Shortly after the jury had retired from the courtroom, Harris asked a *Press* reporter, "Well, what do you think?" The scribe cautiously answered, "It's hard to say." Harris agreed, commenting that the reporter was "about right. I'd say it was a toss-up."

After dining at a restaurant near the courthouse, Harris and his friends waited in or near cars outside the building. As the deliberation dragged on deep into the night, Harris occasionally went back into the courthouse to see if there was any word on the jury. Pearce and Elliott spent most of their time waiting with Cotton in his chambers.

Finally, the suspense ended when the jury concluded more than nine hours of deliberation by returning to the courtroom shortly before four o'clock in the morning of the following day—Tuesday, July 9. Occupying their now familiar seats, the jurors joined Cotton, three of the trial attorneys (Holland had become ill the previous evening and returned to his home in Albion), Harris and a handful of others in awaiting the arrival of a court reporter.

Cotton then asked if the jury had reached a verdict. Its foreman, Sam J. Miller of Fairfield, an electric cooperative engineer, replied, "Yes, we have." He handed the verdict to Cotton, who read it to the virtually empty courtroom.

"We, the jury," it said, "find the defendant not guilty."

18

With Malice toward None

"Oh me, oh my," gushed a joyful Harris after the verdict was read.

It may have been the ungodly hour of 4 A.M., but Harris suddenly was a free man. With his face bearing a wide smile, he moved to thank members of the jury that had acquitted him of the murder of Howard Taylor. But he was restrained from doing it.

However, nothing prevented him from grabbing the hand of Deneen Matthews, the veteran attorney who'd orchestrated his defense. And nothing stopped him from accepting congratulations from relatives and friends in the small contingent present for the announcement of the verdict.

Charlie even shook hands with Judge Cotton, who wasted no time discharging Harris as a defendant and releasing the $50,000 bond through which Harris had remained out of jail since his indictment nearly six months earlier. When Harris thanked Cotton for his umpiring of the trial, the jurist was heard to murmur, "I call 'em as I see 'em."

The judge did not object to Harris making several phone calls from his chambers. One was to his ill attorney, John Holland, who'd departed the scene the previous evening. During a call to a brother in Tulsa, Harris exclaimed that he'd "never had a feeling like this before."

Harris' exuberance carried over in a conciliatory statement that he put out in the wake of the trial. The most eye-catching verbiage—concerning malice—evoked thoughts more of a statesman than an erstwhile gangster turned farmer. Indeed, the very fact that he issued what amounted to a press release reflected some of the public relations moxie once exhibited by Al Capone and southern Illinois hoodlum Charlie Birger.

In an apparent stab at promoting good will, Harris expressed "trust that any malice that may have arisen during and before this trial may be gone with the verdict." He preceded this optimistic note with an offer of his "deepest sympathy for Mrs. Taylor for the most unfortunate incident of January 1963."

He exhibited a touch of histrionics in expressing hope that the trial "may forever be a closed chapter in this, my book of life." In view of the verdict, he had nothing but praise for the jurors and everyone else participating in the proceeding—but omitted mention of Pearce and Elliott. Thanks also were accorded the men who had helped him post bond. He excluded none of them, not even Courtney Meritt, whose son Jerry was a prosecution witness against him.

Harris went so far as to broach the past in saying he was "truly grateful to the people of Wayne County, with whom I pitched my lot back in 1947." This was a reference to the refusal by a grand jury in the county to indict him for complicity in the murder of Carl Shelton that year. Similarly, he later avoided prosecution in the attempted murders of Little Earl Shelton, a nephew of Carl, and Lula Pennington, a sister of Carl, even though he was accused of being a triggerman in both incidents.

One other thing jumped out in Charlie's press release. Holland and Matthews were lauded for "their tireless efforts and manner in presenting the true facts to an all-wise and understanding jury." Harris might have gone even further in showering credit on Matthews for his acquittal.

Deneen's demonstrated knack for lining up juries sympathetic to his clients—no small accomplishment—may have come into play. At least, many knowledgeable persons thought so. They contended that Matthews had succeeded in securing the seating of a woman whose friendship with Harris precluded her from voting for his conviction under any circumstances.

One who believed this was Cochran, who definitely felt that Pearce and Elliott had lost the case in the jury-selection stage. The upshot, in the minds of those sharing this view, was that the solid effort by the prosecutors in lining up forceful testimony against Harris was all for naught.

Jurors who were willing to comment did not agree. One said it was untrue that the panelists initially stood eleven votes to one for the conviction of Harris. Another told the *Wayne County Press* that, even on the first ballot, only six jurors voted to find Harris guilty.

The verdict was met with mixed reactions, as might have been expected. It surprised those who thought the case against Harris was strong, including an attorney who was quoted as saying, "The state presented as fine a case of circumstantial evidence as I have ever heard. I do not see how there could have been an acquittal."

One businessman saw it differently.

"If I had been on the jury, my verdict would have been the same," he said. "The state proved circumstances showing Charlie could have done it, but it wasn't proven that he actually did it."

Just as citizens were divided on the judgment of the jury, their take on Harris himself appeared to be split even more sharply in the aftermath of the trial. A cadre of loyal supporters remained in place, some still mindful of his opposition to the Sheltons and others simply enamored with an individual so outwardly charming.

However, their number did not seem to be on an upswing following the trial. To the contrary, the proceeding appeared to have left many persons even more negatively polarized in their discernment of Harris. Many were convinced that he clearly was guilty of the murder—with the only uncertainty being the unanswered question of whether he had one or more accomplices.

While Harris' public statement was a shrewd gesture aimed at effecting reconciliation between himself and his growing legion of detractors or doubters, chances are it did little to diminish the underlying fear of a man who could go from being Dr. Jekyll to Mr. Hyde in a split second. Too, the trepidation of those skeptical of Harris was underscored by their feeling that the man could get away repeatedly with murder. To them, he was a cat with more than nine lives.

Even his defenders saw a strange, cold excitement in Harris. He had the bearing of a man perpetually on the lookout for trouble. If he didn't find it, then it found him.

Harris began the next chapter of his life a few days after he left the courthouse as a free man. He set out for Phoenix, Arizona, where Betty and Charles Newton and their youngsters had been living for about a year. The purpose of the trip was to convince the family to return to Illinois.

On the surface, it appeared Harris asked the Newtons to come back because he needed Charles to work for him. Before departing Illinois, Newton had handled tasks for Harris at his bootleg place, the Mansion on the Hill. Even though it since had been destroyed by fire, Harris said he was moving ahead with other interests that offered rewarding employment for Newton.

Yet, there was an underlying reason for Harris' journey to Phoenix— his crush on Betty Newton. Relationships with women were a zestful part of Charlie's life. He enjoyed their company, caring not one whit if they were married. His affection for Betty had grown before her move to Arizona, and it had lingered in the months since. He wanted her back in his world.

It was learned later that Betty had little enthusiasm for returning to Wayne County, especially in view of the fact that the reason for relocating in Arizona had been to give her husband a better chance of dealing with his health problems. Nevertheless, Charles Newton succumbed to the persuasiveness of Harris and consented to give Illinois another try.

Further involvement with Harris was a risk he was willing to take.

19

Fascination

Carolyn Sue Newton was fifteen years old when her parents and their five children returned to the Fairfield area after her father accepted the job offer from Harris.

On a steamy July evening in 1963, their "welcome home" consisted of bullets penetrating the autos parked in front of the Hodge Place, the Harris-owned house into which the Newton family was to reside. One of the cars had been driven by the Newtons, and the other belonged to Harris, who happened to be present.

The best guess was that the gunfire came from one or more individuals incensed over the exoneration of Harris in the Taylor murder. Nevertheless, it was a terrifying experience for a family that would soon discover the perils of getting mixed up with Charlie Harris.

Harris' involvement with the family went beyond hiring Charles Newton. Harris had made the down payment on the Newton auto, which was left riddled with bullet holes as a result of the late-night, drive-by shooting. The car was taken to the Williams-Harshbarger Oldsmobile dealership in Fairfield, the seller of the auto. When the repair work was finished, the vehicle was returned to the Newtons. Subsequently, payments on the car were not made, and the dealership repossessed it. Harris then went to Ray Williams, a partner in the car firm, paid the money that was owed, and the auto was returned to the Newtons.

A few Harris partisans aware of this assistance viewed it as typical of his oft-displayed generosity toward his friends. They were inclined to dismiss the notion that Harris had an ulterior motive in making the car payments.

As far as appearances in the mind of young Carolyn, who had plenty of chances to observe Charlie during his visits to the Hodge Place, she still held years afterward that "if Charlie was attentive to my mom, I just didn't notice."

Nevertheless, while acknowledging that Charlie may have been hung up on her mother, Carolyn remained doubtful that Betty returned the affection.

"I did remember," she told the author, "that mom and dad had differences. But, I didn't know that they were over Harris."

Carolyn Sue loved her mother, Betty Newton, and she never accepted the widely held belief that her mom had an affair with Charlie Harris. (FBI agents seemed so sure of it that they labeled Betty a mistress of Harris. There were others in law enforcement and the news business not as blunt. They called her a "girlfriend" or, even more diplomatically, a "woman acquaintance" of Harris.)

Before long, discord cropped up between Charles Newton and Black Charlie. It was enough to prompt life-style changes for the Newtons. After five months in the Hodge house, Charles and Betty moved in December 1963 to Fairfield. Three months later, they relocated to a farmhouse near the Wayne County hamlet of Geff. The moves were accompanied by new employment for Charles.

For Carolyn, the oldest of the Newton youngsters, the departure from Pond Creek meant transferring from Mills Prairie High School to Fairfield High School. As for Betty, the change of scenery did, or should have, put a little more distance between herself and Harris.

However, persistent rumors held that contact between Betty and Harris had not ended. The instigator was thought to be Harris, who adopted something akin to a fatherly watchdog posture in regard to the blue-eyed, full-figured woman thirty-six years younger than him. It may have been a way for Charlie to remain a part of her life, but it was not welcomed by Betty.

As 1964 moved along, Carolyn sensed that her mother increasingly seemed troubled by what she saw as Harris shadowing her. The anxiety was evident to Carolyn in the hours she spent with her mother, such as on those occasions when she tended to the bleaching of Betty's hair from brunette to blonde. Others noticing the apprehension included some in the crew at The Grill, a popular Fairfield restaurant where Betty was a waitress.

With the advent of the long, hot summer, something else was noticed. Almost overnight, Betty was seen keeping close company with Jerry Meritt, the young man who'd had the temerity to testify against Harris in the Taylor murder trial. Although Charlie had professed, after his acquittal, to hold no grudge against Meritt, intimates of Harris found that hard to swallow. They could think of nothing that would be more of a red flag to Harris. If anything could incite him to anger, or worse, they felt it would be the sight of Betty and Jerry together.

Therefore, few were surprised when rumors spread through the grapevine that Harris had declared privately that three persons were not covered by his public pledge the previous year to bear malice toward none. The exceptions were Betty, Meritt and Willard Pearce—whom Harris now reportedly regarded, a year after the fact, as an enemy for prosecuting Charlie in the Taylor slaying.

While this may have been only hearsay, Betty Newton took it seriously enough, recalled Carolyn, to borrow a handgun from a friend at the beginning of August 1964.

"Mom was just really afraid of Harris by this time," Carolyn said. "So, she got the gun, along with bullets, from this friend, and she carried them in her purse. After several weeks, though, she returned the weapon to the friend."

At this stage, Carolyn noted, it was true that her mother frequently was in the company of Meritt, whom she said also was "very scared, very nervous about Harris." Meritt was around a lot, Carolyn said, because her father had entered the John Cochran Veterans Administration Hospital in St. Louis for jaw surgery.

"As I understood it," Carolyn recollected, "Jerry was spending the time with us to protect mom while dad was in the hospital. I never felt that she was having anything like an affair with Jerry. It should be said that my mother loved my father."

A few days before the scheduled surgery, Betty wrote a letter to her husband in the hospital. In it, she related that "we are all fine" except for their ten-year-old son Kenneth, who had "stuck a piece of barb wire in the top of his foot." She said she took Ken to "Dr. Phillips," who gave him a tetanus shot, bandaged the wound and refused to accept any fee.

"It wasn't too bad," Betty wrote, "but I was afraid of blood poison in the summer."

Based on the letter, car payments still were a challenge for the Newtons. She wrote "they came and took the Olds...and stored it" at the Williams-Harshbarger dealership. "They said," the letter continued, "we could pay when our check came, and get the car. So, whatever you want to do."

Changing the subject, Betty asked whether Charles had "talked to the doctor anymore? And, what did he say?"

In closing, she expressed optimism that a friend or relative would bring her to the hospital for a visit within a few days. Until then, she urged her husband to "keep your chin up, Hon, for soon you will be well."

Definite plans were made for the visit to occur the following Sunday, August 16, 1964, the day before Charles Newton's surgery.

It was a Sunday that looked to be normal in Fairfield and Wayne County, with many persons going to church and then heading for family dinners. However, the tranquility was interrupted by a Fairfield radio news broadcast about an early morning fire that had destroyed a vacant house in the Pond Creek neighborhood.

A damaging fire in Pond Creek hardly was earth-shaking news. It seemed to occur with regularity. However, there was an added twist this time.

The radio reported that two charred bodies were believed to have been found in the smoldering rubble.

20

A Grisly Discovery

Vernon Musgrave and his fourteen-year-old son David first noticed the smoke curling into the sky as they stood in the yard of their farmhouse on the morning of Sunday, August 16, 1964. They realized a fire was raging not too far away, but didn't know what was burning.

Their curiosity was answered when Vernon Carter, an acquaintance, and another fellow in a pickup truck stopped to tell them that the vacated farm home of Courtney Meritt was going up in flames. Within minutes, Vernon and David had rushed to the scene.

More than four decades later, David sat in a Springfield, Illinois, restaurant and recounted to the author his indelible recollection of what he witnessed.

By the time the Musgraves arrived, firemen were fighting a losing battle to preserve any part of the house, which was located nine miles southeast of Fairfield on a gravel road running east from the Maple Well corner on the Burnt Prairie Road. In addition, nothing could be done to save a car that was aflame behind the residence when the fire fighters showed up.

David stationed himself next to a red and silver fire truck, and remained there as Fairfield Fire Chief Richard Miller radioed for Wayne County Coroner McNeill and Sheriff Leathers to head out as soon as possible.

Listening to Miller, David never forgot hearing him say something to the effect that "we haven't found anything, but I can smell it."

Later in the day, Miller would tell the press that he knew upon arrival at the house that more than a conflagration was involved. "We had just turned into the driveway, and I smelled the burning flesh and knew there were bodies in that fire," he said.

Vernon Musgrave also realized it. According to David, his father "knew what burnt bodies smelled like" from his participation in the Americans' capture of Guadalcanal in World War II. He said that his dad was repelled enough by the stench to forgo eating the rest of the day.

It took officials a while to confirm that there were bodies—two to be exact—in the ruins. However, the intense heat prevented their removal until nearly three hours after the firemen arrived.

The corpses—or what remained of them—were a ghastly sight.

Each body, one a man and the other a female, was badly charred—with only the head and torso still connected. Legs and arms had been separated by the burning. A search of the ashes revealed one left arm and hand definitely belonging to a woman because of a wedding ring on a finger.

The bodily trunks were discovered between the springs and mattress of a gutted bed in a ground-floor room of the two-story frame house. The man was face up, the woman face down. The bodies lay side by side.

Two major conclusions were reached as the ruins still smoldered. First, both the man and woman were murdered. Before the bodies were removed in canvas bags for transport to a funeral home in Fairfield, investigators saw that each skull had more than one bullet hole.

Secondly, officers at the site voiced certainty that the fire was arson, even though no gas cans or other evidence were found to support the belief. Fire marshals reaching the scene did determine that the destroyed mattress on top of the torsos had been doused with a chemical agent that made it burn intensely.

Because the sheriff had ordered that everybody standing around had to be questioned before leaving, David Musgrave had an opportunity to watch the coroner conduct a cursory examination of parts of the bodies with gloved hands. Official identification of the victims would have to wait, but it was only a formality.

Speculation by those at the fire site—and by persons elsewhere as news of the blaze spread—was that the bodies were those of Betty Newton and Jerry Meritt. It seemed as clear as putting two and two together.

The inseparability of the pair in recent days had become fodder for gossip. The bodies were found in the remains of an unoccupied house owned by Jerry's father, Courtney, who along with Jerry's mother had moved to Fairfield more than a year earlier. The burned auto behind the farmhouse was registered to Betty's husband, Charles. And, the families of Betty and Meritt did not hesitate to say, sadly, that they had no doubt about the identities of the victims.

Not surprisingly, the name of Charlie Harris immediately popped up in conjecture about the murders. Those who tracked such matters natural-ly assumed that the sudden bond of Betty and Jerry had infuriated Harris. However, Willard Pearce, still the chief prosecutor in Wayne County, was quick to insist that the law had no suspects in mind "at this time."

Asked about Harris, Pearce said he presumed Charlie would be avail-able for questioning if necessary. After all, Pearce added, "He's never run away, has he?" The state's attorney may have been unaware of or forgot-ten that Harris had skipped town when a warrant for his arrest was issued following the shooting of Carl Shelton seventeen years earlier.

Black Charlie assuredly was on the minds of Newton and Meritt fam-ily members. They not only instinctively knew who the victims were, but had little doubt about the identity of the murderer. Still, they hesitated to go public with their certitude.

Carolyn Newton was among those who caught the Sunday radio broadcast about the bodies in the burned-out farmhouse.

"I had last seen my mom the day before, but I knew she was sup-posed to be visiting my dad in the St. Louis hospital that Sunday," she said. "Still, a strong chill went through me when I heard that news on the radio."

Not long afterward, her grandfather John Shockley, Betty's father, came with several other persons to the Newton residence near Geff, and took his grandchildren to his home in Fairfield. Carolyn recalled having a "certain feeling, even though nobody had told us anything yet." The suspense ended when Charles Newton, who'd been summoned from the hospital, arrived at the Shockley place later in the day.

"Dad told us that our mom was in that house that burned, and that she was dead," said Carolyn. "Even though I'd had that feeling, I still went into shock."

The next day, John Shockley was quoted in St. Louis newspapers as saying, "I hate to say it, but I am reasonably convinced that this was Betty." For one thing, he noted that his daughter wore dentures, and that he'd been told the woman victim was wearing them.

Mrs. Elizabeth Hodges Meritt, the mother of Jerry, was more outspoken to reporters. Although declining to discuss who may have slain her son, she said that he had been living in fear for his life during the past year. (That would account for most of the time since his testimony against Harris in the Howard Taylor murder trial.)

Jerry had been "scared to death," she said. As a result, she said that he had "stayed at home here with us for nearly a year…hardly ever went up town…was even afraid to take a job." However, she added that Jerry recently had landed a position with a chemical spraying firm after resolving that he "couldn't go ahead living this way."

Questioned about the company he was keeping with Betty Newton, Mrs. Meritt responded, "She was scared to death, too. It is true they were together all the time. He was the only one she had to look to."

Her unmarried son, who was twenty-eight years old, four years younger than Betty, had served in the army with an engineers' battalion as well as with airborne troops. He had no criminal record, but had come to the attention of law officers in recent years as a sometimes excessive drinker and hot-rodder. At the time of the Taylor murder trial, he had been serving a brief sentence for reckless driving.

Assertions of impropriety in the relationship of Meritt and Betty were contested sharply by Charles Newton in an interview three days after the discovery of her body. While acknowledging that the two "were together a lot," Newton said that he'd asked Meritt a month ago, before he entered the hospital, to "look after Betty."

His family and Courtney Meritt's had been close, he said, and "we knew something of each other's problems." He stated that "the Meritt girls and Betty were always good friends" and that "Jerry and I were good friends."

Newton, tall and appearing frail, said he never would believe that his wife "went to the Meritt home of her own wish." He said that Betty either was murdered before "she was taken" to the vacant farmhouse or "was forced to go (there)."

When Betty had accompanied him to the hospital in early August, he said, she mentioned that "she'd been pestered some." Consequently, he said that he told her to notify Sheriff Leathers if "anyone bothered her." He added, "She promised she would."

Newton was poignant in insisting that he "just can't understand" what had happened.

"She adored the children and would never have done anything to embarrass them," he said. Moreover, Newton went on, he and Betty were still in love after seventeen years of marriage.

He wistfully lamented that he was "sorry that I didn't provide a better life for her. We've had to move around so much. A year ago we were in Arizona. I was in the hospital there most of the time." More recently, though, he said Betty liked the place near Geff where they were living. During one of their last conversations, Newton noted, he told her he intended to buy it.

The day after the interview a private service was held for Betty at the Dixon & Johnson Funeral Home chapel at Fairfield. She was buried in the city's Maple Hill Cemetery. The day before, mourners had filled the same chapel for the service for Meritt. He was accorded military rites and buried in the veterans' cemetery near Maple Hill.

Ironically, even though the families of Betty and Meritt had laid their bodies to rest, formal identification of the murder victims still had not been made. Many persons found this hard to believe, even annoying. Just as frustrating to those expecting an immediate arrest in the killings was the seemingly slow pace of the law's investigation. Pearce, the sheriff's office and other inquisitors—including some from the state—were unusually tight-lipped, explaining that the absence of witnesses to the slayings prohibited an easy resolution.

Pearce acknowledged that many individuals were being questioned, but declined to name any suspects. He did allow that the inquiry was likely to pick up steam after reports were made by state crime laboratory personnel, who had sifted through the ruins of the farmhouse and were expected to positively identify the victims and provide more material information on the committal of the crime. Autopsies on the victims before the burials did confirm that each had been shot in the head more than once.

The absence of any word from authorities regarding a suspect hardly dissuaded street talk of Harris. If the prepossession of many folks held sway, he'd already been charged with the murders.

Charlie, himself, may have sensed a shrinking of his old support base in the wake of the killings. While he remained in Wayne County, sightings of him were rare. Those who did make contact found him subdued, far from his normally cocky self. His most public appearance since the murders probably came five days afterward when he went to a funeral home in Fairfield to pay his respects following the death of Mrs. Lelah McKibben, who as Lelah Smith had been his first wife.

While none of those believing Harris guilty of the murders dared confront him face-to-face, there were others paths of retribution. One was old hat in Pond Creek.

Ten days after the farmhouse blaze, arsonists almost simultaneously torched a vacant house and a barn owned by Harris. The home, a little north of the trailer in which Charlie lived, was the old Hodge Place that the Newtons originally occupied after their return from Arizona. The barn was close to the trailer, which was not burned. Nor was a nearby garage-tool shed. When firemen reached the burning barn, they found no spectators—only pigs from the barn lot running loose. Harris never appeared at the fires, which occurred in early morning hours.

A week later, Charlie made the papers again. It was learned that federal agents were conducting their own inquiry into the destruction of the barn because it contained a large amount of corn upon which a federal loan had been secured.

Of more interest, headlines blared that Harris had decided to move the house trailer from his Pond Creek farm to a location in Fairfield. The revelation was bolstered when law officers confirmed that they had received a request to provide protection to persons moving the trailer.

Tongues wagged on whether the move actually would occur. The matter soon was overshadowed, though, by a disclosure that Harris had been questioned for the first time about the double murder. The interrogation by law officers took place in Albion in the presence of attorney John Holland and a court reporter. Holland had assisted Deneen Matthews in the successful defense of Harris in the Taylor murder trial.

Harris was asked about his movements on the weekend of the two murders. He was quoted as denying any knowledge of the killings. Afterward, Pearce insisted that Harris was not queried as a suspect in the case.

The same day, September 9, a Wayne County coroner's jury acted. After interviewing Pearce, Leathers and Richard Miller, the jury returned separate but identical verdicts stipulating that Betty Newton and Jerry Meritt each was murdered by a "person or persons unknown." While the finding hardly was unexpected, it signified that the criminal justice process was gaining momentum.

This was confirmed a day or two later when Pearce announced that a special circuit court grand jury would convene September 16, one month after the murders, to hear testimony and consider evidence in the case.

In the meantime, any possibility of Harris' trailer moving to Fairfield was doused in arson-set fires at dusk on September 12.

Destroyed in the flames were the trailer and the garage-tool shed. A plastic canopy over the door to the trailer was found fifteen feet away, giving rise to speculation that a bomb might have been thrown into the trailer. Officers discovered a bucket near the shed that smelled of kerosene.

They also found an eerie calling card tied to the property's front gate—bed springs believed by investigators to have disappeared from the charred ruins of the old Courtney Meritt home. The bodies of Betty Newton and Jerry Meritt had been found on the missing springs.

No doubt, the torching of Harris' properties since the double murder reflected increased boldness by his enemies. The destruction also brought to mind the "scorched earth policy" waged against the holdings of the Sheltons years before. Harris had been a self-proclaimed aggressor in the drive against the Sheltons, but now he was on the other end of the stick. Not all, but certainly a number of his former allies no longer could stomach him. If the law could not bring him to his knees, they apparently felt, vigilantism could.

But then, the wheels of justice suddenly shifted into high gear.

The special grand jury met under the guiding hand of Pearce for more than eight hours on September 16, sifting through evidence collected by investigators and hearing four witnesses. Besides Leathers and McNeill, they were Charles Spruell, an Illinois State Police investigator, and Emily Hodges, the housekeeper for Harris.

The result of the panel's deliberation may have been anticipated, but it still was a bombshell.

Black Charlie was indicted on charges of murdering Betty Newton and Jerry Meritt and of setting fire to the abandoned farmhouse in which their bodies were found. He also was charged with perjury, an allegation going back to supposedly false statements that he made during his testimony in the Taylor murder trial in 1963.

Emily Hodges also was indicted on charges of perjury. In her case, she was said to have allegedly lied in testimony before the grand jury. She was taken into custody, but quickly released on a $5,000 bond signed by a Fairfield businessman.

Harris was not arrested because he was nowhere to be found. In fact, nobody had seen him for nearly a week. It was thought to be especially strange that he had not surfaced when his trailer and tool shed had burned. The man whom Pearce said had "never run away" apparently had fled.

A bench warrant for his arrest was issued by the court in Wayne County. It was followed by a federal arrest warrant naming Harris as a fugitive attempting to avoid prosecution for murder. It was issued in East St. Louis by United States Commissioner Elvira Fellner, and turned over to the FBI for follow-up action.

As an extended search for Harris commenced, state and county authorities initiated a close watch on the homes of individuals likely to have incurred his wrath. Leathers said the precautions applied to Pearce and certain relatives of the two murder victims. He did not reveal others possibly receiving the special care.

Authorities did receive a tip that Harris had been seen in Evansville, Indiana, after his indictment. Pursuing the lead, officers were informed by an attorney there that Charlie, in fact, had been in his office after the grand jury action and led him to believe that he was thinking about surrendering. Subsequently, patrol cars surrounded a neighborhood in Evansville where Harris reportedly was spotted. It was a wild-goose chase.

While Harris evaded arrest in Indiana, the same was not true for Emily Hodges. The forty-two-year-old woman was charged with bail violation after an arrest at the home of Rena Harris, Charlie's wife, in New Harmony, Indiana. Although she had been free on bond, Emily violated terms of her bail by going to Indiana without court permission.

Three days later, she pled guilty to one of the perjury counts against her and was sentenced to six months in the Illinois reformatory for women at Dwight. After that, Circuit Judge Randall Quindry ordered that she be placed on three years probation.

The count to which she entered the guilty plea was a charge that she wrongfully testified to the grand jury that Harris had been in her presence during the time that Betty Newton and Meritt were slain. Pearce said that this was a false statement intended as part of a cover-up for Harris.

So, while the former housekeeper for Harris and aunt of the murdered Jerry Meritt was shipped off to a penal facility in northern Illinois, the tracking of Charlie was another story. His trail was getting colder as lead after lead petered out.

The only thing for certain about Harris was that the burning of his Pond Creek holdings continued. Before the end of September, arson was blamed for flames that destroyed a frame corncrib and smokehouse used for storage on his farm. A month later, a fire swept across a field and consumed another barn thought to belong to Charlie.

If he had any problem with the unending fires, he didn't show up to protest.

Harris had completely vanished.

21

Stalked by the FBI

J ohn Edgar Hoover took a break from his duties as director of the Federal Bureau of Investigation late in 1949 to engage in the card game Hearts with legendary journalist William Kinsey (Bill) Hutchinson of the *International News Service*. While testing their ability to outmaneuver each other, they discussed additional steps that might be taken to promote the capture of dangerous lawbreakers.

One idea—generating more publicity about fugitives believed to pose the most serious threat to society—was included in a published article resulting from Hutchinson's conversation with Hoover. The story triggered an outpouring of support from law officers and others throughout the country for the heightened publicity concept.

As a result, the FBI announced in March 1950 the official launching of its Ten Most Wanted fugitives list. The faces and descriptions of those cited were tacked up in post offices and other public places from coast to coast. When an individual was removed from the list upon capture or death, a new FBI entry was selected.

On May 6, 1965, a newcomer was described as follows: a white man; five feet, seven inches tall; dark complected with brown eyes and graying black hair; and weighing 148 pounds. He was said to reportedly have three gold-crowned upper front teeth. At sixty-eight years of age, he was one of the oldest—if not the oldest person—to have made the list.

His wanted poster stipulated that Charles Bryan Harris was being sought in connection with a double murder and that he was considered "armed and extremely dangerous."

This was amplified in a corresponding statement released by the FBI that contended Harris "has reportedly vowed to shoot it out with any law enforcement officers attempting to apprehend him, and has been known to be in possession of a valise full of handguns." The statement added that Harris was believed "to often carry a .45-caliber pistol in a cigar box under the front seat of his car, to sleep with a gun and possibly be in possession of a submachine gun."

And, it was added, "Harris is known as an excellent shot with all types of guns."

Labeling Charlie "a veteran and vicious criminal," the statement noted that he "has a reputation of having allegedly murdered several people." Saying only "several" differed from internal FBI documents charging that Harris quite likely had slain "twenty or twenty-five people through the years."

The statement issued for public consumption characterized Charlie as follows:

"He is said to occasionally drink beer and whiskey to excess, enjoys patronizing low-class night clubs, has a reputation as a ladies' man, usually wears glasses while driving and often dresses in a suit with shirt and necktie. He has reportedly employed disguises to evade arrest and gangland reprisals, and has dressed as a woman...."

As for the cross-dressing, an internal document asserted that Harris was capable of appearing like a "little old lady" by wearing women's apparel and "changing his tone of voice." While FBI files not always were free of misinformation, the assertion that Harris went out in a dress and high heels, if true, would have surprised or amazed or perhaps even shocked the folks back in Pond Creek.

How ingenious, some would've said. His survival instinct outstripped any shame he might have felt in donning female garb. It might have earned him a new sobriquet, though. Hardly fond of being called Black Charlie, he'd really have bristled at being dubbed Black Charlene.

The FBI didn't ignore him on men's wear either. For a person who took pride in his sartorial splendor, Harris might have taken umbrage at the

FBI's estimation that he was "a trifle slow on fashion changes, and wears wide ties and wide-lapel coats."

Whether dressed like a man or woman, Harris went from a run-of-the-mill fugitive to a man with a big bull's-eye on his back on May 6, 1965.

An examination of the FBI's internal file on Harris revealed that, when he was placed on the most wanted list, Hoover issued a directive to the FBI's Springfield, Illinois, field office to "insure this investigation receives vigorous, imaginative and continuous attention." The director ordered that, from this point on, he wanted reports submitted daily on the progress of the investigation by both the Springfield and "all auxiliary offices."

Harris was now the target of a full-court press by the FBI, a person in the cross hairs of the most dominant figure in American law enforcement. Even his own agents lived in fear of the extraordinarily neat, intense and disciplined Hoover, a monolithic individual who had made the FBI the nation's preeminent national police force since becoming head of its forerunner in 1924, the Justice Department's Bureau of Investigation.

To a great degree, it was Hoover, more than anyone else, who had brought efficiency, professionalism and centralized control to law enforcement in the United States. Prior to Hoover, law enforcement was mainly an uncoordinated mishmash of county sheriffs and municipal police departments. Hoover, the squat man with a face that resembled a bulldog, was not without his critics. When tracking Communists, saboteurs and—in his later years—some civil rights leaders, Hoover was accused of sometimes abusing his considerable power.

In ordering his agents to pursue Harris with a new vitality, Hoover was giving Charlie a taste of the heat put on name-brand criminals in the past—notable yeggs (robbers) like Dillinger and Pretty Boy Floyd. Harris had not achieved their stature, but he was prominent enough in the Midwest to merit front-page coverage above the fold of the newspaper.

As part of the zeroing in on Charlie, Hoover mandated that "Harris' former associates, relatives and contacts remain constantly aware of his fugitive status." This was a reminder to inform interviewees that harboring or otherwise assisting a federal fugitive could be a law violation.

By the time Harris became one of the Ten Most Wanted fugitives, he had been on the lam for nearly eight months following his indictment the previous September in Wayne County on homicide, arson and perjury charges. Relatives and others questioned about Harris had been of little help during that span. Fear was rampant that reprisals might have awaited those who played ball with investigators.

Throughout that eight-month period, the FBI's Harris dossier revealed, attempts to track him down included nationwide surveillance and follow-ups to purported sightings of the man. All efforts reached a dead end. More than once, agents reacted to false leads that Harris no longer might be alive.

Police in Alton, Illinois, once notified the FBI that a male body found floating in the Mississippi River met "the same general physical description" of Harris. But, the man was not Charlie. Another time, agents were told that something looking like a freshly dug grave in a wooded area of the Pond Creek bottoms might contain the body of Harris.

Before checking out the tip, an agent cautioned in a report to Hoover that "residents of the area quite often bury carcasses of deer which they poach out of season." However, it was added that "this fresh dirt could also possibly be for contraband which Harris has been known to hide in this manner. Harris has at times hidden a cache of guns in a waterproof vault by burying them in the ground." The dirt was dug up, but nothing was found.

Curiously, the FBI received more than one tip that Harris had been murdered by crime syndicate hit men to prevent him from talking to authorities in a bid for possible leniency. This seemed strange in view of Harris' insistence that his days of association with big-time gangsters were long past.

Nevertheless, the FBI did not ignore the speculation, especially when specifics were mentioned. For instance, one report to Hoover said that two mob gunmen trailed Harris to Evansville, Indiana, where they gave him "a concrete suit" followed by a "bath" in the Ohio River. Again, the hypothesis came to nothing.

No tipsters were ignored, though. Not long after Charlie's disappearance, the FBI was contacted by a woman in St. Louis who claimed that a man representing himself as "Blackie Harris" met her in a tavern and then, after "they had drinks," forced her to spend the night with him at a hotel. However, her description of the man did not fit that of Harris. Moreover, agents in St. Louis said they quickly determined that the woman was "a mental case" and a habitué of "cheap taverns."

Agents who were veterans of manhunts had felt from day one that their best bet in pursuit of Harris was to watch the homes of his relatives across the country. They suspected that Charlie was shifting every few weeks from one relative or acquaintance to another.

Special scrutiny also was given to areas with a history of harboring criminals. In the case of Harris, this meant keeping an eye on rural sectors as opposed to major cities like Chicago, where Charlie was deemed a duck out of water. However, one exception was Phoenix, a favorite Harris retreat through the years.

Still, a more likely place to look for Harris was the rugged Cookson Hills region in eastern Oklahoma. It had been a legendary hideaway for fugitives, including a number of the notorious Depression-era bandits.

Not far from the Cookson Hills was Tulsa, where agents maintained close contact with Charlie's brother, Oliver Harris, and Truman Fenton, identified by the FBI as a long-standing friend and nephew of Harris. Both continued to deny having seen or heard from Charlie.

Of course, agents never overlooked the possibility that Harris was hiding in the remote nooks and crannies of Pond Creek or in other parts of southern Illinois—places where friends would be willing to funnel him food and other necessities. The FBI was assisted in its surveillance in this region by Illinois State Police crime section agents, a group that included, off and on, Charles Spruell, Frank Schaefer, Ted Fanos, Eldon Banning and Ed Heyer.

As part of the new emphasis on capturing Harris after he joined the most wanted list, an FBI memorandum to field offices stated that the agency was prepared to pay for assistance leading to his arrest.

If warranted, the memo said, "consideration should be given to requesting (the) Bureau for authority to offer informants, relatives and associates a lump sum payment for information directly leading to subject's apprehension."

The communication acknowledged that the search for Harris had been unproductive. It reiterated that "a possible reason" for the reluctance of people to talk "could be fear for their personal safety." If so, the memo went on, an interview with a person likely to know something should be conducted "in such a manner as to calm his fears and gain his confidence."

Agents were asked to determine "the degree of past association" an interviewee may have had with Harris. This was especially true with women, the memo said, not the least of which were "female relatives" with whom Charlie "allegedly had 'affairs.'" In the eyes of the FBI, according to the memo, these unnamed gals in particular might be productive subjects for "thorough and penetrating interviews."

The files on Harris do not reveal if an interview sparked by the memo was responsible for a long-sought break in the manhunt. The blackout of names ensured anonymity for the man or woman who supplied confidential information to the FBI on June 8, 1965, that led agents to the H-V Motel in Springfield, Illinois.

This time the lead was not a dead end.

The agents were very interested in a man who had checked into the motel on May 21 under the name Fred Elkin, and who gave an address as Rural Route 7, Marion, Illinois.

Shown a photo of Harris, the motel owner and a woman desk clerk positively identified Elkin as Harris. The clerk especially remembered the man who had resided in the room numbered 17 until checking out May 24.

In a report to Hoover, the FBI office in Springfield said the clerk recalled Harris arriving at the motel in a taxi. Dressed in a business suit and wearing a gray hat, he paid for his room in advance. The report quoted the clerk as saying that Elkin/Harris "had been an extremely quiet person, and he never bothered anyone."

The day he left, she related, he had received a telephone call from a man, followed by several more calls. Subsequently, the report continued, she noticed a man sitting behind the motel in an older white pickup pulling a horse trailer the same color. Not long afterward, she saw the pickup with Harris inside proceed south on the Route 66 bypass. However, the woman said she paid little attention to the departure because Harris owed no money on his room.

While the FBI still could not pinpoint the exact whereabouts of Harris, agents had a fair idea after good gumshoe work delivered the pickup driver into their hands. Although the unidentified man professed innocence of any wrongdoing—and apparently never was charged with anything—he admitted responding to a call to pick up Harris at the motel.

In a report to Hoover June 16, the Springfield office said that the man drove Harris to Wayne County and dropped him off on a "gravel road about six miles east and seven miles south of Fairfield." The man told agents that Harris "did not talk too much" on the drive except to say that he wanted to surrender to authorities after contacting an attorney.

However, Harris had done no such thing in the three weeks since his return to Wayne County. And, some of his friends and relatives there still stonewalled agents inquiring about his hiding place. But not all of them kept their lips sealed. Not anymore.

The feds were closing in.

22

An Early Morning Capture

One false move by Black Charlie, like reaching for a nearby loaded rifle, and Agent Charles R. Wood Jr. of the FBI would have fired away. Harris' eyes briefly flickered toward the weapon, but he recognized the futility of challenging the firepower of the posse of G-men that had him trapped.

Instead of the shoot-out predicted by some on the day that law enforcement would catch up with Harris, Wood only heard him utter the words, "I am your man; I am Charlie Harris."

The manhunt for Harris ended at exactly 5:30 A.M. on June 17, 1965. The windup occurred in an unoccupied, two-story farmhouse in Pond Creek, about a quarter mile off a gravel road between Burnt Prairie and the Simpson-Winzenburger Cemetery. Harris had spent the night in the place, which was roughly two miles from the burned-down farm home where the charred bodies of Betty Newton and Jerry Meritt had been discovered ten months earlier.

By ending peacefully, the capture of Harris failed to become part of the bloody legends and lore spurred by the climaxes of some of the FBI's famous pursuits.

It was uneventful in comparison to the fatal shooting of John Dillinger outside Chicago's Biograph Theater in 1934 and the killing of Pretty Boy Floyd in the Ohio countryside the same year. Bullets zinged helter-skelter in the FBI's full-fledged assault in 1935 on the house occupied by Ma Barker and one of her sons, Fred, by Lake Weir at Oklawaha, Florida. Both died in the gunfire.

As with the Harris capture, no weapons were fired in 1936 when agents arrested the long-sought Alvin Karpis in New Orleans. However, the Karpis apprehension received national attention because of Hoover's personal involvement in it.

Even though free of violence, the arrest of Harris merited announcement in an immediate press release by United States Attorney General Nicholas Katzenbach. In addition, the Justice Department notified the White House of the capture in a communication the same day to Marvin Watson, a special assistant to President Lyndon Johnson. The alert to the White House noticeably included the FBI's standard description of Harris as "a veteran and vicious killer" sought on a federal unlawful flight warrant.

Details of the capture, which came six weeks after Harris' entry on the FBI's Ten Most Wanted fugitive list, were spelled out by Agent Wood in testimony at Charlie's trial later in 1965 on charges of murdering Betty Newton and Meritt.

As part of a sweep of abandoned farmhouses in Pond Creek by an FBI contingent supervised by Robert E. Gebhardt, the special agent in charge of the Springfield, Illinois, office, Wood said that he spotted Harris at the break of dawn "on the back porch of a place known as the Higgins property."

A few feet away was a .22-caliber semiautomatic rifle that Harris could have grasped. He eyed it nervously, but made no move toward it. After Wood cautiously took possession of the weapon, he asked Charlie if he had intended to use it against FBI agents.

Harris answered, "No, I wouldn't shoot you fellows," according to Wood's testimony.

Wood, who lived at Centralia, testified that the rifle had one shell in its chamber and ten in the magazine. The FBI also confiscated a pair of binoculars and a toilet kit at the house, Wood said. He added that Harris surrendered his wallet, which contained $116 as well as Charlie's driver's license, a registration in Harris' name for a 1962 Chevrolet truck and other papers identifying the wallet's owner.

The wallet also housed a picture of Wayne County State's Attorney Pearce, whom Harris allegedly had marked for death after the Howard Taylor murder trial. Consequently, Herman Lyle, an agent from Mount Carmel who was present on the day of Harris' arrest, turned the wallet and the possibly incriminating photo over to Wayne County Sheriff Leathers for later submission at Harris' trial as state evidentiary exhibits.

Leathers and other local law officers were not on hand for the apprehension of Harris. FBI records indicated that Wood and ten other agents under the direction of Gehhardt swept through Pond Creek in the early morning hours, targeting abandoned farm homes not far from Charlie's properties. Aside from Gebhardt, Wood and Lyle, the files did not reveal the names of the other agents in the operation. Also absent, understandably, were the names of the one or more individuals who tipped the agents on the places most likely to be harboring Harris.

Since being driven to Wayne County from Springfield late in May, Harris was assumed by the FBI to be roughing it by hiding in the woods during the day and sleeping in deserted, often dilapidated houses at night. Agents surmised that food had been smuggled to him by sympathetic individuals.

Harris looked weather beaten when arrested. Unshaven and grimy, he was wearing high leather boots and a dirty straw hat.

Shortly after being taken into custody, Harris was driven, according to the FBI files, to the Holiday Ranch Motel at Fairfield. From there, still at an early morning hour, he was transported by the FBI under heavy guard to Mount Carmel for arraignment before United States Commissioner George Woodcock on a federal charge of illegal flight to avoid prosecution for murder.

Harris appeared to be in high spirits on arrival at his first stop in Mount Carmel, the Post Office. He apparently had regained his composure from the unsettlement gripping him upon his arrest. Proceeding from the Post Office to Woodcock's office on West Ninth Street, Harris seemed jaunty as he traded quips with newsmen and smoked a cigar.

Harris was joined for his appearance before Woodcock by John Holland, the Albion attorney who had helped to successfully defend him in the Taylor slaying case. With Holland at his side, Harris waived a preliminary hearing and declared that he had no statement to make at the time.

Next, Woodcock remanded Harris to Wabash County Sheriff Wallace Compton after he said he could not post a bond set at $50,000 by Woodcock. Harris no longer was upbeat as he departed Woodcock's office. He was heard asking his FBI captors, "You mean I've got to go to jail?" They responded that he was to be held in Wabash County until authorities arrived to return him to Wayne County, where he was under indictment for murder, arson and perjury. He would be tried on those charges, not the less serious federal charge.

Walking to the Wabash County Courthouse at Mount Carmel, Harris uncharacteristically tried to hide his face from cameras with his straw hat. To one photographer, he finally snapped: "You've got enough pictures of me."

Leathers and a deputy were waiting for Harris when he arrived at the courthouse. Aided by other lawmen, they drove him back to Fairfield in a three-car caravan. Having been permitted to shave and clean up somewhat in Mount Carmel, Harris acted a bit more cheerful as the autos filed into Fairfield.

It seemed at first like old times as a number of townspeople—having by now learned of everything that had transpired earlier in the day—awaited his arrival in the downtown area. Spying some of the bystanders, Harris waved his manacled hands in the manner of a conquering hero.

But, this was a different atmosphere from the days when some greeted Harris warmly after the shooting of a Shelton. On this day people simply stared at him, feeling perhaps that they were looking at a person who'd degenerated into a fallen hero in a low-class B-movie.

The journey from Mount Carmel ended when officers escorted Harris to the back door of the Wayne County jail. Feigning disappointment, Harris cracked to reporters, "You mean we don't even rate the front door."

It marked the start of a lengthy incarceration for Harris, months in which he sat behind bars stewing angrily as the Wayne County Circuit Court refused to allow for bail. Notwithstanding his unrest, one school of thought held that, in regard to his personal safety, Charlie was better off in jail.

Word was out that even a few of his normally supportive relatives no longer were in his corner. To them, he'd become a pariah, an unrestrained outcast. They went along with those in Wayne County who lamented his return to his home ground.

Actually, hardly anyone—including FBI agents—believed that Harris had spent much of his time as a fugitive in his home county, except for his final weeks on the lam. However, speculation about his supposedly far-flung hiding places, and about those persons across the country who sheltered him, remained little more than guesswork. Not even the FBI came up with definite answers.

Years later, in a rare taped interview, Harris was asked to disclose the locations where he had hid as a fugitive.

He laughed, and then replied, "I don't talk about that."

23

Another Trial, Another Jury

Was this the end of the line for Harris? Would he finally be sent up the river for arson and two homicides? Or would he again beat the prosecution and walk out of the courtroom a free man?

The answers didn't come overnight because nearly four months passed between his capture by FBI agents and the October 11, 1965, start of jury selection for his trial.

Before Harris entered a plea of innocent in late August to the charges of murder and arson, his attorneys sought dismissal of the accusations on grounds the indictments were faulty. First, it was alleged that they were signed improperly by the foreman of the Wayne County Circuit Court grand jury in 1964. Secondly, the indictments were said to lack necessary legal details. However, the dismissal was rebuffed by Circuit Court Judge Charles E. Jones, the jurist presiding over Harris' trial.

Besides finding that the indictments were valid, Jones twice rejected defense motions that bond be set in order that Harris might make bail and leave jail prior to the trial. State's Attorney Pearce steadfastly insisted that he would contest any move to free Harris, arguing successfully that Charlie was a proven flight risk.

The decision to keep Harris behind bars differed from the situation in 1963 when Harris was free on bond—set by the court and posted by friends—during the period prior to his trial on a charge of murdering fellow Pond Creek farmer Howard Taylor. In that proceeding, also conducted in the Wayne County Courthouse, Charlie was acquitted by the jury.

Some other things also were different this time, starting with the judge.

Jones, a McLeansboro resident with the look of a bespectacled law professor, had gained wide respect for his courtroom demeanor in the short time since his election as a circuit judge in 1964. A University of Illinois law graduate, he had served in the Army Air Corps during World War II.

The cast of attorneys also included some new faces, two on the defense team and one with the prosecution.

Fletcher Lewis and James Lawder Jr. were Harris' new legal beagles. They were joined by John Holland, the Albion lawyer who helped defend Charlie in the Taylor slaying trial. Lewis, from Murphysboro, was the most visible of the trio, assuming the role of Deneen Matthews, the Fairfield attorney who led the successful defense of Harris in the Taylor case.

In Lewis, Harris had a courtroom warhorse—an accomplished criminal defense attorney skilled in reading jurors and familiar with the tactics of prosecutors. The latter was understandable because Lewis, a son of a locomotive engineer, had been state's attorney of Jackson County.

Lawder, also from Murphysboro, became involved at the request of Lewis. Twenty-eight years old and four years out of law school, Lawder previously had worked with Lewis on a murder case in which the defendant, the person they represented, was acquitted. Lawder had not met Harris before agreeing to go to bat for him, and he didn't think Lewis had either.

Holland, whose courtroom presence was mild mannered, had considered in the months before the trial withdrawing from Harris' defense. Charlie's finances had become tangled because of his absenteeism and fire damage to his properties, and he was limited in his ability to compensate attorneys. In fact, an interesting twist occurred only a few days before the start of the trial when Holland obtained a $4,675 judgment against Harris in Wayne County Circuit Court. The amount represented attorney fees that Holland said Charlie still owed him for his legal work in the Taylor case. It was the third judgment obtained against Harris since his indictment for the murders of Betty Newton and Meritt. One for $4,674 was obtained by the Enfield State Bank for two outstanding notes, and the other, for $3,068, was for money owed George Cullum and Don Lawhead, identified as Fairfield oilmen.

Irrespective of his suit for a judgment against Harris, Holland stayed on board for his defense in 1965.

As for the prosecution, the trial had to be déjà vu for Pearce because it was a second go-around with Harris, a man who single-handedly had made his life as state's attorney very uncomfortable. A feeling of disappointment still lingered with Pearce over his failure to secure the conviction of Harris for the Taylor killing in what some had considered an open-and-shut case.

If that was not worrisome enough, Pearce also had to live with the unsettling realization that Harris, the most dangerous person in Wayne County, hated his guts. Charlie had viewed Pearce, a native of Ohio, as a nice fellow in his early days as a practicing lawyer in Fairfield—a time when he'd even reportedly provided some services for Harris. However, Pearce's prosecution of Harris for the Taylor murder left him persona non grata in Charlie's world.

Like Judge Jones, Willard (Bill) Pearce was a University of Illinois law school graduate who'd served in the Army Air Corps in the Second World War. As pictured by his friend and fellow attorney Richard Cochran, Pearce, a Republican who died in 1989 at the age of sixty-four, was handsome, charming and an "outstanding lawyer" who was "a natural in the courtroom."

Cochran never wavered from his belief that Harris prevailed in the Taylor trial because of the astuteness of Matthews in ensuring the inclusion on the jury of at least one woman who never would have voted to find Harris guilty. It turned out that Cochran had an opportunity to try to prevent that from occurring again because Pearce asked him to assist in the latest prosecution of Charlie.

Back in June of that year, Cochran had been driving across Kansas, returning from a vacation in Colorado, when he heard a radio report that FBI agents had captured Harris in rural Illinois. "Little did I suspect," Cochran said, "that I would be more directly involved later on."

Pearce had been aided in the Taylor trial by the widely known Ivan A. Elliott Jr. of Carmi, whose father had been Illinois attorney general. But this time Pearce wanted Cochran at his side, a thirty-five-year-old attorney who in his six years of practice in Fairfield had yet to gain the name recognition of Elliott. Some thought it was asking a lot of Cochran.

The challenge was compounded by the fact that Pearce approached Cochran for help only a few days before the trial opened.

"Bill called me to his office, which was right above my office on Main Street across from the courthouse," recalled Cochran. "He asked me to get involved in the prosecution and handed me the Illinois State Police file on the Harris case. I told him I'd have to clear this with my older law partner, Kelley Loy."

Loy, who'd represented Harris in the past, urged Cochran to turn down Pearce's request. Expressing a lack of confidence in Pearce, Loy told Cochran, "You'll never get a conviction. You're just asking for trouble."

A factor in Loy's advice may have been concern for the safety of Cochran and his family. At the time, Cochran and his wife Anne had three children: Virginia, seven years old; Richard, four; and Susan, two.

Nevertheless, Cochran said he explained to Loy that if he "could help stop the murders, then I'd like to give it a try." To that, Cochran quoted Loy as concluding, "Well, if that's the way you feel about it, then go for it."

Cochran then told Pearce that he'd join him.

According to a tape-recorded conversation years later between southern Illinois publisher Gary DeNeal and Harris, the teaming up of Pearce and Cochran came as a surprise to Harris. Charlie contended that Cochran had agreed to assist Lewis in his defense.

Harris told DeNeal that "Mr. Lewis wanted someone locally that might help him in a way select the jury because he was a stranger" to Wayne County. So, Harris summoned Cochran to the jail because he "was the only free-lance attorney in Fairfield…and we made a verbal agreement that that's what he would do."

When Lewis next saw him, Harris continued, "I told him about who I had selected." But, Charlie averred, when Lewis "went over to see Cochran," he discovered that Cochran "had turned around and joined Pearce."

All of this was denied by Cochran in an interview with the author on July 11, 2008. According to Cochran, he "never talked to him (Harris) at all on the Meritt-Newton case."

Worry about lining up a favorable jury was only one of the concerns facing Harris' lawyers. The preparation of an adequate defense in itself looked to be a challenge because of what many observers felt, once again, to be a strong case against Harris.

Lawder addressed the matter in a telephone interview October 20, 2008, with the author.

"This was a hard case to prepare for," said Lawder, "especially because Mr. Harris was in jail before and during the whole time of the trial. It is tough to defend a person who is incarcerated. We had to wonder when we were talking to him in jail if the walls had ears. We hoped not. It was not supposed to happen. But, it was, after all, the sheriff's bailiwick. When we wanted to visit Harris in the jail, we always had to make an appointment through the sheriff's office."

Laying groundwork for the defense also was hard, Lawder argued, because "it was difficult to get information from the prosecution.

"As I look back, I thought the state's evidence was completely circumstantial. They didn't have a case on solid grounds. There was no confession, no eye witnesses."

During the pretrial period, Lawder noted, Pearce "made an overture about settling the matter." If Harris would agree to a guilty plea on a lesser charge, such as manslaughter, the prosecution would recommend a lighter than expected prison sentence.

"Mr. Lewis was obligated to discuss this overture with Mr. Harris, and he did," Lawder related. "He recommended to Harris that, in his opinion, Harris should take the offer or deal. This was one strong-willed person making a recommendation to another strong-willed person. But, Mr. Harris did not want to go to the penitentiary, and he said so to Mr. Lewis. He did not want to accept that offer."

Subsequently, after Harris turned down Pearce's proposal, Lawder quoted the defendant as telling him, Lawder, that he was "afraid Mr. Lewis is not very happy with me." But, Lawder added, Harris reiterated that the plea offer was unacceptable because, in Charlie's words, "I did not commit the crimes. I wouldn't have harmed a woman. I never abused a woman." According to Lawder, Harris also remarked: "I wasn't an arsonist either."

Although Harris tried to insist that he was not a fire-setter, someone else apparently was. A week before the start of the trial, arson was strongly suspected in a blaze that destroyed the unoccupied farmhouse, owned by Robert Higgins and his wife, where Harris had been captured by the FBI. Authorities considered the fire to be the latest one related to Harris.

The destruction of the farmhouse further fueled the widespread attention drawn to the soon-to-start trial. Newspapers in St. Louis and Chicago were set to join the local press and the wire services in daily coverage of one of the year's biggest events in downstate Illinois.

Pundits were amazed that excitement over the trial rekindled memories of those persons who eagerly had anticipated the trial of high school teacher John Scopes in 1925 in Dayton, Tennessee, for teaching the theory of evolution in violation of state law. That trial, an outgrowth of conflict between science and religion, featured eminent lawyers on both sides— Clarence Darrow for the defense and, for the prosecution, William Jennings Bryan, the person for whom Charles Bryan Harris was named.

The literary efforts by H. L. Mencken, the satirical sage of Baltimore, and other writers to sensationalize both the trial and the mores of backwoods Tennessee would be paralleled in selected coverage of the Harris trial.

There was no better example than *Master Detective* magazine, which went so far as to trumpet the Harris case as "the most sensational court trial in the state's history." Sparing none of the lurid details that attracted readers to pulp fiction, the magazine chronicled the trial in streetwise jargon that would have made the country's seminal twentieth century mystery writer Dashiell Hammett darn proud.

In a lead-in to its story on the trial by Charles Gibson North, *Master Detective* painted the scenario rather earthily as a "drama of death by bullets and desecration by fire (that) included a former henchman of the infamous Shelton brothers; a sexy blonde with a husband, five children and two lovers; and a crazed vigilante mob bent on vengeance."

While Fairfield denizens considered this depiction a tad over the top, nobody disagreed that Harris again had succeeded in putting his world and its inhabitants back on center stage.

The spotlight was on jury selection as the trial got under way on October 11. (Judicial purists always pointed out that a trial technically did not begin until after the seating of a jury, but the picking of jurors commonly was called the first stage of a trial.)

As the selection process commenced, Harris was his normally jaunty self when he was brought to the courthouse from his jail cell. As he headed up a long flight of stairs to the courtroom, a reporter asked, "Are you all ready, Charlie?"

"Don't know whether we're ready, but we're going ahead," he responded. "Nothing ventured, nothing gained."

While he traded smiles with acquaintances in the courtroom, a reporter complimented him on his gray silk suit, one of two he had purchased during his 116 days in jail. Glancing at the reporter, Charlie quipped, "You always say the nicest things."

More than 400 individuals had been summoned as prospective jurors for the Taylor murder trial, a truly high number, but the total for the Newton-Meritt trial far exceeded it. Nearly 900 men and women were interviewed over a two-week period before selection of the jury was completed. Many of those parading to the jury box were dismissed after stating that they already had made up their minds about the case. Numerous others were excused for medical reasons. Additionally, some were challenged because of a personal or family relationship with Harris.

The attorneys also had the right to utilize a certain number of so-called peremptory challenges to keep prospective jurors off the panel even if they had no reason to believe that the individuals would judge the trial unfairly.

Just as in the Taylor case, it was assumed that the excuses given by a number of those not wanting to serve simply camouflaged intrinsic fear at the thought of having to decide the fate of a person with the reputation of Harris.

The *Wayne County Press* had recognized the trepidation in the air when it editorialized at the beginning of jury selection that serving "on the jury is a job that no one would especially enjoy. But it must be done."

The editorial emphasized that "it is to be hoped that those lacking a fixed opinion will square up to their duties as American citizens" and not use a fabrication "as a means of getting out of an unpleasant job."

One person who did not duck his responsibility was Stanley Peddicord, a Wayne City farmer who was among the twelve men and women seated on the jury. A son, Ron Peddicord, took time in 2009 to express admiration for the jury service of his father, who died in 2007 at the age of eighty-eight.

Ron, a member of the staff in Brookens Library at the University of Illinois at Springfield, said, "Although my father never told me this, I am sure he believed that serving as a juror would be a sacrifice he must endure, and considered it his civic duty just as he willingly served his country with his military service in Europe in World War II."

Since his father probably felt that he "was capable of being a fair and impartial juror," Ron said, he "had no reason to try to get excused from jury duty as many did."

Nevertheless, serving on the panel was "a big sacrifice" for Stanley, said Ron.

"Leaving his wife and two sons alone on the farm for an extended period undoubtedly concerned him greatly. I recollect relatives staying with us at night, and now I understand why the precaution."

His father rarely mentioned the trial through the years, at least not before Harris' death in 1988. Even then, related Ron, "I knew not to ask too many questions."

Young Ron remembered the bailiff who was watchful on evenings during the trial when he and his mother visited the sequestered Stanley at what Ron recalled as the El Rancho Motel at Fairfield. Later on, Ron again saw the bailiff, only then he was dressed as Santa Claus in the "candy cane house" on a corner of the courthouse square.

It was indeed a small world at Fairfield.

The juror eventually serving as the panel's foreman was Charles (Chick) Owen of Fairfield, the manager of a home improvement firm. The defense had taken sharp issue with the seating of Owen, contending that he could have a lawyerly relationship with Pearce; that he already had done work in the homes of both Pearce and Cochran; and that he had or did have a membership in clubs to which each of them belonged. For these reasons, Lewis opposed the seating of Owen on a ground that he would not be an impartial juror. However, Jones denied the defense's "challenge for cause" against Owen, permitting him to serve on the jury.

Besides Owen and Peddicord, other Wayne County residents picked for the jury were Everett Enlow, Alice K. Donnelly, Robert Anderson, Donald Ed Riley, Herbert Lane, B. Nadine Brown, Elinor Bunnage, Alta Fearn, Dolores Clemmons and Ella Weaver. All in all, Cochran had a good feeling about the jury. At least he was positive that, this time, the panel included no one determined to acquit Harris automatically in spite of the evidence.

The jury got its initial taste of the case on October 26 with opening statements by Pearce and Lewis, followed by the first prosecution witness. The jurors were considering only the double murder and arson charges against Harris. (The defense had asked for a separate trial on the perjury indictment alleging false testimony by Harris in the Taylor case, and Jones had granted the request.)

Before Pearce outlined the state's case, Jones made certain that Sheriff Leathers had followed his order for tight security at the courthouse. Adhering to the judge's directive, Leathers had posted either a special deputy or state trooper at the base of each of the two stairways leading to the second-floor courtroom. They were to admit only the number of persons that the courtroom could seat. This differed from previous murder trials when spectators crowded into the aisles and the back of the room during the most interesting sessions.

Pearce wasted no time getting to the gist of the case.

The jury of six men and six women heard the state's attorney castigate Harris as a jealous individual bent on revenge after Jerry Meritt won the affection of Betty Newton, a woman for whom Charlie had fallen "like a ton of bricks." Pearce promised to produce witnesses who had heard Harris threaten to kill Betty and Meritt if he found them together.

Pearce stressed that Meritt and Betty did not die in the fire in an abandoned Pond Creek farmhouse on Sunday, August 16, 1964, that consumed much of their bodies. They were killed before the blaze by bullets to the head, fired by a .25-caliber pistol owned by Harris, he said. He also noted that, in spite of insinuations to the contrary by the defense, there was no doubt that the victims were Newton and Meritt.

"Certain items found with the bodies were identified by relatives as belonging to Jerry and Betty," he said.

Summarizing, Pearce said that Harris had returned from Chicago shortly before the killings with Mary Ann Woods, a great niece of Charlie, and her husband James. After Harris visited the Fraternal Order of Eagles Lodge at Fairfield the night before the murders, the trio drove to several places in Wayne County looking for Betty Newton. However, Pearce noted that Mary Ann and James refused his request to check out the old Courtney

Meritt farmhouse, where Harris suspected that Newton and Meritt might be found.

Although the Woods couple drove Harris to his trailer home in the early morning hours, Pearce continued, he was up by 6 A.M., went to the Meritt place and discovered Jerry and Betty together there.

After shooting them to death, Pearce contended, Harris "went back to his trailer, got an accelerant and went back to Meritt's and set the house on fire, then returned to his trailer, where he destroyed certain evidence."

Contesting Pearce's version of the case, Lewis argued in his opening statement that Harris had been drinking heavily at the Eagles Lodge on the eve of the murders and was asleep when the victims died.

The Murphysboro attorney sought to back up this account by telling the jury that two men came to Harris' trailer about 6 A.M. on the day of the murders to go hunting. He maintained that they found him asleep.

"The men borrowed a shotgun of Charlie's to hunt with," Lewis said. "Charlie remained at his trailer and was still there about 8:30 to nine o'clock when the hunters came back. He had never left."

Lewis insisted that Harris "didn't learn about the fire and the people being killed until about noon that Sunday. He never went to the Meritt house that morning. He never killed them. He didn't burn that house down. He doesn't know who killed Meritt and Betty Newton."

Following the opening statements, Pearce and Cochran put a string of witnesses on the stand whose testimony was intended to corroborate—piece by piece—the case against Harris.

The state's first witness, Dr. Albert W. Radcliff, an Evansville, Indiana, pathologist, said that an autopsy he conducted on the charred torsos of Newton and Meritt the day after the murders confirmed that both had been shot to death before their bodies were burned. He detailed his removal of bullets or fragments of bullets recovered from the heads of the victims. Betty Newton was hit by five shots and Meritt two. Dr. Radcliff said that he gave the bullets, as well as full upper and lower dentures from the female skull, to Illinois State Police Investigator Charles Spruell.

Spruell testified that he handed the dentures to Robert Lee of Fairfield, another Illinois State Police investigator. Subsequent inquiry, which included examination of the dentures by Betty Newton's husband Charles, verified that the dentures were Betty's.

Spruell also testified that he delivered the bullets to Forrest Litterly, the state crime laboratory technician who had been a key prosecution witness against Harris in the Taylor murder trial. Litterly, a fixture in the lab since 1951, testified that the bullets came from the same .25-caliber weapon. Later on, Harley Mayberry of Waltonville, Illinois, a onetime employee of Harris, testified that he sold Charlie a new Browning .25-caliber, pearl-handled, nickel-plated automatic pistol in 1961. Another witness, William J. Russell of Mount Vernon, a brother-in-law of Jerry Meritt, told the court that he saw Harris carrying a .25-caliber automatic weapon as late as October 1963 at the farm home of John Felix, a neighbor of Harris.

As the trial progressed, at least three witnesses were summoned by the state to show that Betty Newton and Meritt were together in the hours before they were murdered. They included: Courtney Meritt, the father of Jerry; Roland Gardner of Springerton, Illinois; and Jimmy Meritt of Fairfield, a cousin of Jerry.

Courtney, Harris' longtime friend who'd left the Veterans Administration hospital at Marion to testify, said he saw his son alive for the last time in the early evening of August 15. Courtney testified Jerry told him that he and Betty were going "somewhere." Courtney added that he cautioned his son to be wary in the outing, reminding him that Betty was married.

Gardner testified that he was tending bar at the American Legion post at Springerton, south of Fairfield, when Betty and Jerry entered the place about 10 P.M. on August 15. He said they stayed about an hour, drinking Falstaff beer.

Then Jimmy Meritt took the stand to say that Betty and Jerry stopped for gas about 11:40 P.M. on August 15 at a Shell service station in Fairfield where he was an attendant. He said they were in a 1955 or 1956 Plymouth being driven by Betty.

Earlier, Spruell had testified that a 1955 pink Plymouth was parked behind the burned-out farmhouse in which the two bodies were found. Following that, Leathers went on record as saying that the auto, also badly damaged by fire, was licensed in the name of Betty Newton—although in the wake of the blaze authorities had said it was registered in the name of Charles Newton.

The testimony of Charles Newton during the trial's second day provided one of the most dramatic segments—as well as one of the more revealing. Spectators in the hushed courtroom, some 300 strong, leaned forward to catch every word of Newton's answers to Pearce's queries.

The defense still had questioned whether the female body found in the destroyed farmhouse indeed was that of Betty Newton. Charles Newton said he had no doubt that it was. He identified a wristwatch and a bracelet discovered in the fire's rubble as belonging to his wife. He also reiterated that the state's "Exhibit No. 24," the dentures taken from the dead woman, were Betty's.

Then, Newton revealed for the first time his account of both his and Betty's relationship with Harris. Some of the testimony was fit for *True Confessions*, a women's magazine launched in 1922 that featured emotionally compelling, often heartbreaking stories about love and betrayal.

Newton related in his testimony the following:

He first met Harris in early 1961. Shortly afterward and for six months, he and Betty ran Charlie's speakeasy, the Mansion on the Hill, in Pond Creek. After leaving that job, the couple lived in the coal mining town of Royalton, Illinois, before Charles' health problems largely motivated a move to Phoenix in the middle of 1962. While there, Harris visited him and Betty twice. In July 1963, the Newtons returned to Illinois because Charles accepted an offer to do general farm work for Harris. The Newtons moved into the Harris-owned house in Pond Creek known as the Hodge Place. Harris' employment of Newton lasted only a short time.

Charles' friendship with Harris ended abruptly after a conversation between the two men, while Betty was present, on December 23, 1963, in Harris' trailer. What Charles Newton heard couldn't have been more disquieting.

Harris, who was armed, told Charles that there was "something I want to get off my chest. You have a perfect right to be suspicious about Betty and me." Harris said that he and Betty had been having an affair for a long time, starting when the Newtons operated the speakeasy.

After the couple moved to Royalton, Harris did not see her again until his visits to Arizona. During those times, Harris said, "Betty often came to his hotel room." It was in Arizona that Harris admitted he once again fell for Betty "like a ton of bricks."

However, Harris told Charles that Jerry Meritt, who'd also worked for Harris, had "run under him (Harris) with Betty's affection and that he,

Charlie, wouldn't bother her any more." (Yet, after the Newtons' abrupt departure from Pond Creek—moving first into Fairfield and then to a home by Geff—Harris still drove past their residence virtually every day.)

Harris' confession let Newton better understand the motive for an incident he had observed in late October or early November 1963 while he and Harris stood in the yard of the Hodge Place late at night. Brandishing a .25-caliber, pearl-handled automatic pistol, Harris fired about seven times at a passing car. He apparently did not hit the auto, which Harris thought was being driven by Jerry Meritt. Later, Jerry told Newton that it was him in the vehicle.

Charlie was the first to tell Newton that his wife and Jerry had become an item. After the murders, other individuals told Newton the same thing. Nevertheless, Newton was proud that he and Betty never were separated.

This was the essence of Charles Newton's testimony.

In an ensuing stage of the state's presentation of its case, the prosecution produced a number of witnesses who swore that Harris, finding himself a jilted lover, posed a dangerous threat to Betty Newton and Jerry Meritt.

Jeanette Russell of Mount Vernon, a sister of Jerry, recalled that Betty was mentioned during a conversation she had with Harris at a hangout in Wayne City in 1963. According to Jeanette, Harris said that he wished "Betty was here."

She said that prompted her to reply: "You must think a lot of her, Charlie." He retorted, she testified, that he was "very much infatuated with her, and I don't want anybody messing with her."

Betty's daughter, Carolyn, who by the time of the trial had married a soon-to-be Vietnam War veteran named Dallas Jelley, testified that early in the summer of 1964 she overheard a testy conversation between her mother and Harris in which he warned Betty that "all that's saving you is those kids."

Charles Felty, an electric power lineman from Fairfield, related to the jury that Harris was on edge during a chance meeting between the two at the Eagles Lodge in the city in early 1964. Harris told him, Felty testified, that he'd recently burst into the vacant Hodge Place in an unsuccessful effort to catch Betty and Jerry together.

Felty quoted Harris as saying, "If they'd been there, I would have shot them both. I would have shot him first, and then shot her in the guts and watched her die."

Just as potentially damaging to Harris was the testimony of Charles Hutchcraft of Golden Gate, Illinois, an oil-field laborer. In a conversation with Harris only a few days before the killings, Hutchcraft recalled Charlie saying that he was "courting Jerry Meritt now."

"Are you going to kiss him?" Hutchcraft said he jokingly asked.

"And what did he reply?" Pearce questioned.

"He said, 'Yeah, I'll give him the kiss of death.'"

Harris' vengeful mood was stronger than ever in the hours before the killings, according to another witness. He was James Woods, whose wife Mary Ann was a daughter of Laverne Slattery, a niece of Charlie. (Harris often was heard to refer to James Woods as a "nephew.")

Woods testified that Harris had confided to him, while the pair was driving in Fairfield during the night of August 15, that "there are three people I got to get rid of." He named Jerry Meritt, Betty Newton and State's Attorney Pearce, whom Black Charlie berated as a quisling.

Having finished their efforts to document Harris' motive and threats in regard to the murders, Pearce and Cochran next moved to undercut the opening statement of Fletcher Lewis that Harris drank heavily the night before the killings and then slept in his trailer home until sometime after the bodies were discovered in the fire.

To counter Lewis' rendition, the prosecution relied on the recollections of individuals who—with one significant exception—had been supporters of Harris in the past. Two of the former allies were Woods and Leo Bell, a nephew of Harris, and another one was Emily Hodges, the former housekeeper and confidante of Charlie.

Woods testified that he and his wife Mary Ann were urged by Harris to drive him around the Fairfield area late on the night before the murders in a fruitless search for Betty. This occurred after Harris had spent considerable time drinking at the Eagles Lodge.

The trio drove by Betty's home at Geff and another location she once had frequented, but James and Mary Ann stopped short of granting Charlie's request to go to the old Courtney Meritt farmhouse. Instead, they saw to it that Harris was in his trailer by an hour or two after midnight.

Before James Woods left Harris in the early morning hours, he noticed a few specks of blood on Charlie's white shirt. A few hours later, when Woods saw Harris at his trailer, testimony revealed he then asked Charlie about the blood. Harris replied that bleeding had occurred when a finger was nicked by a fan the previous evening at the Eagles Lodge.

Woods inquired about the flecks of blood when he and Leo Bell went to Charlie's trailer a little after 5 A.M. on August 16. The two men wanted to go squirrel hunting, and Woods needed to borrow a shotgun from Harris. Both Bell and Woods testified about the early morning visit to the trailer.

Bell said that they looked through a trailer window after their arrival and saw Harris lying on a couch, still clad in his shirt and dark trousers from the previous evening. Bell rapped on the trailer door, bringing Harris to his feet. After he let them enter, they shared coffee with Charlie, Woods testified. Then Harris produced some shells for them and told them that the shotgun Woods sought to borrow was in a garage/tool shed by the trailer.

Bell and Woods found the weapon there under a raincoat and departed in Bell's car. After driving Woods to an area called the "Bell Lease" to hunt, Bell returned to Harris' trailer and parked his car there, but not in a place that would block Harris' white 1962 Chevrolet. Bell testified he then walked away. At this point, it was about 6 A.M.

As he reached a fence on the edge of the nearby woods, roughly eighty yards from the trailer, Bell said he heard Harris' car motor start. He said he could have seen the vehicle if he'd turned around. But he didn't. He proceeded into the woods. On cross-examination, Bell admitted that he did not know if the car went anywhere.

When Bell went back to the trailer about 9 A.M., he saw that Woods already had returned. Bell did not enter the trailer this time, but testified that he was told by Woods that Emily Hodges had joined Harris in the residence and that there seemed to be friction between the two.

This observation by Woods was a prelude to later testimony by Emily that the prosecution believed to be crucial in attempting to show Harris' guilt. However, before calling her to the stand for what the state intended to be a knockout punch to Harris, Cochran was responsible for producing a witness who turned out to be just as damaging to the defendant.

He was John Felix, a seventy-nine-year-old farmer and neighbor of Harris in Pond Creek and a person who no longer hid his dislike for Charlie—whom Felix said he had known for many decades.

The heart of Felix's testimony was that he saw Harris make two round-trips between his trailer and the nearby Courtney Meritt farmhouse in the early morning hours before the discovery of the fire and the two bodies on August 16, 1964. Without this testimony, the state's case was not as strong. However, Felix would not have taken the stand if not for Cochran.

Felix at first didn't want to testify about what he observed because of bitter resentment over the acquittal of Harris for the murder of Howard Taylor, whom Felix called his best friend. Based on the outcome of that case, Felix was skeptical about the likelihood of Pearce getting a conviction in the current trial. Thus, he was hesitant to become involved.

Law enforcement officials "knew that John had seen something that morning," Cochran told the author, "but he wouldn't talk to them."

Realizing Felix's potential importance to the prosecution, Cochran visited him soon after agreeing to assist Pearce.

"I probably spent two hours, maybe more, sitting on John's back porch talking to him, and trying to get out of him what he knew," said Cochran. "Every time I'd get around to quizzing him about what he had seen that morning, he'd change the subject.

"Finally, after a long period of that, I said, 'John, I've got better things to do than sit here and visit with you. We've got to prepare a case, and I really need to know what you know.'"

Still, Felix held out, emphasizing his lack of confidence in Pearce. This prompted Cochran to ask Felix to put his faith in him. Reminding Felix that "I'm in it now," Cochran assured Felix that "we're going to get a conviction if at all possible."

Cochran's pledge was followed, he said, by "a long period of silence." But then, he said, Felix "opened up, and told me what he knew."

The *Wayne County Press* wrote that the state was rolling out "its heavy artillery" when Felix hobbled to the witness chair—a difficult undertaking that required him to use a cane and crutch.

Felix, whose home was on the south side of Harris' place and not far north of the Meritt farmhouse, insisted before a jammed courtroom that— between 6 and 7:15 A.M. on August 16—he twice saw Harris driving his car south toward the Meritt property. Each time, Felix testified, Harris returned minutes later over the same road toward the trailer. The Meritt house was found afire about 8 A.M.

Asked to elaborate during direct questioning by Cochran, Felix said he arose very early on the fateful Sunday morning because his "varmint dog had been barking half the night over something he had treed." Felix said he got into his pickup to find the dog and drove about 150 yards south of his house before stopping at a gate. He said that from there he had a clear view of the gravel road that went toward the Meritt farmhouse.

Then, Felix testified, "I heard Charlie's car coming over the hill after a while, and I thought it was awful early for him to be up. So I looked to make sure it was him. It was. He was driving fast for him. He slowed at the curve, then went on south toward the Meritt place.

"About ten or fifteen minutes later, he came back, going toward his trailer, still going unusually fast for him."

At that time, Felix had yet to find his dog, which had stopped barking. Thinking of another place where the dog might be, Felix moved to a spot a little north of his barn. About ten minutes later, he saw Harris driving south again in his white Chevrolet.

"Then I saw the varmint my dog had treed," Felix said. "I shot it, and it fell to the ground." Felix thought the animal may have been a possum, but said he wasn't sure of it. "My dog got to it," he said, "so I didn't go look at it."

Not long afterward, Felix said he saw Harris drive by again, heading north toward his trailer.

The testimony of Felix was intended by the state to substantiate its contention that Harris, on his first trip to the Meritt farmhouse, discovered Betty and Jerry together in bed and proceeded to shoot both to death. Or, as North writing in *Master Detective* put it in the manner of Hammett's gumshoe Sam Spade, Charlie "filled their heads with lead." On his second trip to the house, the state held, Harris took kerosene or another accelerant to burn the bodies.

The defense stridently sought to discredit Felix as a witness. For instance, Lewis got Felix to acknowledge that a move by Harris to buy Felix's farm had ended up in an argument, a dispute in which Harris lost a $3,000 down payment.

Lewis also pressed Felix on whether it was true that he still believed that Harris had murdered Howard Taylor.

"I still say it," Felix replied.

Felix's eyesight was questioned during the defense's cross-examination. This prompted Felix to tell Lewis: "Got one eye good as yours. Can't say that about the other eye."

Lewis also asked Felix to say what Harris was wearing when he drove by Felix's place. The spectators laughed when Felix replied, "Don't know, don't know if he had any clothes on." That brought a slam of the gavel from Judge Jones, and a warning against further laughter.

Felix then was asked to give the date of his birthday. When he did, Lewis queried, "How old does that make you?"

"You figure it out," Felix replied.

His answer triggered more laughter, and a stern admonishment from Jones. If there was another outburst, the judge said, "I will clear this courtroom, and we will proceed only with the press present."

There was no laughter as the prosecution climaxed the presentation of its case with the testimony of Emily Hodges. The expectation was that she'd deliver the coup de grace to Harris. If it was accurate that Harris really had a hit list, she'd have been on it after her testimony.

Acquaintances of Emily maintained that the slender brunette, who said she'd worked as a housekeeper for Harris "off and on for five or six years," had written off the friendship after the double murder. While Harris was a fugitive, she had served six months in prison in Illinois after pleading guilty to perjury in testimony to the grand jury that indicted Harris. Her false testimony was that Harris had been in her presence when Newton and Meritt, a nephew of Emily, were killed. Friends said that she later regretted telling an untruth.

Emily, who was living in Milan, Illinois, at the time of the trial, told the jurors that she had spent the night before the murders at the old Hodge Place. She said she had somewhat angrily declined an invitation to accompany Harris and one or two of his relatives or friends to the Eagles Lodge because "they were already drinking, and I didn't want to be around them."

The next day, she said she drove Charlie's pickup to the trailer between 8:30 and 9 A.M., unaware of the fire at the farmhouse. She said she found him in bed in pajamas. She threw a pet Pekingese on the bed beside him before sitting down on the bed herself.

"Charlie asked me if I was still mad, and I told him, 'No, just tired of being pushed around,'" she said. Then, she testified, he patted her hand and told her, "No more."

Soon, Woods returned to the trailer, and Bell came not long afterward. Emily said she made coffee for everyone, but Bell did not enter the trailer. Before the two men departed, Emily said she started to straighten up Charlie's bed. First, though, she had to pick up his clothes lying on it. It was then, she said, that she saw, while Woods was still present, quite a bit of "real dirty" blood on his shirt.

"I asked him (Harris) if he'd been in a fight the night before," Emily testified. "He and Jim (Woods) said he'd cut his finger on a fan at the Eagles." Emily proceeded to put the shirt in a washing machine in the garage.

Later, Harris asked her what she did with the shirt. When she told him, he ordered her to destroy it, "but not here," she testified. She said she took it away and burned it.

Emily said that at some point in the morning she did notice smoke in the air south and west of the trailer. She wasn't aware that it came from the Meritt farmhouse until a nephew stopped by the trailer at noon and mentioned the location of the fire and the bodies.

After the nephew left, she said that she asked Harris if he was responsible for the fire. She said that he responded by putting his finger to her mouth and saying, "Shush."

On another matter pertinent to the case, she told the court that, up until a few days before the fire and murders, she often had observed Harris in possession of a .25-caliber automatic pistol that was pearl-handled and nickel-plated. After the murders, she questioned Harris about the weapon. She testified that he replied, "It is not here."

During cross-examination, Emily said she had known since 1961 about Harris' affair with Betty Newton. Lewis contended this had spurred antagonism by her toward Betty, and he succeeded in getting Emily to admit that she and Betty came to blows in a knockdown fight in 1962. Emily said her clothes were torn off in the fray.

The encounter was "for a number of reasons," Emily testified, but mostly because of Harris.

Emily also told Lewis she was aware of Betty's relationship with Jerry Merit, but did not know "where they were meeting."

After Emily's testimony, the state rested its case. As in the Taylor trial two years earlier, the prosecution felt it had shown convincingly that Harris was guilty. Many who listened to the state's witnesses opined openly that the testimony of Felix and Hodges especially put Harris in a difficult box. The observers now anxiously awaited the rebuttal testimony of Harris, which came on Monday, November 1, three weeks after the start of jury selection.

Harris took the witness stand in one of his fashionable gray suits, and immediately adopted the warm and folksy mannerisms that jurors in the Taylor trial had seen. However, he did not stray from the defense's opening statement by Fletcher Lewis that held he could not have committed the murders and arson because he was sleeping off a binge when the crimes occurred.

Harris said he normally was not a heavy drinker, but that he did over imbibe on Seven Crown Whiskey mixed with 7 Up soda during several visits to the Eagles Lodge on the night of August 15, 1964. A band was playing, and Harris—although saying that he was getting woozy—hit the dance floor.

"Once when I was dancing backwards, I knocked into a floor fan, and it started to fall over," he testified. "I grabbed it with my hand, and I cut my thumb. It started bleeding. I got some blood on my shirt."

As Saturday's late-night minutes turned into Sunday's early morning hours, Harris testified about the efforts by James and Mary Ann Woods to get him home. "I don't know what time we got there," he contended, "(but) it seems to be established it was about 1:30 or 2." He said he had no recollection of first asking them to drive him around in a search for Betty Newton.

He did recall that when he got out of a car at the trailer, he started to walk off.

"James asked me where I was going, and I said, 'To the trailer,'" Charlie related. "He turned me around, and said, 'It's that way.'"

Harris said he stumbled into the trailer and dropped onto a davenport without undressing. "Like any drunk, I went to sleep," he said.

The next thing he recalled was pounding on the trailer door by Woods and Bell. He said that he'd talked with them the night before and knew they were coming to go hunting.

Harris continued, "James asked if I had a shotgun he could use, and I told him there was one in the garage. I don't know what time it was they got there. It was daylight, I know, and I thought it was kind of late to go hunting. I mentioned that. I gave them some shells for the gun. I perked some coffee for them—perked about 10 minutes—and they stayed long enough to drink it."

After the two men left, Harris told the jury, he took off his clothes, put on pajamas and went to bed. He slept until the Pekingese brought to the trailer by Emily Hodges licked his face, he said.

To the best of his memory, he said, it was around 10 A.M., some two hours after the fire was discovered, that he stepped out of the trailer for the first time since he had arrived home in the early morning hours. He insisted that he did not learn about the blaze until a little past noon, after he and Emily had gone peach-picking at the Hodge Place.

Harris branded as untrue Felix's testimony that he saw Harris drive to and from the area of the Meritt farmhouse twice early on the morning of the murders. He added that the court should know that Emily had a key to his car and that she drove it any time she desired.

Charlie denied ordering Emily to dispose of his shirt, contending that he was angry with her when she allegedly did that on her own accord. After all, he argued, it was not true that there was more blood on the shirt in the morning than from the night before. And, he said the blood was his own.

Harris denied owning a .25-caliber pistol at the time of the murders. One that he bought in 1961, he claimed, was confiscated by Leathers when he searched Charlie's trailer after the Taylor murder. However, when Leathers returned to the stand after Harris testified, the sheriff denied that a .25-caliber pistol was among the weapons he confiscated from the trailer after the killing of Taylor.

Before Harris left the witness chair, he denied that he engaged in a conversation with Charles Newton on December 23, 1963, in which—

according to Newton—Charlie admitted having an affair with Betty New-ton. On cross-examination, he did acknowledge that he had been "out with Betty Newton" and that "my acquaintance with her was that we were pretty friendly."

Harris also flatly refuted the testimony of James Woods, who claimed to have heard Charlie threaten to harm Betty, Jerry Meritt and Pearce. When asked if he had held any grudge against Meritt for testifying against him in the Taylor trial, Harris replied: "No. His testimony didn't hurt me one iota. I wasn't mad at him for that or any other reason."

A touchy exchange occurred before the conclusion of Harris' testimony.

The prosecution asked him if he ever had been convicted of a felony. Before Harris answered the question, Lewis objected and asked Jones to declare a mistrial. After Jones held a conference with the lawyers in his chambers, he denied the motion for a mistrial, but directed Pearce not to make any further inquiry about a prior conviction.

Pearce said that the question was not intended to bring out details of an earlier conviction, but simply to permit insertion into the record of proof of Harris' counterfeiting conviction in federal court in Detroit in 1927. Nevertheless, Jones instructed the jury to disregard the question.

(Interestingly, nothing in the record of the trial indicated that any ref-erence was made to Harris' conviction in Arizona in 1918 for the stabbing of a Phoenix police officer, a felonious assault.)

Finally, on Wednesday, November 3, eight days after the beginning of testimony, the case went to the jury. The panel retired to deliberate the fate of Harris after hearing ardent closing statements or summations by the attorneys.

All three of Harris' lawyers fervently appealed to the jurors to find that the state had not proven without a doubt that Harris was guilty of murder and arson. Holland led off by stating that it was incredible to believe that Harris "would go around telling everyone" that he intended to harm three persons.

Next, Lawder joined Holland in attacking the testimony of John Felix. In Lawder's words, Felix was a "bitter old man out of step with society, determined to get Charlie Harris out of the picture."

After assessing the credibility of the numerous witnesses against Har-ris, Lawder exclaimed that there obviously was a vendetta against the defendant. For emphasis, he struck a fist on the table before him and again proclaimed, "A vendetta!"

Lawder said that it was hard to believe the great degree of "hate in Wayne County." He added, "I've seen it on the streets, on the farms, in this courtroom. I've heard it in that witness chair."

In concluding the defense's summation, Lewis took particular aim at Emily Hodges. First, he expressed amazement that the state would put her on the stand since she was an admitted perjurer. Beyond that, though, he went so far as to insinuate that she may have committed the murders.

"I wonder if any investigation was made of her and her activities that night and morning," Lewis said. "She had a motive herself. She had come to blows and fought with Betty Newton herself. We have only her word she was at the Hodge Place all night. The fact that a .25-caliber pistol was used sounds more like her, not Charlie. She had a motor vehicle at her disposal that night.

"You know that old saying, 'Hell hath no fury like a woman scorned.' Emily Hodges had been Charlie's housekeeper, and knew about him and Betty. She had opportunity to kill Jerry and Betty. I think it's as reasonable to suppose she did it...."

In his testimony, Harris had said that, in addition to employing Hodges as a housekeeper, he had "associated with her socially." He pointed this out after saying that his wife Rena by then was living apart from him in "a rest home" in New Harmony. According to his testimony, Rena was "practically an invalid, and has been for the last five to seven years."

Lewis reminded the jury that the state was obligated to show Harris was guilty beyond all reasonable doubt. "There is no burden on Charlie," he stressed, "to prove himself innocent."

In his final words to the jurors, Pearce defended Hodges and Felix.

"If there is a red herring in this case, it is Emily Hodges, the way the defense has attacked her," argued Pearce. "She has come before this court, has been sentenced and served her punishment. That's more than the defendant has done."

As for Felix, the state's attorney said he was proud that the elderly farmer "had the courage to come forward and tell his story. We need more to come forward. More, not fewer."

Pearce harked back to Lawder's mention of a concern as to whether justice for Harris was possible in Wayne County.

"There is justice in Wayne County," declared Pearce. "There are good people who want nothing more than to work and earn their living and raise their families in peace." As for Lawder's perception of "hate" in the county, Pearce said that what really existed was fear of Harris. However, he emphasized, the jury had an opportunity to end a reign of terror by the defendant.

Contending that the state clearly had proven Harris committed the crimes, Pearce told the jurors that he expected a guilty verdict. "The people of Wayne County demand that you find him guilty," he added.

"We are not asking for an eye for an eye, a tooth for a tooth," said Pearce in an apparent reference to the fact that the prosecution had not sought the death penalty for Harris. "We ask only that you put Mr. Harris behind bars, where he can't hurt anyone else."

With the final words of the attorneys fresh in their minds, the jurors filed out of the courtroom a few minutes after two o'clock in the afternoon to try to reach a decision. The lawyers, reporters and spectators scattered. Harris was returned to his jail cell. Hardly anybody expected a verdict for hours. Some thought there might not be a verdict, that a hung jury was likely.

After the jury retired, Pearce and Cochran slipped away to the nearby Elks Club. Sitting down at the bar, each ordered a beer. It may have been a welcome respite from the pressure-cooker atmosphere of the courtroom. But, there was no shedding of stress, knowing that the outcome of their effort now was in the hands of twelve men and women and that the uncertainty might be prolonged.

However, the two attorneys were only partly through their beers when the bartender answered a ringing telephone. He then delivered a message to the pair.

"The judge wants everybody back at the courtroom."

24

The Verdict

The jury was out only seventy-three minutes.

Bailiff G. E. Jackson heard a rap on the jury room door at exactly 3:20 P.M. Quickly responding, he heard the prolific words, "We have a verdict." They triggered a rapid reaction.

Judge Jones ordered the summoning of Pearce, Cochran and the defense attorneys. Leathers was directed to get Harris back in the courtroom pronto. The defendant, like everybody else, was surprised that the jury had reached a verdict so quickly. He'd taken off his suit and was settled in his cell for what he expected to be a lengthy wait.

Returning to the courthouse in shirt sleeves and carrying his suit coat, Harris endeavored to appear unflappable, as always. But the sheriff later remarked that Harris barely could hide his anxiety.

The courtroom was an armed camp. Twelve or thirteen law officers were stationed at strategic positions, including one by each door and three behind the railing near the defendant. They were ready to combat any disturbance because certain folks continued to insist that Harris would not get out of the courtroom alive if he was found innocent. There was no telling how many weapons were being concealed by spectators who'd managed to reenter the courtroom for the big moment.

One lawman assigned to the case took a stab at it when he sat with *St. Louis Post-Dispatch* reporter James Sprehe at a large table in a Fairfield restaurant after the trial had ended.

"If we (had) collected all of the guns from men's pockets and women's purses in that courtroom," the officer said, "we couldn't get them on this table."

Pearce and Cochran were among those armed. They'd carried handguns throughout the trial, and now, at perhaps its most dangerous moment, there was no thought of putting them down.

After scurrying back into the courtroom, the two prosecutors asked Jones if they could sit apart from Harris and his attorneys during the reading of the verdict. Only one table had been provided for all the lawyers and Harris. That suddenly became a concern for Pearce and Cochran.

"There were a lot of very high feelings at that time," said Cochran. "We, Bill and I, asked Judge Jones if we could have permission to sit away from Harris and his attorneys, out of the possible line of fire in the event of a not guilty verdict. But, the judge refused our request."

A glance at the reassembled crowd in the courtroom revealed that a number of Courtney Meritt family members had taken seats. At least a half-dozen newspersons occupied the front row, each poised for a hurried exit once they heard the verdict. Newsrooms at many papers awaited a call from Fairfield on the fate of Harris.

The two major St. Louis newspapers were prime examples. The *Globe-Democrat*, a morning paper, was likely to get the scoop on the trial's outcome story because the jury was revealing the verdict after the final deadline of the day for the *Post-Dispatch*. However, this did not diminish eager anticipation at the *Post-Dispatch* to learn the verdict. City Editor Selwyn Pepper anxiously awaited word from Sprehe, who was covering the trial.

Editors in Chicago also were looking for news on the verdict, some over the news wire service tickers. The *Tribune* always had kept a close watch on Harris, and the *Sun-Times*, incredulously, had taken to calling him "the patriarch of crime in southern Illinois." Too, *Chicago's American*, which sensationalized the news, naturally considered Harris hot copy.

The most stellar coverage, by far, was right at home where the *Wayne County Press* had detailed in words and pictures every lurid aspect of the whole proceeding. Now, with the end of the trial at hand, *Press* editor T. O. Mathews, and his right-hand man and ace photographer, Jack Vertrees, were ready to put the finishing touches on the paper's comprehensive reportage. They just needed to know the jury's decision.

As the jurors filed into the courtroom, Jones gaveled for order. Within seconds, the room was deathly still. Nevertheless, to ensure decorum, he ordered that, irrespective of the verdict, no outcries would be tolerated. Violators of the order were to be taken into custody and held in contempt of court.

"We want silence," he warned.

Finally, Jones turned to the jury and asked if it had reached a verdict. Charles (Chick) Owen, the jury foreman, rose and answered in a clear voice, "We have."

Tension in the courtroom approached a flash point as Jones directed Owen to "read it."

Pearce, who felt he had lived with this case for an eternity and who had faced threats to his life, dropped his face into his hands. The eyes of Harris, known for coldness, were glued on the jury.

"We the jury," Owen read slowly, "find the defendant guilty."

Harris was found guilty of each charge—two for murder and one for arson.

A hush settled over the courtroom with the disclosure of the verdict. Some strained to look at Harris' face, and those who succeeded said that he appeared crestfallen. Other spectators observed expressions of relief on the faces of Meritt family members—although there was no visible gloating.

One Pond creeker summed up the feelings of many of his neighbors when he smilingly commented, "We can plug up our artillery now." Another predicted there would be "a lot of guns for sale." Still another concluded, "We can go home and dismiss the guards now."

Harris may have been downcast upon hearing the verdict, but it didn't seem to last very long. As Leathers began to escort Charlie out of the courthouse and back to his jail cell, the sheriff told him that several reporters wanted him to comment.

"Goodness," he remarked with a smile, "they've covered the trial from the beginning. They know as much about it as I do." Nevertheless, one scribe got close enough to ask him for his opinion of the verdict.

Harris didn't stop walking, but did shoot back an answer over his shoulder. "It's just one of those things. I'm just riding out the storm."

As opposed to the aftermath of the Taylor murder trial, Harris would not issue a public statement or quasi-press release seeking to assure the public that he bore no ill will toward anybody. Mustering such magnanimity now apparently was out of the question.

True to form, defense attorneys did not hesitate to poll the jurors on their decision. Each one expressed satisfaction with the verdict. Nevertheless, Holland told reporters afterward that the defense planned to ask for a new trial. If that was not granted, the outcome of the trial would be appealed to a higher court, he signified.

The judge urged the jurors before their departure not to discuss the case outside the courtroom. Conversing with the attorneys was another matter.

Looking back years later, Cochran said that "we couldn't be positive that we had that good of a jury, but it turned out that we did."

Cochran and Pearce touched base with Owen after the trial, and Cochran recalled the foreman relating the following:

"Chick told us that as soon as they retired to the jury room, the first thing they did was elect a foreman, which was Chick.... It was a sequestered jury from day one, and everybody was tired. He suggested that they take a quick straw vote and see how far apart they were. Well, the first vote they took was unanimous for guilty on all counts. The only thing left to decide was whether or not to recommend the death penalty. There were a couple of people opposed to that, so they just decided to return guilty without recommendation of the death penalty."

Speaking for the defense lawyers, Lawder said decades afterward that "we were disappointed with the verdict, of course. We worked hard on that case. Maybe, we might have done some things differently, but nobody knows."

"It was a defensible case," Lawder added, "but you never knew what a jury was going to do."

Jones did not sentence Harris until more than a month after the trial, but that didn't deter rejoicing by more than a few persons after the announcement of the verdict.

Master Detective wanted the world to know that "news of the conviction, which editors at the *Press* scrawled on long sheets of copy paper and pasted in the window frontier-style, touched off wild jubilation. Through the tiny (Fairfield) business district, voices could be heard shouting: 'Hoo-ray!'"

The *Wayne County Press* opined that the verdict was what "the people wanted" in an editorial the day after the trial ended. As a result of the conviction, the editorial held, "public morale is lifted, confidence is restored in our courts, and it is shown once again that a Wayne County jury can return a verdict of guilty when the evidence indicates it.

"Now there is hope that a new era of law and order beckons for Pond Creek and Wayne County. Maybe, over the years, our community will recapture the better name that it deserves."

The foremost thanks for the resolution of the case "goes to those neighbors, relatives and erstwhile friends of the defendant who had the guts to take the witness stand and tell their stories," the editorial continued. "It was a brand of courage the likes of which we haven't seen in a criminal case in court here for a long, long time."

The editorial also applauded the trial work of Pearce and Cochran, as well as the efforts of law officers who dealt with the latest Harris episode from its start.

Some of those lawmen joined Pearce and Cochran at a celebratory house party in the hours after the verdict was rendered. The party continued the next day at a farm south of Wayne City. As it progressed, someone set up a target on a tree, and every attendee—including the FBI agents present—tested his marksmanship.

The outing offered an opportunity for individuals long preoccupied with the Harris case to let off pent-up steam. Cochran also remembered an ironic, if not humorous, note about the gathering.

A few days before, when the Harris trial was still ongoing, a bank had been robbed in the village of Mount Erie, northeast of Fairfield. On the day of the victory celebration at the farm, Cochran said a news report proclaimed that FBI agents were investigating the heist "without letup."

Well, Cochran mused, at least two of them, Charles Wood and Herman Lyle, both involved in the tracking down of Harris, were not because both were at the party.

Moreover, as the get-together was breaking up in the evening, Cochran recollected a comment by Wood in reference to the investigation.

"I hope nothing happens tonight because I'm out of ammunition."

25

No End to the Saga

Harris was sixty-nine years old—an age at which many persons were retired and able to travel, play with grandchildren and pursue other pleasures of the commonly called "golden years." But Charlie's future looked to be a living hell, far removed from being enjoyable.

Nothing had changed his fate since his trial and conviction on charges of two murders and arson. He was back in the Wayne County jail, which had been his residence in the months before the trial. Since he was being held without bond, he was not likely to be leaving his cell until his sentencing and departure for what was expected to be a lengthy prison stay.

Judge Jones had put off sentencing to give Harris' lawyers time to submit motions for a new trial. They intended to seek a retrial on grounds that Harris wrongfully was denied bail after his capture in June, and that his defense had not been permitted the necessary number of peremptory challenges of prospective jurors. However, legal analysts said there virtually was no chance that Jones would approve another trial.

While Harris waited, he received another slap in the face from Emily Hodges, his former housekeeper and a prosecution witness.

A week after his conviction, she filed a petition in Wayne County Circuit Court seeking a $20,540 judgment against him and his wife Rena.

Hodges said the money was owed for maid services that she performed from 1959 to August 16, 1964, the day of the slayings for which Harris was found guilty. She was not the first person to go to court for a judgment against Harris. But, the sum she sought was the largest.

No doubt, Harris was in a stew over Emily, whom he considered a turncoat because of her damaging testimony against him, when his mind turned to a more pressing matter on December 10.

On that day, Jones—after rejecting the motions for a new trial—sentenced Harris to serve sixty to seventy-five years in prison for the murder of Betty Newton and the same term for the murder of Jerry Meritt. The sentence for the arson conviction was ten to fifteen years. All were to run concurrently.

Fletcher Lewis still contended that Harris had not received a fair trial and served notice that Harris' conviction and sentencing would be appealed to the Illinois Supreme Court. Nearly two years would pass before the tribunal ruled on the appeal.

More than a few persons breathed a sigh of relief on December 22, the day Harris was taken from the county jail before dawn for the ride to the Menard State Prison at Chester.

Jack Vertrees of the *Wayne County Press*, who had a penchant for recording history, requested permission to accompany Harris on what some hoped would be his final departure from Fairfield. Neither Harris nor Sheriff Leathers objected. Vertrees made the trip in the front seat of the sheriff's car. Leathers was driving, while Charlie sat in the backseat, handcuffed to Harry Lee, a sheriff's deputy. Following the vehicle was an Illinois State Police car manned, as Vertrees recalled, by troopers Robert Lee and Harold Jones.

Vertrees later recounted that, after obtaining consent from those in his auto, Harris puffed on cigars all the way to Menard. While gazing at Christmas decorations in Mount Vernon and other areas through which the small convoy passed, Charlie drifted from one subject to another.

He did not think the death penalty was a deterrent to crime, and he thought it was a shame that the American farm boys serving in wars received training in weaponry that turned them into killers. He opined on the nation's space exploration program and vented his views of preachers and heaven. He brought up the Sheltons too, repeating his claim that they nicknamed him Black Charlie—which he still saw as an attempt to dispar-age him.

When the law officers were escorting Harris to the front gate of Me-nard, Vertrees retrieved his camera from under his seat in the car and cap-tured one last photo of the old gangster. Vertrees later was to find out that Charlie did not appreciate the picture one bit.

After the gate closed behind him, Harris became inmate No. 33156. He officially had commenced his third and final prison stay; the first in his home state.

Charlie entered Menard at a time when the institution was gripped by unusual tension. Only a month before, three guards had been stabbed fatally and a number of others wounded in a dining hall riot. William Bas-sett, one of the four inmates charged with the murders, was from Fairfield and another, John Stamps, from Granite City, Illinois. The uprising raised questions about security procedures at the penitentiary and bolstered crit-ics of Ross V. Randolph, the state's public safety director and former war-den of Menard. Randolph, a highly respected penologist, was continuing to reside at the prison when Harris arrived.

In spite of the impact of the riot, Menard still retained a reputation for having a more hospitable environment for inmates than Illinois' other maximum security prisons. Menard had been built in 1877, and its build-ings reflected a quasi-Civil War style of penal architecture, a far cry from the updated designs of most other Illinois prisons.

Menard also had a unique setting. Nestled in bluffs where the Missis-sippi River flowed by Chester, the prison occupied a natural rock setting that created what penal authorities called "an illusion of quiet isolation—like an island posed in a sea of silence."

The arrival of Harris at Menard prompted an oft-heard question. Did it signal the end of his saga?

Not quite.

Harris' story would continue. The appeal of his case to the Illinois Supreme Court was pending. The charge of perjury against him still was outstanding. Several of the prosecution's key witnesses at his trial soon were to be back in the news. And Charlie apparently was not going to let his incarceration stop him from trying to get Willard Pearce bumped off.

Shortly after Harris' imprisonment, Pearce and Cochran moved early in 1966 to prosecute him on the unresolved charge of perjury returned by a Wayne County grand jury at the same time it indicted him for the two murders and arson in 1964. A trial on the perjury indictment had been deferred at the request of Charlie's attorneys.

Harris had committed perjury, the grand jury concluded, when he testified falsely in 1963—during his trial on a charge of murdering Pond Creek neighbor Howard Taylor—that he had not owned or possessed a .45-caliber handgun, a weapon used in the shooting of Taylor. Harris was acquitted at the trial.

Cochran was asked years later why the perjury charge was pursued in view of the fact that Harris already was in prison. The attorney replied that, since there was a chance that the Supreme Court might uphold Harris' appeal of the outcome of the 1965 trial, "we wanted something that would hold Harris in prison. Otherwise, he would be freed."

As it turned out, the trial on the perjury allegation would not be held until the summer of 1967, roughly three months before the Supreme Court ruled on his appeal. By then, other chapters in the Harris narrative had been written.

In early March 1966, Carl H. Wittmond, a Democratic Illinois state representative from Brussels in Calhoun County, was involved in steps to acquire Harris holdings. Wayne County officials said deeds had been filed by Wittmond giving him title to about 1,000 acres of land owned by Charlie and Rena. Some of the property was believed to be tied up by judgments obtained against Harris by John Holland and others. Circuit Judge Randall Quindry, whose court had issued the judgments, said that issues surrounding the tied-up acres had to be worked out between Wittmond and Harris' creditors.

Years before, Wittmond, a farmer, merchant and hotel operator, had purchased at auction considerable acreage in Wayne and Hamilton counties that had been owned by Carl Shelton. Even though he'd experienced great difficulty in getting persons to work that acreage because of threats from Shelton enemies, Wittmond apparently was not dissuaded from buying more land from another gangland figure.

In an interview in 1988, the year of Harris' death, Wittmond said that Charlie "always was a friend of mine...until he got it in for everybody...."

Later in March, Harris was returned to Fairfield briefly for a hearing on the attempt by Emily Hodges to obtain a $20,540 judgment against him. The session in Wayne County Circuit Court mainly dealt with a requirement that she testify to the worth of her maid services, which she valued at $10 a day during her six-year stint in the job. A few days after the hearing, Quindry awarded Emily $600, a sum far below what she sought. However, sources said that, through a separate proceeding, she was awarded another $1,400 of the amount she claimed Harris owed her.

While in Fairfield for the hearing, Emily purchased a 1966 Chevrolet from a Carmi auto dealer. She considered it part of the new life she was seeking to build in Milan, where she had moved and obtained a job at the Miller Container Company in nearby Rock Island.

The following month, Emily was driving her new car near Milan when an auto driven by Kelsey Gosa of Rock Island crossed the centerline and crashed head-on into her vehicle. Suffering head and chest injuries, she was pronounced dead on arrival at a Rock Island hospital. Gosa died at the hospital a short time later.

Emily Belle Hodges was only forty-four years old when she was buried at the Union Cemetery southeast of Fairfield. The words "Safe with Jesus" were inscribed on the stone at her grave.

Three months after Hodges' death, John Felix passed away. The elderly neighbor of Harris whose eyewitness testimony was crucial for the prosecution died in San Antonio, Texas. He was there visiting a daughter, who was identified by the *Associated Press* as June Ladzinski.

The next death of a prosecution witness was the most shocking. James Leo Bell, a nephew of Harris whose testimony helped convict him, was discovered dead in his home southeast of Fairfield on October 10, 1966. Bell, whose pajama-clad body was found lying with a shotgun by its side, was a son of Charlie's sister Mabel, who had died two years earlier.

Authorities said that the gun's muzzle was near the left side of Bell's neck, under his chin. His head rested in a pool of blood. They said the death appeared to be a suicide, possibly a result of Bell's medical problems. However, a number of persons close to Bell suspected that he'd been murdered. These individuals noted that a dwindling but still visible cadre of Harris loyalists was known to resent greatly what they considered Bell's betrayal of his uncle.

Bell, an army veteran wounded in action in World War II, was forty-seven years old. He was buried in Union Cemetery, only a few steps away from the grave of Emily Hodges. Nothing ever came of the suspicion that he might have been murdered.

As for Harris, himself, he was back in Fairfield in August 1967 for a trial on the perjury charge. A jury of five men and seven women found him guilty after former acquaintances testified that Harris did possess a .45-caliber handgun, a weapon believed to be used in the shooting death of Howard Taylor. (Charlie had denied under oath in 1963 that he had such a gun.)

Subsequently, Harris was sentenced by Associate Circuit Judge William Eovaldi to a prison term of seven to twelve years for the perjury conviction. But, the sentence was to run concurrently with his other prison terms.

Charlie felt that his prosecution on the perjury count was overkill since he already was behind bars for murder and arson. His distaste for Pearce never had been a secret, but seldom had he criticized Cochran. However, he served notice to Cochran, during a time-out in the trial, that he now was on very thin ice.

While the other lawyers were taking a break, Harris looked across the counsel table into Cochran's eyes and remarked, "I guess you're pretty proud of yourself, the way you have jackassed me around."

Cochran returned the stare, and replied, "Charlie, I don't think I've done anything to you. You've done it all to yourself."

That prompted a quick rejoinder.

"I'll get you, you son of a bitch," threatened Harris.

Cochran never became aware of any attempt by Harris to harm him. The same was not true for Pearce, providing a young felon named Glenn Totten was to be believed.

As recounted by Cochran, Totten was paroled in 1967 from Menard, where he had been serving time for a robbery at Mount Erie. He disappeared after his release; a violation of his parole. He was found and arrested in a western state, and brought back to Illinois for a return to Menard. However, he became unglued at the thought of going back to Menard, contending that it would mean his death. Consequently, he was placed in the state prison at Pontiac.

Totten's reasoning was taken seriously enough by the Illinois State Police to trigger a call to Pearce. What Pearce was told prompted the state's attorney, who was a pilot, to fly with Cochran to Pontiac in his Piper Cherokee, which he kept at Fairfield.

Sitting down with Totten in the Pontiac warden's office, Pearce and Cochran took a statement from Totten in which he revealed a purported role in a dubious plot.

He said he had made a deal with Harris before his parole from Menard. He agreed to assassinate Pearce for $5,000. He was to contact a Harris confidant in Evansville to receive a down payment on the killing, with the rest to be paid after the murder. Totten did meet with Harris' friend and was handed the first installment of the promised money. But, he didn't perform his end of the deal.

"Totten said he never intended to kill Bill, but he agreed to do it because he needed the money," Cochran said. "However, after Totten reneged on his agreement with Harris, he begged them not to put him back in Menard, knowing that he'd be killed by Harris."

No follow-up action was taken against Harris as a result of the Totten matter. It certainly was a reminder for Pearce that he was not safe from Harris' wrath, even with Charlie in prison. However, Pearce, and Cochran found their solace in knowing that—because of Harris' conviction and sentencing on the perjury charge—he'd remain in prison even if the Supreme Court overturned the outcome of his double murder and arson trial.

In the meantime, Harris had obtained new representation before the Supreme Court—Robert H. Rice, a seasoned and politically astute attorney from East St. Louis. Observers did not feel that the appeal of Harris' conviction for murder and arson had a good chance of success as the prosecution had presented such a solid case for his guilt. Still, it was unnerving given that the court was capable of surprising decisions that defied conventional wisdom. Nothing was certain until the tribunal's opinion was handed down.

That occurred on November 30, 1967.

In line with the customary procedure, the reporters in the Statehouse pressroom assembled in the ornate Illinois Supreme Court Building on South Second Street in Springfield for the periodic release of multiple opinions. As always, Kenneth Watson, the veteran political columnist for the *Illinois State Journal*, gave each reporter an opinion to digest and summarize. The reporter who was handed the one on Harris soon was tapped on the shoulder by Charles Whalen, the longtime chief of the *Associated Press* bureau in the Capitol.

"What's the ruling on Black Charlie?" Whalen asked.

"The court upheld his conviction," the reporter replied.

"Well, let's hurry to get it out," Whalen urged. "There are a lot of people interested in this one."

The opinion upholding the conviction had been delivered by Justice Byron O. House of Nashville, who represented the court's southernmost district on the seven-member panel. In the opinion, the tribunal refuted arguments raised initially by Lewis, Holland and Lawder and later pursued by Rice.

Their contention that the circuit court in Wayne County erred in denying Harris' request for bail prior to his trial was viewed by the court as invalid.

"Defendant makes no claim that his conviction was in any manner affected by the denial of bail, such as depriving him of an opportunity to prepare for trial," the court said in its opinion. "Under these circumstances, the purpose of bail could not be accomplished by now reversing the order denying bail."

In addition, the court stated in its opinion summary that law "excepts from the right of bail persons who are accused of an offense punishable by death, and the proof is evident or the presumption of guilt is great...."

Harris' appeal went on to argue that the seating of juror Charles Owen deprived him of a right to trial by an impartial jury. It was contended that Owen automatically would favor the prosecution because of business and social ties to Pearce and Cochran. But, the court ruled that "if a juror meets the statutory qualifications, the determination of whether a challenge for cause should be allowed rests within the sound discretion of the trial court...." A reading of the trial record "convinces us," the court said, that Jones "did not abuse his discretion in finding Owen to be an impartial witness."

The justices next held that Harris was not entitled, as his counsel claimed, to an extraordinary number of peremptory challenges in jury selection because he was being tried on three charges at the same time.

Here, the court relied on case law in citing statutory language which held that "if several charges against a defendant or defendants are consolidated for trial, each defendant shall be allowed peremptory challenges upon one charge only, which single charge shall be the charge against the defendant authorizing the greatest maximum penalty."

The appeal also contended that the trial court erred in admitting into evidence photographs of the torsos and heads, as well as X rays, of Betty Newton and Jerry Meritt. The objection was that the exhibits inflamed the jury while not resolving any issues in the case. The court disagreed, ruling that the photos confirmed the great challenge in visual identification of the victims.

Too, the opinion added, the exhibits "showed defendant had executed his plan in the manner he said that he would" by attempting "to destroy all evidence as he had said he would."

In conclusion, the justices held that "we are of the opinion that defendant received a fair trial."

The importance of the Supreme Court's decision was underscored about a year later when the Illinois Appellate Court at Mount Vernon reversed Harris' perjury conviction. The court ruled that the prosecution had failed to prove how his allegedly false testimony, in retrospect, was material or important.

Had the Supreme Court not upheld his murder and arson conviction, the appellate court decision most likely would have made Harris a free man—pending possibly further judicial action.

Charlie would have been back on the street.

26

Having His Say

Gary DeNeal was his normal, vigilant self as he sat in a cafeteria at the Vienna State Prison on July 3, 1979, for the wrap-up of a rare and informative undertaking. It was his final day of recording conversations with an eighty-two-year-old inmate who'd led a life with more curves and twists than a roller coaster.

The hands of the interviewee, who was dressed in street clothes instead of penal garb, were busy continuously folding, unfolding and refolding a paper napkin. As he had in the earlier tapings, the man portrayed politeness to the point of delicacy. DeNeal also noticed that he referred to himself as "Little Charlie," but never Black Charlie or Blackie.

DeNeal, a folk writer, historian and poet residing near the Shawnee National Forest hamlet of Herod, had persuaded Charlie Harris to sit for the recordings—four in all. They were part of DeNeal's research effort for his authoritative biography of southern Illinois gangster Charlie Birger.

Harris was of minimal help on Birger, but he had much to say about people who had figured heavily in his own past. For a man who usually had exercised considerable restraint in public comments, Harris came close to letting his hair down with DeNeal.

The conversations did not produce any mea culpa or confession to one or more of his misdeeds, but Harris had choice words for the state's parole system, some Illinois Supreme Court justices and, of course, Willard Pearce. He also took a shot at T. O. Mathews, who'd left the post of *Wayne County Press* editor in 1977. On the other hand, Richard Cochran surprisingly was not castigated.

By the time of the final interview, Harris had served about five years at Vienna. A minimum security facility for trusted inmates that opened in 1965, it was situated near the deep southern Illinois city of Vienna, the county seat of picturesque Johnson County. The atmosphere there had earmarks of a country club in comparison to the punitive environments at Menard and Stateville, the places of Harris' previous confinement in the Illinois penal system.

In a letter dated November 12, 1974, to outgoing Wayne County clerk and friend Jack E. Copeland, Harris compared Vienna to "an old folks home." But, he added, "I am a bit on the old folks side at that…a little disfigured, but still in the ring."

The worst place for Harris had been Stateville, where he was moved from Menard in late 1967 or early 1968. It mattered little to Charlie that Stateville was the state's most prestigious prison.

Located at Crest Hill, just north of Joliet, Stateville was Illinois' version of a "big house"—similar in reputation to two other signature state prisons, Sing Sing in New York and San Quentin in California. Recognizable by its round cell houses, Stateville was known for its authoritarian administration and incarceration of prominent Chicago gangsters.

Although he was not mistreated by the guards, Harris never adjusted to Stateville, complaining that a cell he shared with another man was ridiculously small. He objected to the long hours of confinement in his cell—tedious periods interrupted only for short recreation periods, meals and visits to a commissary to obtain smokes and small necessities. He was resentful that Stateville officials had refused his request to attend the funeral service for his wife Rena, who died February 19, 1968.

After he was transferred from Stateville to Vienna in 1974, he became a favorite of the new guards he encountered. Some visitors went so far as to say he appeared to enjoy celebrity status. One reason for this, if true, may have been Vienna's location in a part of the state where Harris was a household name.

Judy DeNeal, Gary's wife, found Harris exceedingly charming when she attended a taping at the Federal Courthouse in Benton, Illinois, the only one of the four interviews not conducted at Vienna.

"Really, he was like a well-mannered, grandfatherly sort," she said. "He would say, 'Give me five,' and put out his hand to be slapped."

Her intuition told her that Harris was "a womanizer—a man who knew how to make a woman feel appreciated." She recalled him lamenting that a major negative of prison life was the absence of "women to sleep with."

"Of course," Judy noted, "I was thinking…when he picked out or had a gal, it could be bad if she didn't stay faithful to him. I also remember thinking that there had to be a touch of arrogance in a man who felt it was okay to sleep with another man's wife."

Delving into the moral makeup of Harris was a tricky proposition. For one thing, modes of conduct to which he subscribed, as he made clear late in life, were not tied to theology. Gary DeNeal concluded that Harris was "an atheist who felt the Old Testament was written by bloodthirsty tyrants. Organized religion to him was a lot of hokum."

Nevertheless, DeNeal noted that Harris said he did attend church services at Vienna "because he wanted to help make the young minister feel appreciated."

While religious parallels hardly were featured in the tape recordings, Harris' unrelenting ire toward Pearce was harsh enough to put the former state's attorney in the company of Judas Iscariot—the apostle who in the Gospel accounts betrayed Jesus. Forgiveness was out of the question for Pearce, the onetime Harris friend who prosecuted him twice for murder.

Harris denied that he had asked a young felon being paroled from Menard in 1967 to murder Pearce for $5,000. (The parolee, Glenn Totten, had related the request, which he did not attempt to carry out, in a statement to Pearce and Cochran.)

"I talked to lots of men in Menard while I was there," Harris was taped as saying. He conceded that he might have met Totten, but insisted that he did not "remember the boy."

Obviously, Harris' scorn for Pearce was not shared by the many persons who gave him high marks for eventually putting Charlie back behind bars. Pursuing legal actions against Harris had been part of his job, but doing so had required Pearce to summon courage and professional stamina that put considerable strain on his health and career.

Mathews was another of those categorized by Harris as a friend turned antagonist. In gibes at T. O. and others at the *Press*, Harris contended in the tapes that he only got a fair shake from the newspaper when the Sheltons still were in Wayne County.

"But, once the Sheltons were gone out of the community…they turned on me," he said. From then on, he argued, the paper never wrote one thing about him "that wasn't detrimental." Mathews in particular, Harris maintained, "always had his two-cents worth in there" because—once the remaining Sheltons had fled—the editor was "against me from the jump go."

Harris' take was out of sync with the views of others. Out-of-town journalists at his murder trials had found the *Press* articles, at least during those proceedings, to be balanced as well as impressively detailed. This was an interesting observation because coverage of Harris on his own doorstep had entailed challenges of a personal nature for a small-town paper like the *Press*. Visiting journalists did not have to hang around afterward.

It may have been faint praise, but Cochran was one of the few persons to receive some kind words in DeNeal's recordings.

"Cochran is a straight-up, law abiding citizen," Harris said of the attorney who helped Pearce send him to prison. "To the best of my knowledge, he has lived a clean life, devoted to his family."

However, DeNeal asked Harris if it was true he had threatened Cochran during Charlie's trial for perjury. Harris said that was a fabrication, but added a curious observation that might have made Cochran uneasy.

Declaring that Cochran had been "worrying about whether I'm going to ever see the free world or not," Harris tacked on the following:

"If he has done something to me that warrants annihilation of him, then am I supposed to suffer while he's enjoying the free world?"

Harris may have referred to the strong opposition by Cochran and Pearce to Charlie's desire for parole. Since becoming eligible in 1975, Harris' bids for release repeatedly had been turned down by the Illinois Parole and Pardon Board. A main reason for the denial, the board explained, was the unwillingness of persons in his home community to accept his return.

A key factor when considering parole was the board's need to feel assured that an inmate would remain at liberty without violating the law. In the case of Harris, the panel had been contacted by individuals who feared that he still constituted a threat to a number of persons in Wayne County.

Asked by DeNeal to comment on concerns raised by persons fighting his parole, Harris replied that he did not "know how they get the idea that I would retaliate. I never did. And, if their consciences are bothering them, I can't help that."

A shortcoming of the parole system, according to Harris, was that a bid for freedom could be sabotaged by "one person, regardless of how lowly he is, writing one lousy letter against you."

"Ten angels can't overcome that," he said.

In his words, the board was "just as useless as tits on a boar pig."

His taped remarks also revealed frustration with the state's criminal justice system.

He remained convinced that jury selection in his 1965 trial was rigged against him by the exclusion of persons who knew Harris. Judge Jones was said to not be his own man. Instead, Charlie saw him as "putty" in the hands of Pearce. The Supreme Court's rebuff in 1967 of the appeal of his conviction turned out to be hypocritical, Harris asserted, in view of the scandal that engulfed the court two years later.

Charlie well was aware of an unsavory situation that brought disrepute to the court and led to the resignations of two of the panel's members, Chief Justice Roy J. Solfisburg Jr. and Justice Ray I. Klingbiel. The pair was found to have violated judicial canons of ethics by secretly receiving stock in a Chicago bank before or during the time the court was considering a case involving a top officer of the bank. Subsequently, Klingbiel wrote an opinion that upheld a lower court's dismissal of criminal conflict of interest charges against the officer.

After listening to Harris' grievances, DeNeal thought it appropriate to query him on what he thought was the likelihood of ever getting out of prison.

"Nil," Charlie responded into the recorder. "The opposition's purpose...is to keep me here until I die."

* * * * * *

Charles Harris did not breathe his last behind bars. In December 1980, state officials announced their intention to parole him. They said his age and time served were factors in the decision. Records of the Illinois Department of Corrections revealed that the parole occurred February 3, 1981, a little more than fifteen years after he began serving his sixty to seventy-five year sentence.

In 1990, DeNeal utilized the tapes and other communication with Harris to profile him in *Springhouse*, a magazine on southern Illinois history that DeNeal edited and published with assistance from his wife. DeNeal concluded that Black Charlie, like some other widely known scofflaws, was an enigma.

DeNeal said Harris came across as "meticulous, full of years, full of laughter (and) full of stories big on mistakes, false friends and hairbreadth escapes." But, DeNeal also recognized that "others, with good reason, saw him as a killer cold-blooded enough to make icicles jealous."

Harris' darker side surfaced, DeNeal wrote, in his notion that "killing a man was actually letting him off easy."

"If you really want to hurt somebody, hurt him bad enough so he has to think about you every time he wakes up and feels the pain," uttered Harris.

He followed this chilling pronouncement to DeNeal with a little laugh.

Two Towns

E vents long characteristic of life in America were ongoing during a warm June evening early in the twenty-first century. One was a stirring band concert in Fairfield, while the other was a festival in Elkhart, Kansas, celebrating a slice of the nation's legacy.

The Fairfield City Band, under the direction of a pretty young woman with sandy blonde hair, concluded its program with a rousing rendition of "El Capitan," one of John Philip Sousa's traditional marches. An appreciative audience on the lawn of the Wayne County Courthouse showed that some places still had an idyllic side.

Simultaneously, many miles to the west, the Grassland Heritage Festival was in full swing at Elkhart. Through drama, dance and traditional music, the historic culture of southwestern Kansas was brought to life by artists and a multitude of visitors, many of them Santa Fe Trail enthusiasts. Travelers and commerce on the trail—long romanticized in western lore—had left a lasting influence on the area.

The festival also focused attention on the nearby federally administered Cimarron National Grassland, a vestige of the parched Dust Bowl of the 1930s that had been converted into a major recreational area. Twenty-three miles of the Santa Fe Trail ran through the grassland. At one point on this stretch, a person would be within walking distance of the museum-like home of Bea Riley.

She was the reason for a common thread between Elkhart and Fairfield—namely her uncle, Charlie Harris. After his parole in 1981 from the Vienna prison in Illinois, Harris spent the last years of his life living on Bea's property a few miles northeast of Elkhart.

Known as Jakie Bell when she grew up in Pond Creek, Bea had built a new life for herself in the so-called cornerstone of Kansas—the region where the southwest corner of the Sunflower State converged with Oklahoma and Colorado.

Harold Riley, the husband who'd brought her to his home area of Elkhart in the early 1950s, was long out of her life before his death in 1982. On her own, she'd become a highly respected member of the community while working as a hospital nurse and then as a private care nurse in homes. She also made time for other undertakings, such as raising burros and organizing trail rides. She occupied a seat on the board of directors for the Morton County Historical Society Museum, which she helped establish in 1987 while Harris still was alive.

The Chamber of Commerce in Elkhart, the seat of Morton County, named her its woman of the year in the late 1990s for her leadership in civic activities. In the same span, Bea was honored by the Pride Committee of Elkhart for service to the community.

As if these honors were not enough to set her apart, the woman recognized for wearing her long black hair in Indian-style braids also had a unique residence. A year before Harris came to live with her, Bea purchased a vacant Methodist church building. Two years later, she had it moved five miles to a site on fifty-three acres she owned in the national grassland. Her land was not only in the proximity of the Santa Fe Trail, but also near the usually dry bed of the Cimarron River.

Harris had questioned her sanity when he learned of the church acquisition. Bea recalled him telling her that she never would be able to make it habitable. But, when she did, he allowed that he was proud of her.

"As the church was moved," Bea related to the author in 2008, "Charlie insisted on walking behind it the whole five miles. The going was slow, and he made it. I just thought it was his way of trying to show he wanted to be part of what was happening."

Afterward, he lent a hand on some of the work needed to get the church into a livable state. His carpentry skills came in handy, most notably in a loft he built above the altar to support a bedroom.

When finished, "The Plantation"—the name given by Bea to the church and her acreage—was a showpiece. The inside of the home resembled a museum, housing arrowheads and other Indian artifacts, cowboy paraphernalia, skulls, mounted game, western movie mementos and trinkets galore from the Santa Fe Trail. The surrounding yard contained conical teepees, a log cabin and relics of pioneer days among sagebrush, cottonwoods and yucca plants.

Behind her home was something that probably meant little to the individuals and groups from the area who led tours to The Plantation. A visitor from Illinois might have felt differently. It was a cell door from the old Wayne County jail, a building where Harris knew every nook and cranny.

Some unknown person or persons had gone to a lot of effort to transport it—a haunting reminder of a violent past—from Fairfield to Kansas. However, hardly anyone who came to The Plantation in the 1980s envisioned the thin, elderly little man living there as anything but a courteous gentleman. People in that remote section of Kansas were not aware of Charlie's background. And he, of course, didn't bring it up.

Harris resided in a white, two-bedroom trailer a short walk from Bea's home. He was not its first owner, a reason perhaps that he was able to buy it for about $3,400. Bea said he loved the trailer, avidly read newspapers there and stored some of the items he picked up at a junkyard a few miles away.

"He was always going to fix stuff up with those pieces of junk he brought back," Bea remarked. "He said going to the junkyard was 'his thing.'"

As in the old days, Charlie still refused to wear jeans to town, only trousers and clean shirts. Some older women, Bea observed, "still found him attractive."

Riding with Charlie at the wheel was not desirable, though. Bea was on edge when accompanying him in one of the two used Ford LTDs he owned during his Elkhart years.

"I didn't like riding with him," she stated. "When you saw him coming, you'd better get over. He had become a poor driver."

One clue to his past—in case anybody had noticed—was Charlie's required visit once a month to a parole officer in Hugoton, Kansas, a few miles from Elkhart. As a condition of his release from prison, Bea explained, he was not permitted to visit Illinois while on parole. Although

Illinois corrections department records indicated that he was discharged from parole on November 24, 1982, at the age of eighty-six, Bea did not remember his parole ending that soon.

Harris did return to Wayne County for a few visits in the 1980s. Each time, though, he expressed no hesitancy about getting back to Elkhart and his trailer in the grassland. Kansas had become his adopted home state in the twilight of his life.

Even though Elkhart was not as populous as Fairfield, the cities shared many similarities.

Each still embodied the tone and rhythm of small-town America where life moved at a slower pace than in the big cities. While neither one was divorced from the massive tides of a changing nation, the townsfolk refused to surrender their allegiance to holidays, parades and to what urbane individuals may have labeled as "simple joys."

As William Schmitz soon recognized after moving to Fairfield in 1989, the townspeople also were allegiant to each other.

"One thing about Fairfield," Schmitz pointed out, "the people take care of their own. They try not to let you go to waste or go down. They don't let their own get thrown under the bus."

The Elkhart that Harris came to know might have been one of the small Kansas towns depicted in the fictional works of Pulitzer Prize-winning playwright William Inge, a native Kansan who brought to the stage and screen the hopes and heartaches of people in small places.

His play *Picnic* captured the pulse of small-town Kansas in the early 1950s as local beauty Madge shakes up her community with her passion for handsome drifter Hal. In *Splendor in the Grass*, a 1961 movie based on a story by Inge, a Kansas town in the late 1920s was the setting for the unforgettable love, sexual repression and eventual grief experienced by teenagers Deanie Loomis and Bud Stamper (played respectively by Natalie Wood and Warren Beatty).

Black Charlie did not encounter famous actors in Elkhart, but he did find, as in Fairfield, a good number of farmers and oil-field workers. Similar to numerous Illinois towns in Harris' memory, the Elkhart skyline was defined by towering elevators used for storing grain grown in the area.

Sustaining agriculture had been no easy task in that part of Kansas, as a brochure at the Morton County museum at Elkhart made clear.

"Pioneers who came west to Morton County…searching for free land struggled against the extremes of 'Mother Nature'…freezing blizzards, instant dust storms, flash floods, grasshopper invasion, drought and prairie fires," the brochure related. "They literally 'carved' homes out of the land, only to have their dreams destroyed by the elements…but, still they stayed, and survived."

Antique tractors were among the many exhibits in the museum, which the National Park Service designated as an interpretive center for the Santa Fe Trail. Its counterpart at Fairfield would be the Hanna House Museum of the Wayne County Historical Society, opened long after Harris had left the county for prison.

Fairfield exhibits featured old embalming instruments and fluids for the years when many funerals were held in homes. And there were reminders of the oil boom days in Wayne County that included a Pure Oil Company film of life in an early oil camp. Hard to miss was the stuffed head of a fanged "Pond Creek swamp monster," an evil-looking creature every bit as scary as the gunmen who'd roamed Pond Creek.

Judith Puckett, a teacher and Fairfield civic leader who was instrumental in the opening of the museum, did not ignore the county's criminal history. An exhibit that brought to life the Sheltons also included the FBI wanted poster on Harris and a transcript of Charlie's trial for the two murders and arson.

Like it or not, it seemed Harris almost always ended up being a center of attention.

28

No Regrets

U nderworld characters quickly learned never to sit with their backs to anything but a wall.

Richard Cochran may not have known that because he was a respected attorney in Fairfield, not a crime figure. However, a few tense moments on a day in the mid-1980s convinced Cochran that it was a good plan to follow. He reached this decision in a most unlikely place—Cy's ice cream and coffee shop in downtown Fairfield.

His back was turned to the front entrance of Cy's when one of the friends he'd joined for coffee, a person who was facing the front door, suddenly signaled with his eyes that Cochran should look behind him. Complying, Cochran immediately spied Charlie Harris standing at the counter glaring at him.

No words were spoken, but Cochran stared back at the man he'd helped send to prison some two decades earlier. The standoff ended when Harris, without taking the ice cream he'd ordered, turned and left the shop.

"It was the last time I ever saw him (Harris)," Cochran said. "I really was not afraid of him because I'd determined long ago not to let fear ruin my life." But, he added, "I did make a point after that to not sit with my back to the door."

The brief encounter occurred during a month-long visit by Harris to Fairfield after his discharge from parole. It well may have been an isolated incident because, according to various other people, Harris was well received as he reconnected with old acquaintances in the area.

He first stayed near Fairfield at the farm home of his nephew, Virgil Harris, and his wife Imogene. They chauffeured him as he made his rounds because his drive from Elkhart to Fairfield had convinced him that his eyes no longer were sufficient for piloting an auto outside the familiar roads at Elkhart.

It may have been a miracle that Harris, only a year or so from his ninetieth birthday, had even made it to Fairfield.

Bugged by prostate problems as well as fading eyesight, he had struggled along in his 1979 olive green Ford LTD, a four-door vehicle with a black vinyl top. The only positive note was the company of his new love, a little Shih Tzu appropriately named Danger.

A last leg of the lengthy drive had been made a bit easier because of a chance meeting at a truck stop. Harris struck up a conversation with the driver of an eighteen-wheeler bound for Fairfield. The man suggested he run interference for Charlie by having him closely tail the big rig. The strategy worked, and Harris cruised into town.

However, Charlie had decided he would not be up to driving his car back to Kansas. He summoned Dalene McCoy, a daughter of Bea Riley and a nursing assistant, to come to Fairfield from her home at Elkhart to herd him around Wayne County in his LTD and then drive him back home. Halfway through Harris' four-week visit, McCoy took a bus to St. Louis, where she was met by Harris, Virgil and Imogene.

For the next half month, she drove Charlie during the days and spent the nights in an apartment at Grayville, Illinois, a town on the Wabash River southeast of Fairfield. The apartment was owned by Margaret Bell Vaughan, a niece of Charlie and half sister of Bea. It was next to a popular restaurant-tavern operated by Margaret that was known for its Wabash River catfish dinners, corn on the cob and the beveled glass behind the bar.

Years later, Dalene vividly recalled the only time she saw Harris enter the restaurant while she was staying at Grayville.

"When Charlie made his appearance, the bar was crowded and noisy," she related. "Then, suddenly, it became so quiet you could hear a pin drop. Believe me, everybody knew who'd just come in. Pretty soon, though, people began to greet him, and he went around for thirty minutes shaking hands and visiting. Many wanted to buy him a drink, but he turned them down.

"Watching the way he was received, it was pretty obvious that he was somebody. Say what you want, he had a presence about him."

Harris continued to make that presence known on the drive back to Elkhart—an undertaking described by McCoy as "the wildest trip ever." To begin with, Charlie and a new passenger, Rachel Hallam of Fairfield, another of his nieces and a half sister to Bea, bickered constantly over politics, Fairfield gossip and other weighty matters.

"They just always disagreed," Dalene said, "although some of it was good-natured."

However, Harris was anything but good-tempered when a crisis erupted not long after leaving Fairfield. It couldn't have been worse because it involved Danger.

During a stop at a gas station in St. Louis, Harris was asleep in the backseat, where he was riding with Danger. By the time Harris awakened, Dalene already had driven several hundred miles west of St. Louis.

"Where is Danger?" he asked immediately.

Dalene suddenly became mortified when she realized the little dog was not with her and Rachel, who occupied the front passenger seat. There was just one answer. Danger must have slipped out of the car at the station, the day's only stop thus far. Neither she nor Rachel had noticed the dog was missing.

After she sheepishly told Harris that Danger apparently had escaped at the station, he ordered Dalene to stop the car. She said he told her in no uncertain words to "turn this SOB around and go back to find my dog."

"So," she said, "we drove all the way back to the gas station and, hard as it was to believe, found Danger sitting by a pump. He was whining, no doubt for Charlie."

After that, Dalene noted, "we drove straight through to home, stopping only a couple of times for bathroom breaks. And believe me, we carefully counted heads each time before going on."

* * * * * *

Danger remained at Charlie's side the rest of his days. If Harris' wish had been fulfilled, the dog would have been put to sleep after Charlie's death and buried with him. However, the sharing of a casket with Danger was not allowable.

Harris died on June 20, 1988, thirty-six days shy of his ninety-second birthday and a little more than seven years after his last release from prison. He exhibited mental and physical vitality until the end, which came on one of those sunbaked Kansas days.

Perhaps he had been outside too long because when he walked to Bea's house for dinner, she sensed that he was unusually tired. She became convinced of it when he defied his normal routine by not taking off his shoes before laying on a couch for a short rest prior to the evening meal. Bea also noticed Charlie didn't have his teeth in his mouth.

With the time for supper drawing near, Bea dispatched her grandson to get the teeth from Charlie's trailer. When the boy returned, Harris raised his head a little and said: "Son, put the teeth right there." Complying, the youngster placed the dentures on a coffee table by the couch.

Charlie would utter no more words.

Attempts to awaken him were unsuccessful, and Bea sensed he was gone after she could not detect a pulse. Nevertheless, an ambulance was summoned, and he was taken to the Morton County Hospital at Elkhart. He was pronounced dead after entering the emergency room. Bea later was told that he died of a brain hemorrhage.

Following a visitation at an Elkhart funeral home, the Reverend Earl Chestnut of the Church of God in the city presided at a grave-site service in the Elkhart Cemetery. Scriptures were read for Harris, in spite of his skepticism about religion.

"Charlie questioned whether there really was a heaven or hell," said Bea. "He'd often ask, 'Has anybody been to one or the other and come back to tell us about it?'"

While he did not have Danger in his vaulted casket, he was granted his request to be buried in a new pair of pajamas with a handkerchief. As explained by Bea, he "wanted it to look like he'd just gone to sleep."

He was interred next to his wife, Rena, who had lived her last days at Bea's until her death in 1968. Engraved on their gray granite tombstone were the words, "Together Forever."

Charles Bryan Harris' final resting place under a spreading cotton-wood was very serene for a person whose life was anything but placid.

It was peaceful for a man who'd stressed to Bea Riley that "there is a difference between putting a bullet in an animal and into a human body."

It was peaceful for a man who, near the end of his life, remarked to her that he "never killed anybody who didn't deserve to get it."

Bea, who knew her uncle better than anyone else, was convinced that "he had no second thoughts, no regrets in looking back."

"He had," she said with utmost certitude, "no conscience qualms about his misdeeds."

None at all.

Select Bibliography

Allison, Lelah. *The History of Leech Township*. Fairfield: The Wayne County Record, 1954.

Angle, Paul M. *Bloody Williamson*. New York: Alfred A. Knopf, 1952.

Brownell, Baker. *The Other Illinois*. New York: Duell, Sloan and Pearce, 1958.

Casey, Robert J., and W. A. S. Douglas. *The Midwesterner*. Chicago: Wilcox & Follett, 1948.

Courtaway, Robbi. *Wetter Than The Mississippi*. St. Louis: Reedy Press, 2008.

Demaris, Ovid. *Captive City*. New York: Lyle Stuart, 1969.

DeNeal, Gary. *A Knight of Another Sort: Prohibition Days and Charlie Birger*. Carbondale: Southern Illinois Univ. Press, 1998.

Gentry, Curt. *J. Edgar Hoover: The Man and the Secrets*. New York: W.W. Norton & Company, 1991.

Hallwas, John E. *The Bootlegger*. Urbana: Univ. of Illinois Press, 1998.

Hamer, Richard, and Roger Ruthhart. *Citadel of Sin: The John Looney Story*. Moline: Moline Dispatch Publishing Company, 2007.

Helmer, William, and Rick Mattix. *The Complete Public Enemy Almanac*. Nashville: Cumberland House Publishing, 2007.

History of Wayne and Clay Counties, Illinois. Chicago: Globe Publishing, 1884.

Howard, Robert P. *Illinois: A History of the Prairie State*. Grand Rapids, Mich.: Eerdmans Publishing, 1972.

Jacobs, James B. *Stateville: The Penitentiary in Mass Society*. Chicago: Univ. of Chicago Press, 1977.

LaMaster, Kenneth M. *U.S. Penitentiary Leavenworth*. Arcadia Publishing, 2008.

Life and Exploits of S. Glenn Young. Herrin: Crossfire Press, 1989.

Martin, John Bartlow. *Butcher's Dozen and Other Murders*. New York: Harper & Brothers, 1950.

Meritt, Fred. *Memoir*. Springfield: Sangamon State Univ. Oral History Office, 1974.

Mills, Randy K. *Troubled Hero*. Bloomington: Indiana Univ. Press, 2006.

Nunes, Bill. *Southern Illinois: Amazing Stories from the Past*. St. Louis: Corley Printing of Earth City, 2008.

Pensoneau, Taylor. *Brothers Notorious: The Sheltons*. New Berlin: Downstate Publications, 2001.

The Kefauver Committee Report on Organized Crime. New York: Didier, 1951.

Wittmond, Carl. *Memoir*. Springfield: Sangamon State Univ. Oral History Office, 1988.

Index

A

Adams, Joe 29
Adams, Kate J. 50
Allison, Lelah 6-7, 9-10
Altgeld, John Peter 12
Anderson, J. C. (Blackie) 62, 93
Anderson, Robert 200
Andrus, Lucile 50
Armes, Monroe (Blackie) 46, 68, 69
Armes, Roy (Tony) 69, 95-96
Arnstein, Julius (Nicky) 45
Associated Press 226, 229
Atkins, Ellen Merritt 53-55

B

Bailey, Harvey 44-45
Baker, Olen 81
Baldwin, Carl R. 69, 70-71
Banning, Eldon 185
Barker, Arthur 45

Barker, Fred 45
Barker, Herman 45
Barker, Lloyd (Red) 44, 45
Barker, Ma 45
Bassett, William 224
Bell, Beatrice (Jakie). *See* Riley, Bea
Bell, James Leo. *See* Bell, Leo
Bell, Laverne 83
Bell, Leo 121, 206, 207, 211, 213, 226-227
Bell, Mabel. *See* Harris, Cora Mabel
Bell, Margaret 87
Bennett, C. A. 41
Bills, J. D. 85
Birger, Charlie 27-29, 71, 231
Bixby, F. Lovell 55
Black Charlie. *See* Harris, Charles Bryan (Charlie)

Walsh, Patrick 36-37, 39
Watson, Kenneth 228-229
Watson, Marvin 189
Wayne County Press 102, 103,
  105-106, 107, 108, 109, 135,
  144, 145, 154, 162-163, 166,
  199, 208, 218-219, 220-221,
  223-224, 232, 233-234
Weaver, Ella 200
Whalen, Charles 229
Williams, Freeda 9
Williams, Ray 9, 168
Wilson, Bob 112
Wilson, Russell 144, 157
Windlan, Emma Lee 38, 39
Windlan, Fred 38, 39
Windlan, Ivan 38, 39
Wittmond, Carl H. 225
Wolfenden, Thomas 36
Wolff, David A. 54
Wood, Arthur D. 53

Wood Jr., Charles R. 188, 189,
  190, 221
Woodcock, George 190-191
Woods, James 159-160, 201-202,
  206-207, 211, 212, 213, 214
Woods, Mary Ann 201-202,
  206-207, 212
Woltman, George 109-111
Wortman, Frank (Buster) 44, 46,
  64, 66, 67-72, 74-75, 83, 87, 89
Wortman, Ted 71-72
Wylie, Dellos 98

Y

Young, Seth Glenn 26-27
Young, Walter 81

Z

Zelko, Molly 94
Zerbst, F. G. 51
Zuber, James Shelton 107-108

Photo by Sarah Pointer

Taylor Pensoneau, onetime Illinois political correspondent for the *St. Louis Post-Dispatch* and a former president of the Illinois Coal Association, is the author of biographies of former Illinois governors Dan Walker and Richard B. Ogilvie, and Illinois Senator W. Russell Arrington, a state legislative leader. (The Walker biography was coauthored by Bob Ellis.) Pensoneau also is the author of *Brothers Notorious: The Sheltons* and *The Summer of '50*, his first work of fiction. He lives at New Berlin, a village west of Springfield, Illinois, with his wife Elizabeth, retired editor of *Outdoor Illinois* magazine.

Back cover photograph courtesy of Beatrice Riley